Héloïse Goodley was a city banker until she made an impulsive decision to join the army in 2007. Commissioning into the Army Air Corps, she has completed two operational tours of Afghanistan and currently holds the rank of Captain as Adjutant of an Apache helicopter regiment.

An Officer
and a
Gentlewoman

Héloïse Goodley

CONSTABLE • LONDON

CONSTABLE

First published in the UK by Constable,
an imprint of Constable & Robinson Ltd., 2012

Published in this paperback edition by Constable, 2013

3 5 7 9 10 8 6 4 2

A CIP catalogue record for this book
is available from the British Library.

ISBN: 978-1-4721-0217-1

Printed and bound in Great Britain by Clays Ltd, St Ives plc

Papers used by Constable are from well-managed forests
and other responsible sources

MIX
Paper from
responsible sources
FSC
www.fsc.org   FSC® C104740

Constable
An imprint of
Little, Brown Book Group
Carmelite House
50 Victoria Embankment
London EC4Y 0DZ

An Hachette UK Company
www.hachette.co.uk

www.littlebrown.co.uk

This book is dedicated to my grandfather,
Llewellyn Williams.
An author and true soldier.

NOTE FROM THE MINISTRY OF DEFENCE

The author attended officer training at the Royal Military Academy Sandhurst in 2007. Since this time the Academy has undergone what has become known as a 'quiet revolution'. Since 2009 this has witnessed a dramatic change in both what and how Sandhurst trains cadets. The effect of these changes is that Sandhurst is now commissioning a different junior officer from that of four years ago. This process is evolutionary and will continue to change and adapt. Sandhurst now ruthlessly seeks to become a 'Centre of Training Excellence'; exploiting new technologies to enhance learning and setting the standards which newly commissioned second lieutenants will take on to the Field Army: in essence demonstrating to the Army 'what good looks like'. This is at the very core of the requirement for the team at Sandhurst. It will ultimately be the lasting legacy of Sandhurst in the formation of an Officer Corps adapted for the unknown pressures and complexities of the twenty-first century.

AUTHOR'S NOTE

The following account is based on the author's own
experiences at the Royal Military Academy Sandhurst and
provides an accurate depiction of what it was like to
undergo officer training there in 2007. However, in
recounting some of these experiences, fictional licence has
been applied as one person's account is simply not
interesting enough to pen an entire book about. In a few
instances it has been necessary to change the names of
certain individuals, whilst other characters have become
purely fictional representations and bear no resemblance
to their actual counterparts. The Royal Military Academy
Sandhurst has been educating and training army officers
for over two centuries and the staff and instructors who
serve there are at the peak of their profession.

CONTENTS

'Every man thinks meanly of himself
for not having been a soldier . . .'

Samuel Johnson

1

IN THE GRAVEYARD OF EMPIRES

I am sitting in near darkness, my seat belt fastened firmly around my waist. All the lights have been dimmed and the window shutters pulled tightly shut. To the outside world we have become just a distant black noise in the heavens above. I put on my body armour and helmet, securing the buckle and affixing Velcro straps. I'm not sure why we have to do this; if the Taliban are lucky enough to shoot the plane out of the night sky, a simple piece of Kevlar on my head isn't going to prevent a jihadist jackpot; but I'm in no position to question, and do as I am told. The aeroplane swoops and yaws, starting its descent, forcing me downwards into my seat as we plummet out of the blackness towards Kandahar Airfield below. We list left then bank violently right; twisting and dropping on a roller coaster ride in the sky.

Without lights the RAF pilot is flying by night-vision goggles, the world below him illuminated in shades of neon green. Normally at this point on a flight everyone with a window seat would be peering out, those in the middle craning their necks to study the outline city lights of our destination below, but instead we are sitting in neutral silence.

Suddenly the background throb of the engines is replaced with a dull thud and squealing rush as the landing gear drops ready to touch down. The cabinful of troops sit in an eerily still darkness, senses heightened by the Blitz blackout. I feel a whiff of fear and nervous trepidation creep in. I have wanted to come to Afghanistan since I joined the Army; this is the war of the moment, of my time. I want to do my bit, experience the machine of battle and finally put all that training to some use. But as I had packed my bags and bid family and friends farewell tiny doubts squirmed in the pit of my stomach, and a solicitous fear fluttered in my chest. It felt like peering over the edge of a high diving board or withdrawing money from a cash machine at the dicey end of town; I was aware of a danger but unsure of the reality of the threat. I had been trained for what lay ahead. I had been readying myself for two years; but no training can prepare your emotions. None of my training could steady the churning I now felt in my gut or the cold clammy sweat in the palm of my hands.

It was the early hours of 10 January 2009. Ten hours earlier I had left a grey drizzly Saturday behind at RAF Brize Norton, boarding the Royal Air Force plane to Afghanistan. On the outside, the plane had been a huge gunmetal-grey hulk, lacking any of the brightly coloured livery of commercial airliners, but on the inside it was identical to a British Airways cabin, because it had once been so (the RAF Tristar fleet were bought from British Airways in the early eighties). The only difference was that where first class should have been there were six stretcher hospital beds instead, ready to evacuate wounded soldiers from the battlefield, serving as a bleak early reminder that this was not a charter flight to Minorca. Unlike British Airways, lunch wasn't served with candy smiles and silk neck scarves, but by RAF stewards wearing khaki all-in-one coveralls. They pushed a trolley up and down the cramped aisles handing out small white cardboard boxes containing an apple, a stale sandwich, a packet of crisps and a Mars bar, pouring jugs of sweet orange squash into paper cups.

Today this is how troops go to war.

My ears popped as we continued our descent. A cabin of sitting ducks, waiting patiently. Incognizant of the world outside, my fate lay in the pilot's hands. Outside there was a whoosh and a hissing sound as flares were dispensed into the darkness around the aircraft; then, moments later, a squealing bump as the wheels touched terra firma. The aircraft fuselage vibrated madly as the engines were thrown into reverse and we made our bumpy way along the runway. I drew in a deep breath; this was it, I had arrived at Kandahar International Airport.

Around me the cabin lights came on as the aircraft taxied to a parking bay and there was the usual clamber for items from the overhead lockers. Passengers filled the aisles readying to get off, as others stood at their seats, their heads crooked by the low ceiling above. At the front of the aircraft the doors opened, and a metal staircase was manoeuvred into position for the slow queue to filter forwards and disembark. As I reached the front and stepped from the plane, a smell hit me like a vicious slap, an overwhelming noxious miasma pervading the airfield: the shocking stench of human faeces. When the breeze blows in the wrong direction, which tends to prevail, a pong of poo lingers over Kandahar, picked up at the 'poo pond', a large open liquid sewage pit.

Welcome to Afghanistan.

(Popular rumour has it that a soldier once swam across the 'poo pond' for $100.)

At Kandahar the air is filled with noise too, like Kafka's Castle; a cacophony of helicopter blades, jet engines, propellers, growling vehicles and shouting continues around the clock, all part of the war effort. It was in such stark contrast to the tranquil snowy Oxfordshire fields and dying Christmas lights I had left behind only hours earlier.

Once outside the aircraft and on the dispersal, the passengers climbed into a convoy of beaten and neglected buses for the winding journey from the aircraft to the 'terminal', a dusty tent lined with wooden waiting benches. Coughing and wheezing veils of black smoke, the buses made their way past the Taliban's Last Stand – a crumbling building riddled with bullet marks, shrapnel scars and a bomb hole in the roof where an Allied raid ended the Taliban's reign in Afghanistan in 2001. The visible proof of battle damage suffered in their final fight gave a meaningful reminder that Kandahar is the spiritual home of the Taliban, and defeat in 2001 has not yet led to Allied victory.

I spent that night at Kandahar, rolling out my sleeping bag on the bottom bunk of a bed in the anonymous rows of bunks in a 600-man transit tent. Fortunately the jet lag and early start helped send me straight to sleep, because otherwise worry would have left me lying awake in the unfamiliar darkness, listening to the new sounds of war and the rustlings in the bunk next to me. The following evening I would be flying to Camp Bastion in Helmand Province, a place that would be my home for the next four months.

Constantly building and growing, Kandahar Airbase is the hub of NATO's mission in southern Afghanistan. The machinery of war is well established in this sprawling city of tin hut and tent headquarter homes where rear-echelon decision-makers and support staff do their bit. The skyline is dotted with fluttering multi-national flags; Italian, Dutch, British, Australian, American, Romanian and Afghan soldiers all contribute to their effort in the coalition force. Among the offices and sleeping tents there is a central public square, called the 'Boardwalk', which provides recreational luxuries that soldiers fighting daily on the ground can only dream of. Along the Boardwalk's wooden parade a fashion show of foreign uniforms can be seen as soldiers queue for pizza from Pizza Hut, visit the Canadian doughnut house, Dutch coffee shop, Korean takeaway or French Patisserie. In the centre of the Boardwalk, American Marines whoop and high-five as they play ice hockey on a full-sized concrete hockey pitch, while Danes shoot hoops on the basketball court. Around the airbase Filipino and Sri Lankan civilians empty bins, sweep roads, wash laundry and clean the toilets while bearded

KBR[1] contractors talk into walkie-talkies; these are the people who are really winning from this war.

Among the eateries there are gift shops too, selling Afghan rugs, fake Oakley sunglasses, mosque alarm clocks and other curios at rip-off prices to soldiers on their return home. It was all far removed from the scene of war I had been expecting. And with this almost holiday camp atmosphere of pizzerias and iced cappuccinos it could be quite easy to be lulled into a false sense of safety at Kandahar, but the mortar alarm resounds regularly, causing people to scurry for cover as the base is often rocketed by the Taliban hiding in the surrounding hills, determined to win back their heartland.

The next evening I was back at the terminal tent again to board a Hercules flight to Camp Bastion, the main British base in Afghanistan. Flying around in the dark of night like this is a necessary precaution in Afghanistan to keep out of sight of the Taliban threat and it means that a lot of the RAF Hercules pilots rarely see daylight during their time in Afghanistan. At a painted wooden desk a female soldier found my name on a piece of paper and ticked it off, checking me in, and I carried my rifle through the scanner into the departure area (airport security restrictions are a little more lax here than they are at Heathrow). In the departure area I sat on a long wooden bench and flicked through old magazines and out-of-date newspapers, killing the time until my flight by reading last year's news and drinking a warm bottle of water from the broken fridge. There was little else to do but wait and the dusty concrete

---

1   KBR is an American private military engineering and construction company.

floors were lined with soldiers sleeping, their heads propped against their body armour. I scanned the room, taking in the different groups of people. Some soldiers were gathered around a Nintendo DS, while others with headphones sat alone listening to music. There were two soldiers with straggly beards and shaggy hair standing at the back in black North Face jackets, trying to look inconspicuous, but obviously Special Forces. I could spot those who had been here before and experienced this many times – they had a nonchalant air and confident manner about them, as they headed to the coffee area and bagged the best spots to sleep, tucked out of the way and beyond the whirring generators. That would be me next time, but for now, I was on edge, the nerves in my stomach had yet to settle as I worried about what lay ahead. Eventually an RAF soldier wearing a yellow bib and green ear protectors stood in the doorway to the tent and hollered for us to gather our things ready to depart.

Boarding the Hercules felt far more like a real act of war. The rumbling engines blasted out scorching hot air and billowing dust as I walked towards the tail ramp, causing me to shield my face as I stepped up onto it. I shuffled around metal pallets of netted cargo to find a seat and strapped myself in, propping my rifle between my knees and donning helmet and body armour once more for the hour-long flight to Camp Bastion, where the fate of the twenty-first century world security is being decided.[2]

---

2 In December 2006 on a visit to Camp Bastion, Tony Blair told British troops that 'here in this extraordinary piece of desert is where the fate of world security in the early twenty-first century is going to be decided'.

Camp Bastion is the biggest British-built base since the Second World War and home to almost 4,000 troops. The camp occupies a rectangle four miles long by two miles wide in the southern Afghanistan desert. This vast and growing town of tents, barbed wire and huge steel shipping containers is set in a parched dusty moonscape, overswept by sandstorms. The soil here is so arid that not even a weed will grow, but just a few miles to the east meanders the Helmand River, weaving a lush nourished ribbon of green through the desert like Egypt's Nile. The fields and orchards of this Green Zone are where the drug barons and warlords are, where the fields of opium poppies grow, where the Taliban choose to pick their battles and where British ground troops are based to fight them. Camp Bastion is located here in the neighbouring desert to support them, sending forward food, water, ammunition and equipment; launching helicopters and tending to the wounded in the state-of-the-art field hospital. It also provides a stop-off for battle-fatigued soldiers going home after months of fighting. And at Camp Bastion they stagger off helicopters into an oasis of Western civilization emerging from their feral FOB[3] existences into Willy Wonka's chocolate factory. Eager for normality, they dump weapons and heavy body armour and head straight to the computer room to check Facebook and football scores, while in the dining tent these gaunt teenage soldiers fill their plates with steak and

---

3 Forward Operating Base, the small football-pitch-sized fortified compounds from which infantry ground soldiers patrol in the Green Zone, where the food is in ration packs and there is often no running water.

imported military cheesecake, and in the showers months of grime and dust are scrubbed away.

I arrived at Camp Bastion by night and the following morning woke early. I slid out of bed, grabbed a quick shower and dressed in the dark: T-shirt, shirt, trousers, socks, boots, a jumper for the January chill. I brushed my hair and teeth, adjusted the beret on my head and stepped outside into the still morning air. It felt fresh with a bitter bite that woke me as I wove my way through the rows of tents and blast protection walls to the Joint Operational Command (JOC, the decision-making nerve centre). Inside the night shift were still in, manning the bank of radios and monitor screens, getting updates on current events across the province. In the corner a large flat-screen television provided live Predator[4] feed, the flickering black and white images prying into a suspicious Taliban compound. For now life was quiet across the region; a few infantry foot patrols had gone out on the ground from their FOBs, but there was no sign of the Taliban. In the background a generator hummed, powering the whole operation. Maps and boards with plans and timelines hung around the room, while empty paper coffee cups piled high in the bin. This is the brains of British helicopter operations in Afghanistan.

I had arrived for the morning brief and, as it finished a shout came in: 'Nine-Liner!'

---

4 Predator is an Unmanned Aerial Vehicle (UAV) – a remote-control plane that circles high above Afghanistan watching, piloted by someone sitting in an air-conditioned office in Las Vegas who clearly has the right idea for earning his war medal.

A request for urgent medical assistance. A Royal Marine had stepped on a home-made bomb in Sangin. He was critically injured ('Category Alpha') and needed urgent medical help.

Suddenly the relative morning calm was shattered. Land Rovers raced through camp, sirens wailing and blue lights flashing, as the emergency response team surged into action. Down at the helicopter flight line they came screeching to a halt, disgorging bomb disposal experts, nurses, doctors and pilots into the back of a Chinook. Among them, a consultant who could start life-saving surgery on the casualty in the back of the helicopter, bringing A&E to the frontline. The rotor blades were already turning, slicing the air with a low thwack, thwack, thwack. Ground crew soldiers ran around detaching fuel nozzles and removing wheel chocks, readying the aircraft for lift-off; and within moments the Chinook and a supporting Apache helicopter were off the ground and on their way, disappearing in a loud collision of dust, noise and haste.

The whole scramble had taken less than ten minutes.

It was a slick and well-rehearsed operation. The entire focus was about getting to the soldier and saving his life, bringing him back to the field hospital at Camp Bastion where he stood a good chance of survival. Soldiers on the ground in Afghanistan are guaranteed to be at the hospital within ninety minutes of wounding, most make it within forty-five, some as quickly as fifteen. Medical emergency and saving lives are the absolute priority here, money and resources are no object.

I strolled back to the JOC comforted by the knowledge that help was on its way and the soldier, though injured, would be OK. Inside I flicked on the kettle, watching BBC Breakfast television on the British Forces Broadcast Service (BFBS) while I waited for it to boil. As I poured the boiling water into a paper cup a radioed update arrived: the soldier's status had changed from 'Category Alpha' to 'Category Echo'. He had died.

My body went numb.

Slowly stirring my coffee with the plastic teaspoon, something between my stomach and chest turned over. Just like that. I had been in Afghanistan for less than forty-eight hours and already a British soldier had paid the ultimate price. I had never met him. I didn't even know his name. I knew nothing about him, but it struck me. I continued to watch Sian Williams and Bill Turnbull on their red sofa talking about the recession and snow that were bringing the UK to a standstill. Somewhere back home someone else was probably doing exactly the same routine as me: sipping a fresh cup of coffee and watching the early morning news, getting ready for the day ahead. Except they were about to get a knock on their front door that would shatter their lives and change it for ever. A mother, father, wife, sister, brother, daughter, son, grandparent, friend. Things would never be the same for them. He was gone. Another solemn hearse travelling through Wootton Bassett.

Death is routine in war, but these were the emotions I was not trained for. I had never been so close to death. The Royal Marine was the first of nineteen soldiers to die in my four months in Afghanistan. Each of the nineteen repatriated home in coffins draped with a Union Jack. Each remembered in prayers uttered by the padre at vigil ceremonies, the whole of Camp Bastion gathering, heads lowered, looking at boots in the dust. Each death was saddening but they became a fact of life out there, as British soldiers paid daily with life and limb.

Outside I watched the helicopters return, and wondered how I had come to be in this corner of a foreign field. Just two years earlier I had been a suited civilian, commuting to a desk with the rest of the rat race. Now I was actually at war. Not part of the gritty infantry combat on the ground, but still here, smelling it, tasting it, feeling the emotions that newspapers, books and television screens simply cannot convey.

As the coffee passed through me I walked across the dirt road to one of the Portaloos in the line of blue phone-box-like Tardis (or 'Turdis'). I locked the door behind me and held my breath as I lifted the lid to reveal the horrors within. Inside the Portaloo the plastic walls were covered with graffitied gallows soldier humour and I smiled to myself as I sat down and read the comment on the door in front of me: 'Thank you for your application to RMAS'. RMAS – the Royal Military Academy, Sandhurst, the British Army's officer training academy.

That was how I had got here.

2

OUT WITH THE SHARP SUIT, IN WITH THE MARCHING BOOTS

I had managed to go through life in the right order. I worked hard at school, got GCSEs, A-levels and went to university, where after three years of avoiding serious responsibility I graduated and took a job at a bank in the City that paid well and made my parents proud. I bought sharp suits, wore power heels, sat finance exams and spent two hours of my day at the clemency of London Transport on the Underground, commuting to a desk in the shiny glass and chrome of Canary Wharf.

It was utterly soul destroying.

I went along with it for a while and played the City game. Squandering my enviable wage in bars and clubs on the King's Road, soaking up the bright lights of London with little to show for it. At university I'd known no alternative. All the big, powerful City firms had come through on their milk round, seducing us with flash PowerPoint presentations and sharp pinstripe suits, and we students clambered over one another to be there. To be plied with their free booze, queuing to schmooze potential bosses and slip CVs to the recruiting girls. And I allowed myself to be swept along like everyone else, as these big names brought big promises. Investment banks. Management consultancies. Accountancy firms. Insurance brokers. Law firms. What these companies propositioned was temptingly sweet: the offer of a student-loan-busting starting salary and juicy joining bonus. It was what everyone wanted.

Wasn't it?

I interviewed with a few and after a couple of rounds of sweaty-palmed cross-examinations, secured a job with an investment bank. And so, with the ink barely dry on the dotted line, I cashed my first giddy pay cheque as graduation mortar boards were being flung into the air. I felt ready to start working life. I'd had enough of lectures and exams, and I wanted to start doing something other than just learning and running up debts. Of course I would miss the irresponsible, laissez-faire, carefree student life, but not the essay deadlines and baked bean meals. I packed up my poky student digs, to find an even pokier flat in London which I moved into, unpacking my belongings into clever IKEA storage solutions in a bijou box room, ready to start my new City life. A grown-up life. A life of smart suits and shirts. A life of Oyster cards and Underground maps. A life of fiddling with cufflinks and understanding the *Financial Times*. With my final exams out of the way, furrowed brows, bleary eyes and caffeine became replaced with client meetings, ticking deadlines and even more caffeine. It was a whole new world. A world without daytime television and duvet days spent sleeping off hangovers. A world that didn't stop for sport on a Wednesday afternoon nor care for my late essay excuses. It was a world of client dining and corporate dinners, not cheese on toast. It was a world of money and finance inside the Square Mile. Of backstabbing and office politics. It was a heartless world filled with pretension and greed, because what wasn't revealed in the flashy milk-round presentations, nor handed out with the corporate freebies was that in return these big firms wanted my soul; and 'what shall it profit a man, if he shall gain the whole world and lose his own soul?'[1]

I hated it. I lacked any passion for it and slowly the life began to seep out of me as I became trapped. I was wasting the best years of my life caught in a City spiral. Waking each morning from a disturbed night's sleep two hours earlier than my body wanted to, to join the rest of London's commuters, fighting delays on the District Line, so I could be tied to a desk, staring square-eyed at a computer screen all day bored by Excel. The coveted job: it turned out I didn't want it. But what did I want? I didn't want to be here, I knew that, surrounded by grey drudgery, in a grey City with grey depressed drones. I didn't fit. I couldn't settle down. I used to have energy, drive and ambition. Now I craved daylight and a bit of variety.

As the months rolled into years I began to realize that there had to be more to life than spending eighteen hours

1 Mark 8:36.

in the office enslaved by a highly paid job. I felt as if I was staring at the blank wall of a dead end, but what were the alternatives? I was tired of living for my holidays, weekends and the hope of escaping beyond the M25. But I wasn't qualified to do anything else. If I wanted to move on I'd have to land on a snake and slither back to the start, before climbing the ladders up to where I wanted to be. I would need to retrain but it was a leap I was increasingly prepared to make. I was single and unattached, and I was free to make that leap; I had no commitments and no baggage. No serious boyfriend, no mortgage, no pulls or ties. I started considering my options, and the choices available to me. Which doors were still open and which were now closed? Sitting on the train to a client meeting I scrolled through my BlackBerry and looked for Life Plan B.

Four years after this highly paid despair set in, I found myself seated at a dinner next to some ghastly hedge fund manager, listening to him braying about his assets and how fabulous he was. The arrogant buffoon bored me to pains with spiel of how much money he had and spent; the costs of private dining in Scott's, how eye-wateringly big his bonus was, that he'd just bought his second Ferrari and an expensive new kitchen despite being uninterested in cookery. Everything about his life revolved around money, and he was happy because he was making it and flashing it. As I listened to him I realized that his heart was beating to market movements, they were his raison d'être, while my heart didn't so much as flutter to the FTSE. And he wasn't the only greedy, contemptuous tosser at the table; I was surrounded by them. People whose priorities in life focused solely on pecuniary gains. People who were driven by materialistic competition, by the greatness of their wealth and an insatiable thirst to make more money than their neighbour. Their pallid lifeless faces, overworked bloodshot eyes and thinning stressed hair revealed that their bodies as well as their personalities were destroyed by their jobs. For these investment bankers and fund managers, bond traders and brokers, their measure of success in life was money. But what is money? Bob Dylan said something along the lines of a man being a success if he gets up in the morning and goes to bed, and in between he does what he wants to do. And I knew I wasn't doing what I wanted to do, and I'm not convinced everyone else was either.

But I felt compelled to persist because of my privilege. I should have been grateful for what I had. Many of my fellow students weren't swept up in the university milk rounds. The City has a reputation as a ruthless hire-and-fire world and, as a woman with a job in a bank other than at the secretary's desk, I'd broken through the glass ceiling. But I wasn't grateful. I didn't want it. I didn't want to compete. I didn't care about the flashier car, bigger house or five-starred hotel. I didn't want a basement conversion in Fulham, Michelin-starred meals or bespoke suits. I wanted to break free from it all and do something completely different with my life. I wanted to run away and join the circus, but what is the educated girl's circus?

I wasn't afraid of long hours and hard work. And I was happy for my job to become my life. I wasn't put off by having to hold my own in a testosterone-filled environment, but it had to be worth it. And right now it wasn't. I would love to lay claim that in 2006 I sensed the approaching economic apocalypse and recessional doom, that I was running away from pending fiscal tragedy but I didn't. That was pure luck.

There was another dinner guest that night who didn't fit in either. But he didn't seem to care. Robyn was the younger brother of our host, in town fleetingly before heading to Iraq. He was incredibly confident, exuding vitality and an excitement for life. Upbeat and intrepid, his ruddy, tanned face had a healthy complexion at odds with the rest of us City folk. He was fresh, bright-eyed and energetic. His eyes sparkled with a cheerful joie de vivre because he wasn't spending his days shackled to a desk like the rest of us. His different, refreshing perspective was the result of a career choice that didn't involve fighting District Line delays, sacrificing your soul and sucking up to arrogant humourless clients. His days weren't spent surrounded by hideous capitalist greed and dreadful brash bankers, because he was in the Army and had a different Zen.

Later, over coffee, between dull discussions of offshore banking and first-class lounges, Robyn entertained with exciting stories of his life in the military, his time in Kenya, Brecon and Basra. Listening to him I realized what work should be about. He relished what he did, with a thrilling zest and zeal. His job seemed so varied and exciting and he had a passion I lacked. He did a job he clearly loved and I was envious. Very envious. As the wine bottles emptied, we clambered into a taxi to continue the night at a Mayfair club. Sitting in the back of a black cab watching the lights of London whizz past me, my life whizzing past me, I listened to Robyn regaling us with a story about his time as a cadet in training at Sandhurst. As he talked on, delivering another humorous punchline, he leaned towards me and casually tapped my knee.

'Héloïse,' he said with a cheeky grin, 'you should join the Army.'

'Really? Oh no I don't think so. I'm not suitable for that sort of thing.'

'Not true. You'd be surprised,' he said, leaning back into his seat. 'You strike me as exactly what the Army are looking for.'

The Army? It was something I had never before considered. Were there even women in the Army? Weren't they all butch lesbians? I knew no one in the Army. I knew nothing about it. But I'd had enough of the City and knew I had to get out, and with that innocent throwaway comment from Robyn the die was cast.

When I left school most of the Army was still off limits to women and joining had simply never been presented to me as a career choice. The RAF recruited boys from my school, but that was it, just the boys. At university I had met a few students who were in the OTC,[2] but they weren't cool and the idea of spending your weekends cold and piss-wet through when you could be warm and sleeping off a hangover was a simple decision for my student self to

---

2 Officer Training Corps.

make. But now, staring down the barrel of a bleak unfulfilling City existence, I was curious.

Still thinking about Robyn's comment the following week I ventured to my nearest Army Recruitment Office, tottering down High Holborn in my suit, having sneakily escaped from the captivity of my desk with some mumbled excuse about a client errand. As I stood on the pavement outside, I gazed up at the posters hanging enticingly in the window. Images depicted soldiers looking wary in combat face paint, driving tanks across open plains and marching proudly with bearskins perched on their heads. Each had that twinkle in their eyes I lacked. It all looked very different to my average day in the office. I pushed open the glass door and stepped in, instantly feeling out of place in my suit among the forces uniforms. A young soldier in combats approached me and offered his help. He started by asking my age, never a good opening line with a woman, especially if it is to lead to an ageist rejection, because unfortunately at twenty-seven, he informed me, I was already too old for most of the Army's career opportunities.[3] And with that the wind was blown from my sails. Any small fantasies I had had of swapping sharp suits for marching boots crumpled, withered and died. I was too late. But what the recruiting soldier had failed to identify was that my plummy accent and tertiary education might make me eligible for a career as an officer rather than a soldier, and my abject ignorance of the Army's apartheid structure meant I didn't realize either. As

---

3 The Army has since increased the maximum age limit for soldiers to thirty-three.

I walked back out, stepping into the pedestrians of High Holborn, the glass doors closed behind me and the opportunity was missed.

Months passed and I continued to look for alternative uses for my life, keeping my eyes wide open and prejudices at bay. I now felt galvanized to make the change but was lost for what to do. I knew that when I reached old age it would be the things I didn't do in my life that I would regret rather than the things I did, and right now I had to do something else. Thanks to my City salary I'd paid off my student debt, I had qualifications to fall back on and a small property investment. I was free to try something completely new. But now with a blank sheet in front of me I had no idea how to fill it. The world was my oyster and it was more daunting than the most important client meeting.

But my interest in the Army didn't go away and, as if fate was hunting me down, I bumped into Robyn again on the Tube.

He chuckled at my naivety. 'I meant for you to apply to Sandhurst,' he said. 'Not join as a "Tom".'

I gave him a look that showed I was still a little less than understanding.

'It's where the Army do their officer training,' he offered. 'It takes a year. And at the end of it you get the Queen's Commission and go off to command the soldiers.'

He was still very enthusiastic about me joining and convinced I'd be perfect for the military. So a week later, on his recommendation, I found myself on the doorstep of an address in Greenwich, where I could be successfully channelled into the Army's recruitment system. Inside I sat waiting in a foyer that had all the bland, sterile charm of a dentist's waiting room, with a corner stack of tattered old magazines and a floor of rough blue carpet tiles. I flicked through an old copy of *Soldier* magazine as I waited, reading with curiosity advertisements for 'ballistic underpants' (saving Ryan's privates) and '1,000 mile socks'. I was here to meet the woman responsible for London army officer recruitment. After a while a soldier in uniform showed me to her office where she welcomed me with a nod and motioned for me to sit in the low chair opposite her desk. Her manner was formal and gruff as she interviewed me, and seated above me at her desk her size was exaggerated from my low perspective. I was surprised to discover that she had actually been in the Army herself and even more shocked when she asked me whether I had a boyfriend, because, 'Everyone knows that Sandhurst is widely acknowledged as the country's biggest dating agency.'

An interesting recruitment pitch.

Above her computer screen sat the evidence from which she made her claim – a photograph of the husband she herself had ensnared there. But she seemed to think I possessed the qualities sought in a Sandhurst hopeful and completed the requisite forms, stamped the paperwork and sent me packing with a glossy brochure and date for my first officer assessment.

Unsure exactly of what I had just done, I stood on Greenwich Station platform waiting for the next train back into central London with Status Quo's lyrics circling around in my head: 'You're in the Army now/Oh, oh, you're in the Army now.'

The next step on the road to Sandhurst was to attend a 'selection briefing': a two-day filter held at Leighton House in the little town of Westbury on the edge of Salisbury Plain, the Army's heartland. Set in forty acres of parkland straddling the main road from Bournemouth to Bath, Westbury camp is surrounded by tall, moss-clad stone walls and comprises a collection of cheerless redbrick buildings around a handsome Georgian mansion called Leighton House. Originally the residence of the Lord Lieutenant of Wiltshire, the property was requisitioned by the War Office at the outbreak of the Second World War for convalescing soldiers and it is here now, among the assault course and trout lake, that the Army Officer Selection Board seek out the enigmatic qualities of army leadership.

I arrived nervously on a Monday, and reported to the Camp Guard Room. Inside, a pinched, smoke-aged man with a wrinkled-up face ticked my name from his list and handed me a vehicle pass and directions. I climbed back into my car and made my way over the speed bumps that dotted the road winding its way through the camp, and entered the car park at the far end. I found myself a parking slot and gathered my bag of belongings, then carried it across the gravelly square to a set of shabby squat buildings and dumped them on a bare spring bed in an open shared room. Paint was flaking from the walls, mirrors were cracked and in the corner a chest of drawers was missing handles; it felt distinctly unloved. The room that the toilet occupied was even still painted in the bright cobalt blue colour, last popular in the seventies, and not updated since. Everything about Westbury felt frayed and underinvested, nothing like the shiny glass and chrome newness of Canary Wharf. But I wasn't here for an assessment of the interior decor.

Ahead of me lay a day of briefs, discussion groups, aptitude tests and my first taste of army food, abrasive blankets, cold showers and wholly unnecessary shouting. For my time here I wouldn't be known as Héloïse, nor even Miss Goodley, I became just a number, and was handed a yellow bib with it on to wear over my suit. I became number one, and the first to be called forward for everything. There were seventy other potential hopefuls along with me at the selection briefing, representing a cross section of serious wannabes: serving soldiers; career changers like myself and floaters looking for something to do after graduating from university. Among them there were plenty who were even more unsuitable for military life than I felt. One, a Malaysian mathematics PhD student, barely had a grasp of the English language, and had been sent to try to join the army by his university careers advisor, in what was probably last-bid desperation. Another, a tiny, painfully thin, fragile girl, who couldn't have fought her way out of a wet brown paper bag, refused to eat anything but the cereal bars she had brought with her, and cracked to tears under the slightest examining pressure.

As number one I was first to be called forward for my interview with the Colonel that afternoon and after being directed along a series of corridors I came to a small room where a man in uniform was waiting for me. He looked old and weary and as I entered I felt as though I was distracting him from the books and disarrayed papers that were piled high on his desk. As I took a seat on the plastic chair opposite him I didn't recognize his rank, and didn't understand the military rank structure, so my overfriendliness and casual manner were instantly construed as a rude lack of deference. Paying me no welcoming compliments, he took a yellow folder from the pile beside him and opened the cover of it, quietly perusing the paperwork inside, which I guessed to be my application form.

'Hmmm. I see you were house captain at school,' he finally said after a long silence, looking up at me for the first time. 'And how was that?'

What? House captain. That was almost ten years ago. I was twenty-seven now and had done plenty of more significant things since leaving school. It may have been a relevant question for a recent school leaver or university student, but I barely remembered it now.

'Oh I loved it,' I said, stretching my memory back and looking for some relevant tangent to joining the army. 'I really enjoyed the responsibility of looking after the younger girls,' I added, grasping at a potential crossover skill for an officer.

'Hmm,' he said, before going quiet again and looking back down at my file.

'And I see you played first team hockey at school too. Jolly good,' he said without enthusiasm, still not looking up from my papers. 'And what about now? What sport teams do you play for now?'

I was flattered that he was still impressed by my distant school-day glories but I didn't have time to play for sport teams any more. I was at the mercy of my City employers now, shackled to my desk for eighteen hours a day. There wasn't any time in my life to put on shin pads and race across the AstroTurf, as much as I would have loved to have done so.

'Regrettably my current job doesn't allow me the time to commit to sport teams any more,' I said, knowing he wasn't going to warm to my response. 'I like to run a lot though,' I said, trying to smooth over my lack of team spirit.

'Oh.' He nodded. Giving no emotion away. I could tell he didn't like me. There was no rapport between us and as I left with a last-ditch attempt cheery smile I wasn't confident he'd seen in me what Robyn and the Army recruitment woman had.

That night we slept on our squeaky iron-sprung beds in bleak dorm rooms of six, listening to the sound of others snoring. In the morning, I tiptoed along the long draughty corridor with my wash bag and towel to the showers at the opposite end, shivering or scalding under its temperamental drip. It certainly wasn't the accommodation of client expense accounts.

I spent two days at Westbury, being put through my paces. My mental aptitude and physical abilities were scrutinized, my political acumen tested and grasp of

English examined. And although I might not have impressed the colonel, the Army liked what they saw and I passed, receiving an invitation to come back for the Main Board assessment a few months later.

So far I had kept all this discreetly to myself. Such an enormous career U-turn was likely to draw strong views from my friends and family. A daughter in the Army was hardly something my mother would be boasting about in the staff room at the school she taught at in Kent and it would take me over a decade in the army to climb back to the City wage I was currently on. Joining the army was not a decision to be taken on a whim, but, honourably or naively, I believed there to be more to life than the disproportionate sums of money I was being paid and a life surrounded by material greed. So I continued to proceed with the recruitment process in secret, deciding to tell friends, family and my employers if or when I was successful.

By now it was summer 2006, the hottest on record, and as I enjoyed lazy days in the sunshine, passing the few months until my second assessment at Westbury, headlines began filtering into newspapers of the intense fighting soldiers were embroiled in in Afghanistan. It had been three years since the second Gulf War had started and words like 'car bomb' and 'Baghdad' on the news channels were becoming so trite the public consciousness barely registered, but Afghanistan was supposed to be a low-level peacekeeping mission not a full-blown scrap. The words of war in the media were beginning to change as reporters brought our attention to Sangin, Kajaki and Musa Qala, where soldiers were holding their own in ferocious fighting in relentless Taliban attacks. The baton in the war on terror had been passed and al-Qaeda's central front was shifting from Iraq to Afghanistan. Nevertheless, as I spent summer evenings drinking Pimm's with friends by the river in Putney, I somehow failed to register the connection between Robyn, my trips to Westbury, what I was signing up for and the photos of mentally and physically shattered soldiers with thousand-yard stares spread across the pages of the *Sun* newspaper. Somehow they didn't apply to me. I was joining a different army. The ferocity of war and the fact that the British Army was now fighting two of them was completely lost on me, because no number of embedded journalists in their blue-flak bulletproof vests can truly bring war into our living rooms; the full gritty reality is kept comfortably at a distance.

The months eventually passed and I was back down to Westbury for the full four-day Army Officer Selection Board (AOSB, not to be confused with ASBO!). This time the bar had been raised, the standard was much higher and the testing more demanding. It costs £100,000[4] to recruit and train an Army officer and the selection process is scrupulously thorough and equally equivocal. The aim of AOSB is to assess for the mystical officer quality, the potential to command and lead soldiers after a year of

---

4   *Defence Recruitment & Retention in the Armed Forces*, a study by the National Audit Office, November 2006.

Sandhurst moulding. And despite making it to university and fumbling my way into a City job, I wasn't sure whether I actually had this essence of officership. I could hold my own in a boardroom, but what about on the assault course?

The first morning started with a fitness test. A running, press-ups, sit-ups, heaves test. The army is pretty keen on being fit, so it was no surprise that those who failed would be eliminated in the first round, packed off home again. The bus that brought people from the train station even waited around ominously to make the return trip. Again wearing the bizarre combination of suit, heels and a netball bib with my candidate number on I spent the rest of the day frantically being assessed with essays, interviews and exams. Then after another squeaky and snore-filled night's sleep, I swapped my suit for ill-fitting green overalls and gathered with the others outside for the 'outdoor command tasks'. These involved trying to negotiate a number of different *Crystal Maze*-style timed challenges using barrels, ropes and planks, all slippery wet from the misty rain. We worked in teams of eight and, as people found themselves precariously suspended at the end of a plank, every muscle straining as the clock ticked down, true personalities emerged unguarded for the assessors. Not all the tasks were apparently even achievable and I hoped to God this was true as we disastrously dropped our petite, pint-sized comrade on her head whilst offering her forwards to bridge a gap six feet above a muddy puddle.

Next to the assault course for a sort of Crufts meets *Krypton Factor* affair, where there were tunnels to scurry along, windows to dive through, walls to scramble over and ropes from which to swing. All against the clock in the fastest time possible. There is only one way with which to successfully approach an assault course, and that is at pace without thought, hurling yourself at each obstacle mindless of the consequences. Any consideration or hesitation will add unnecessary seconds on the clock and you'll still reach the finish line in the same amount of pain with equal bruising. For added effect the rain came down hard that afternoon and as I stood there shivering, rain dripping from the end of my nose, my T-shirt sticking, cold, wet and clammy to my skin, I questioned my motives for wanting to run away from the City; maybe it wasn't so bad to be clock-watching in a warm, dry office after all. I knew I wanted to change my life but now, with wet pants, broken nails and muddy feet, I was considering less gritty career alternatives. Perhaps after four years in the City I was too soft and precious for the Army. Maybe it was too late for me to roll up my sleeves and get stuck in with the rough and tumble. Could I really swap the flat-lining heart rate of fiscal exertion for the high pulse of physical exertion?

Since the events of September 11, army recruitment has been on the rise, whether it is the notion of fighting Blair's war on terrorism or the fact that there now is a tangible war to fight at all, as opposed to killing time in Germany, sitting out the Cold War and waiting for the Russians. The global recession has also contributed to an increase in recruits. Every year over 4,000 hopefuls attempt the selection challenges at Westbury, hauling themselves around the assault course and doing press-ups in the rain. Competition is fierce. Which is why, two days later, I was astonished and relieved to receive a brown manila envelope 'On Her Majesty's Service' congratulating me on successfully being selected. I had secured a place at the Royal Military Academy Sandhurst (RMAS) and would start next winter.

Until now, I had still kept the whole process a secret, unconvinced that I would actually be selected and make the radical career leap, but I couldn't conceal it any longer and had to tell my parents. My brother and I chose to share the parental wrath and selected a common day on which to deliver the bad news. So, as Tristan arrived home with a tongue piercing, I phoned to tell them that I was throwing away a perfectly respectable City career to enlist. There was a deathly silence at the other end of the phone while my father pulled himself together, but as a daddy's girl I soon won him over and he became more preoccupied with my brother's swelling mouth. My father is of the generation where people joined a company for life and reaped the pension reward at the end of it, and with the army now to be my fourth employer he hoped my career flip-flapping soul search might finally be over, plus he knew that the military pension is still a good one. My mother, ever savvy and in touch with today's youth, was more worried I was a lesbian (I'm not) than about the potential dangers a military career could put me in. No one in my family had ever been in the armed forces, with the exception of my grandfather who fought in the army during the Second World War and never spoke of it. My parents didn't have military acquaintances either so their understanding of what I was letting myself in for was rather limited, as was mine.

Back in London, as I enjoyed my final few months of freedom amidst the comforts of a frappucino lifestyle, it became entertaining to shock friends and work associates with the news that I was abandoning the rat race to join forces in the war on terror. People couldn't believe I was giving up my coveted lucrative career to fight real wars not just price ones. My grandmother thought I'd meet Prince William at Sandhurst and marry him; my boss said he'd be recalling my killing skills back to the boardroom while my dear friend Deborah was excited by the prospect of lots of hunky men in uniform.

But I most enjoyed the smugness of informing my employers.

Banks are used to the drama of people throwing a bonus strop and handing in their resignation, using the bargaining promise of a job offer from a competitor to squeeze yet more cash out of their employers. No City firm is ever for life and omnipresent greed drives fickleness among City employees who switch allegiances as readily as secretary affairs. But leaving the Square Mile altogether, they didn't know what to make of it. It didn't compute. Why would I want to do that? I hadn't even made my first million yet. None of the usual bargaining arsenal had any value, as their offers of more pay or a different position fell on mind-made-up ears.

My flatmate Ann however did have a strong view on me joining the Army. She was far more sceptical about the whole idea and put forward an argument I struggled to counter. Ann is a bright cookie: she read politics at Oxford and has an educated conscience. Her objection was the prospect of me, under orders, having to fight a war I might not believe in. And she had a good point. Serving in the army I might have to. I was informed enough to have reached an opposing opinion on the invasion of Iraq, but if I were to join the army this opinion would have to go unheard. I could conscientiously object, but you need a pretty convincing ethical or moral reason to do so and a simple hunch that Saddam Hussein might not actually have weapons of mass destruction was unlikely to be a solid enough excuse to abstain; although bizarrely in reverse it was a perfectly good enough reason to invade. The British armed forces are strictly apolitical and service personnel are forbidden from taking an 'active part in the affairs of any political organization'. Instead, forces personnel rely on the British electoral system and the power of their vote[5] to make sure Ann's worst fears don't happen. In any case it could be argued that I was already directly contributing more to ruining people's lives through my nefarious employment in the City than any subsequent actions I might have in Afghanistan.

As I enjoyed my last remaining plump pay cheques in Fulham's bars and restaurants, I received the joining

5   UK Armed Forces personnel are entitled to vote either in their hometown or the constituency in which they serve. Those deployed away on operations are encouraged to vote by post.

instructions for the Royal Military Academy Sandhurst and the commissioning course; immodestly described as 'the finest command and leadership training course in the world'. The accompanying glossy recruitment literature brought evidence of the stark reality of what I was embarking on: photographic images showed cold, sweaty and tired people, exerting themselves in various muddy and uncomfortable situations, heaving heavy tree logs and scaling mountains with large backpacks on, while the pages talked of the hard work and long hours involved in making the transition from civilian to soldier.

These sweaty and out-of-breath people were also accompanied by threatening words of the need to be in 'top physical shape' for the 'very physical demands' of the course and to assist with this physical preparation there was an enclosed video, Fit For the Best. Thankful that I hadn't disposed of my redundant video-player when DVDs caught on a decade earlier, waiting for a moment like this when an outmodish organization like the army might necessitate it, I invited Deborah around and we watched intently over a bottle of wine as muscle-sculpted men in tight white T-shirts demonstrated techniques to improve 'stamina and strength'. Probably not the sort of viewing set-up the Army had intended it for, but the video had the desired effect as I was motivated to join a gym while Deborah went home having borrowed it and my video-player.

With £250 joining fees and £70 monthly membership, I have always thought membership at one of London's pretentious City gyms a ridiculous expense for something

I'd probably visit once. I preferred to be outside, gulping fresh air, running up and down the Thames towpath to keep the calorific effects of client dinners and happy hour cocktails at bay. However, this alone was not going to ready me for Sandhurst. I was fit by civilian standards, and had even recently run a few half-marathons, but the Army wanted more than that. Much more.

Before Westbury I had never done a press-up. Never. Not one. And attempts at heaves involved me dangling from a pole by my pathetic chicken-wing arms and flailing helplessly in the air. So to build up a bit of muscle and upper-body punch I enlisted the services of a personal trainer at my local gym to instruct me on how to develop biceps, without turning my size 8 frame into that of a shot-putter's.

I joined my local Fulham branch of Holmes Place Fitness Centre, where before work fellow gym-goers could be found on the reclining bike reading the *Financial Times*, while stylish women in the latest coordinated Stella McCartney gym fashions walked on the treadmills gossiping into mobile phones and yummy mummies dropped off young Harrys for swimming lessons. To boost motivation there were music videos of the Pussycat Dolls prancing about on the bank of enormous flat-screen televisions, to remind me how tight and small my bottom could never be if I was committed enough and ignored the ice-cream counter by the exit. I worked through my training programme, progressively lifting heavier weights with my gnat's limbs until I could execute press-ups without collapsing to my knees. And as the months before

Sandhurst turned to weeks and days I ran further and further, regularly completing over forty miles a week. By Christmas I was pretty fit, the fittest I've ever been, but no amount of time in Fulham's Holmes Place would fully prepare me for the 'physical demands' of the commissioning course, as I was soon to find out.

My arrival date at Sandhurst was now looming large and I was still remarkably naive about the place. Unlike school and university where I had been with my parents to look prior to applying, Sandhurst continued to be a mystery. My only knowledge came from the glossy brochures I had been given and stories in the press about Princes William and Harry who were both there.

So, with a month to go before I was due to start my new life, I was invited, along with some of the other new recruits, to attend a familiarization visit to the Academy. After my brief exposure into army establishment at Westbury this presented another opportunity for me to experience army food, scratchy blankets and unnecessary shouting whilst also being sized up for the new uniform. Whilst there I was also issued with a new pair of military black leather boots to take away and wear in, so that when I came back a month later to start the commissioning course my feet would already be blistered and raw. As a girl I would never reject a new pair of shoes, but these were not the latest Christian Louboutin killer heels and I've never been less excited to receive new footwear. Big, heavy, clumpy, Doc Martenesque boots. No fine styling and flattering cut. No soft Italian leather. We were shown like four-year-olds how to lace them up (there is a specific technique to reduce pressure and injury) and sent home to break them in.

This Sandhurst visit also gave me my first exposure to marching. An experience that ended in naive catastrophe.

While at Sandhurst all recruits are required to march. Everywhere. At all times. Arms are to be out straight, swinging shoulder high, legs should mark a good pace, as no ambling or bumbling are permitted. Cadets are marched around the Academy in orderly rank and file as a squad with a shouty sergeant at the back barking commands.

Left, right, left, right, left, right.

Arms and legs ticking like a metronome. Heels drilling forcefully into the ground, which for me literally happened as I discovered, in a wobbly, scratchy totter, that you cannot march in high heels.

There was a lot of City girl in me that was going to need transforming into soldier.

The visit concluded with a question and answer session about what to expect at Sandhurst, including lots of helpful little tips like 'bring lots of sports bras' and featured my favourite question of all time: 'Can I bring my horse?'

The answer to which was an even more surprising 'Yes'.

Along with new boots I had also been given an extensive and detailed packing list, so as my days numbered I began to assemble the items on it, plundering supermarket aisles for cleaning products. It soon became apparent that Sandhurst was going to involve a fair amount of scrubbing and polishing. The longest section of the list came under the heading 'Cleaning Kit' and included an exhaustive catalogue of items: Flash, Cif, J-Cloths, Brillo pads, furniture polish, dusters, glass cleaner, Duraglit, Brasso, a Selvyt Silver cleaning cloth, brushes, cloths, black shoe polish (plain and parade gloss), brown shoe polish, tan shoe polish, an ironing board and a good quality steam iron. I began to think that employment as a cleaner at Sandhurst was probably one of the easiest jobs in Surrey, with the cadets doing all the work for you. While the hairnets, hairpins, grips, plain slides, black elastics, strong hair spray and hair wax on the specific females' packing list didn't fill me with joy either.

As the weeks ticked down the new military boots I had been issued remained in their box, laced according to the specific instruction. But I had to get them on and break them in, so Deborah and I packed our warm clothes, Gortex, a thermos flask and a map and headed west to the Brecon Beacons in South Wales, which, when suggested over a couple of drinks in the pub, seemed like a good idea.

Deborah and I have been good friends since university, where she was a member of the mountaineering society. Each term she used to disappear off on weekend expeditions to the Lake District or Snowdonia to get piss-wet through, sleeping in a tent, while I preferred the warmth and comforts of the university's indoor swimming pool, my own bed, four walls and a roof over my head. But Debs loved it; she was an outdoor enthusiast and knew what she was doing when it came to mountains and harsh conditions. I didn't. During our summer holidays she had spent weeks in the Arctic sampling ice cores and lichen, while I sought the beaches of Thailand. Deborah had trekked in the jungles of South America, the Alps and Himalayas, while I preferred to bob about in a boat instead. And she had all the gear too: down jacket, gaiters, Scarpa boots, GPS. She was the perfect companion for a boot-breaking mission to Brecon. But Brecon is a formidable part of the country whatever the season, and in late December it was particularly austere; these hills are not used as the selection ground for the Special Forces for no reason, and only a matter of contours up Pen-y-Fan it soon became apparent that the slopes of South Wales's highest mountain were an ill-advised terrain choice for breaking in my brand-new boots. So with blisters forming, we had to retreat back to the burger van and after a bacon sandwich and a shoe change, we managed a happy day in the hills but my primary aim still remained unachieved, as the boots remained in their box in the boot of my car.

There are many theories on how best to break in new boots. The favourite and widely practised is to tape up your feet with medical tape, letting the tape take all the painful rubbing rather than tender skin; some wear two pairs of socks for the same reason, or socks over tights as one soldier once advised me, although I suspect this has more to do with the wearing of ladies' hosiery than blister prevention. Alternatively there are those who try to soften the leather by standing in the bath or use leather conditioner, Dubbin, or urinate in them. The privileged few could ask their manservant to wear them in for them or alternatively, if the whole process is simply too painful, there is always the Navy, where they wear shoes.

As my arrival date at Sandhurst grew closer and the career switch more of a reality, the complete transformation I was embarking on became increasingly apparent. Around me I saw life choices I would no longer be able to make. Doors shut on expensive beach holidays, Alpine chalets and the dream of owning a big country pile. I would no longer be able to afford my shoe and handbag habit, as my spending would have to adjust. As I downsized my car and mortgage, I realized that money meant more than just the materialistic greed I despised in the City. It meant not being able to provide for my children as my parents had for me. No head start with a public school education.[6] No far-flung family holidays. No large home. Having been in a position where I could provide all this for my progeny, was I now being selfish in giving it up? I began to recognize the enormous gravity of what I was doing and, as the importance of this sank in, I had doubts.

But if I didn't go to Sandhurst now I knew I'd regret it for ever, so I packed up my Fulham flat and moved my worldly possessions into my parents' attic (where far too much of it still lies), and, on the first Sunday of 2007, with boots broken in, countless cleaning products packed, City

---

6 The Army do provide financial support for boarding school education as a 'continuity of education allowance', which ensures that the education of forces children is not disturbed when their parents are continually posted and move. However, this expensive provision is increasingly under budgetary threat.

job resigned and my name removed from all social activity lists, I was as ready as I could be to drive to Sandhurst.

And what lay in store for me was beyond even the wildest of my preconceptions.

THE SHOCK OF CAPTURE

I woke shortly after five o'clock on my first morning at Sandhurst instantly regretting the folly of decisions that resulted in my being there. My alarm clock rang out a digitized bleep that couldn't be ignored, so I crawled out of bed and the sheer enormity of what I'd done overwhelmed me like the January frost encrusting the parade square outside. Suddenly the prospect of ironing a work shirt, putting on a suit and enduring whatever delays the District Line had in store wasn't so unappealing. Outside it was still pitch black and would remain so for a further three hours until the bleak winter dawn, but already lights were flickering on in windows across Old College as the Sandhurst inmates began their day. I would happily have swapped my night of fretful sleep and the twisted knot of apprehension weighing heavily in my stomach for all the stresses of my old life that Monday morning, but there was no time for me to dwell and rue, because in the echoing corridor voices could be heard shouting with urgency.

'Get on parade!'

I shuffled around my room, putting on slippers and dressing gown, drifting bleary eyed into the stark fluorescent lighting to line up for the 'water parade', something that was to become ritual over the next five weeks.

I couldn't believe I was actually here.

'Shit.'

*

I had arrived at Sandhurst the previous afternoon in my small Volkswagen Polo. The car was crammed with belongings – ironing board, crates of cleaning products, sports equipment and things I misguidedly thought would be useful – leaving a small space on the passenger seat for Deborah who was coming along to check out the men under the guise of moral support. She successfully distracted me on our drive south with jelly babies and Girls Aloud's *Greatest Hits* and, before I knew it, I had driven through Staff College Gates and taken directions to park on the parade square.

I found an empty space, pulled on the handbrake, switched off the ignition and gulped in a deep breath. Inside my chest my heart began a gut-wrenching thump as I realized my vision had become overwhelmingly obscured, for there in front of me rose the intimidating splendour of Old College. A striking piece of military architecture, its sheer scale and grandeur were truly terrifying. Magnificent tall Doric columns framed the portico of the Grand Entrance, which was keenly watched over by Mars and Minerva, the gods of war and wisdom. And on either side of the main entrance steps sat six polished brass cannons that had been captured from the French at the Battle of Waterloo. It was enormously impressive and the building's imposition reminded me of a dictator's palace, where indeed the corridors and rooms subsequently proved to house a number of malign despots too.

By the time I reached the main entrance my nerves had me in a full, cold sweat despite the bitter January chill. At the top of the steps stood a tall impressive man in exceedingly smart uniform, his shoes polished to mirrored perfection, brass buckle and buttons gleaming in the winter sun. He stood with proud poise, every vertebra extended to the fullest, his chest puffed out, exuding gravitas and importance. Towering over me, he swallowed my tiny palm as I shook his strong bear paw of a hand. Welcoming me to the Academy he ushered me inside. A seasoned warrior with a chest of campaign medals, this was one of the most senior soldiers in the British Army, the Royal Military Academy Sandhurst sergeant major; a man to be equally respected and feared.

Once inside I joined a queue of other fresh-faced, apprehensive individuals while Deborah gathered with parents and the Academy commandant for biscuits, tea and a welcoming address, frantically waving away people who mistook her for another one of the new recruits and thought she was in the wrong place. I joined the tail end of a queue and stood silently in the corridor, waiting my turn to register, shifting my weight uncomfortably in my heels, as I felt awkwardly out of place. I listened to the only noise echoing from those high corridor walls – the icy sound of metal-tipped boots clacking on the worn stone floor as another stiffly smart uniformed man paced back and forth with slow foreboding.

Clack . . . Clack . . . Clack.

I thought about turning to flee.

Standing in the still silence of that corridor, I felt as though I was about to be thrown into the lions' den for a conclusive mauling. This was the calm before the storm. The sergeants circled the queue, eyeing up their new prey like vultures picking off the lame. And as soon as check-in was complete, they gathered the new recruits up, and marshalled them away, herding them along the warren of corridors and staircases that led to the rear of the College.

As we stood quietly in the queue, one sergeant pointed his shiny brass-tipped pace stick at the chest of a wide-eyed suited young man, barely older than a boy. 'Wave goodbye to Mummy and Daddy,' he said. 'You're all mine now.'

Dawdling and happy to wait my turn, I eventually reached the front of the queue, which had wound its way inside a formally decorated room where a desk was positioned, behind which sat a stern-looking lady, also in uniform, hunched over sheets of paper and name badges.

'Name?' she snapped at me, without looking up from her pieces of paper.

'Héloïse. Héloïse Goodley,' I said, forgetting that the army don't use first names.

'Miss Goodley.' She ran her pen down the page, hovering over the names until she found mine. 'Imjin Company. Yellow badge.' And with that she crossed my name from her list and the sergeant next to her handed me a yellow pin badge with the name 'GOODLEY' printed on it. I took it and vacantly looked around the room for where I should go to next.

'Follow Staff Sergeant Cox,' she chipped, with a karate-chop point of her hand, directing me towards another woman now standing by the door and dismissing me to make way for the next person in line. And with that I was swept up, chivvied through a side door and bundled back onto the parade square to get in my car and move it away from the grandeur at the front of Old College and around to the functioning business end at back. Away from the imposing columns and cannon to the rear quarters. Away from the calm and formality of the grand portico, and the polished, pressed perfection of the Academy sergeant major, to my new life. To board the Sandhurst roller-coaster. And there would be no stopping, no let up and no going back. I didn't even get the chance to say goodbye to Deborah who, having drained her china cup of tea, had to find her own way back to London, wandering through the streets of Camberley until she found the train station. She left me a lasting voicemail message of encouragement and luck on my mobile phone.

There is significance to this arrival at Sandhurst, walking up Old College steps and through the Grand Entrance, since the next time cadets do this is amidst great pomp and ceremony eleven months later when they commission from the Academy into the army as officers. Until then the doors are closed and the steps strictly out of bounds (unless maybe you've attended a fancy-dress party in roller skates, it's dark and no one is looking).

Over 800 cadets a year walk up Old College steps and assemble for the commissioning course; split annually into three intakes (the mustard-keen straight-from-university crowd tend to join in September, while the sunshine intake go in January when the big field exercises fall in the summer months and the laissez-faire faction take the plunge in May having avoided the previous two). Each intake is sorted into three infantry style companies of ninety, named in memory of famous battle honours. My Commissioning Course, the first of 2007 (CC071), would be named in recognition of post-world-war encounters at Malaya, the Falklands and my own easy company, Imjin. Ahead of us were Ypres, Somme and Gaza for the bloodbaths of the First World War and Normandy, Burma and Alamein, a reminder of the ferocity of the Second World War.

For me, as I walked up those steps the umbilical cord was cut; over the next few months I was about to be delivered into the military and my midwife for the traumatic process was a female staff sergeant, the pugnacious SSgt[7] Cox. On the whole, senior ranking female soldiers are a frightening breed. They joined the army in the days when women didn't and have tenaciously fought their way to the top of their game, repeatedly fighting to prove their worth. This has hardened them, stamping out all empathy and compassion, the ideal prerequisite for effectively inducing civilian girls into the military at Sandhurst.

---

7 The accepted abbreviation for staff sergeant.

Those first few days at the Academy became a total blur and my memory of them is selectively imperfect. I found myself gripped by the shock of capture amidst a haze of finding my way and uncomfortably wading out of my depth as the Sandhurst machine rapidly cranked into action, dragging me disorientated with it. The conversion from civilian to soldier is a painful one and the initial five weeks are particularly hard. They are designed to mimic the basic training that thousands of young men and women recruited into the soldier ranks undergo at various training establishments around the country annually; except soldiers admirably complete a full fourteen weeks of the ceaseless hell. This initial basic training involved a strict draconian regime of continuous harassment and borstal-like practices. Discipline would be harsh and sleep at a premium, as our days were consumed by hours of toil: cleaning, ironing, scrubbing and polishing.

It was intense and deeply dispiriting.

My femininity was stripped away from me, as tailored suit was replaced with drab khaki coveralls (until my uniform would be issued), my long hair was scraped and pinned back into a face-liftingly tight bun, while jewellery, perfume and make-up were gravely forbidden, consigned to my civilian persona, which would not be seen for a while.

I was one of thirty-two girls who started Sandhurst that winter, assembled together into a platoon known as Eleven Platoon. We comprised a motley collection of predominantly university graduates, some school-leavers, ex-serving soldiers, two foreign cadets and me.

I was the only military debutante among this number, everyone else having either attended the Officer Training Corps[8] at university, the Army Cadet Force,[9] Welbeck[10] or served with the Territorial or regular army as soldiers. I had no prior military experience and in those first five weeks I was enormously disadvantaged, relying heavily on the kind patience and generosity of the others to guide me.

We represented a broad spectrum of individuals, from plump to petite, wealthy to working class. Almost a foot in height separated the tallest and shortest among us. There was a wide range of physical abilities too, with no common physique on display to typify the Army girl. Some could run the mile-and-a-half army fitness test in just eight minutes while others took over twelve. But what was quickly apparent was that we all shared a common courage and mental resolve. A tenacity and a will to keep going. Those that didn't wouldn't survive.

Initially everyone was very friendly, in that way people are when they join a new group. Slightly false and overly keen to quickly make new friends. I went around introducing myself, shaking hands and hearing everyone's name, later forgetting them all, and thankful for the nametags that we had to wear. Despite the high concentration of women in close proximity there was no

---

8 University Officer Training Corps (OTC) is an army club where university students can pick up all their bad habits before they go to Sandhurst.

9 The Army Cadet Force is the 50,000 strong army youth organization for twelve-to eighteen-year-olds.

10 Welbeck Defence College is a mini Sandhurst where sixth-form students can study for their A-levels while also marching and being shouted at.

time for bitchiness at Sandhurst. We all had to get along together over the next year or we would fall apart, and if there was someone you didn't like it was just going to make life harder.

The indignities of this basic training saw my humanity stripped to its bare essentials, as life became a daily struggle for survival under the oppressive regime. Almost every action seemed punishable as I became moulded from a carefree civilian into a soldier. We marched everywhere, even inside, up and down the corridors, slouching was forbidden, no hands in pockets, no leaning against walls, only speaking when spoken to; being late was the most grave of offences. Press-ups were the favoured tool used to teach most of these lessons, and as the weeks went by I got quite good at them.

As well as years of beating men at their own game SSgt Cox had been further hardened by her northern roots and Hull upbringing. She implemented a painfully strict reign and the first of her repressive rules was the banning of chocolate and mobile phones. The implication of doing this to a group of girls was catastrophic, and with the joy of texting and the serotonin release from a bar of Cadbury's Fruit & Nut unattainable, morale quickly plummeted. This became further compounded when we realized that we were interned at the Academy for five long unremitting weeks until we could demonstrate the requisite standard of marching skill to 'pass off the square' and would be allowed home for the first time.

Although not very tall in stature, SSgt Cox more than compensated for this with a powerful punch and terrifying pitch in her raised voice, which could make hounds whimper and hide. Her uniform was always pristine and immaculately pressed, her boots (though only about a size three) were polished to perfection, while her dark hair was always gelled flawlessly to her head, and wound up at the back into a firm bun, with never a stray hair free to flutter in the breeze. A career spent surrounded by men in the army had sharpened her tongue to a razor wit too and she could cut down any male who dared to stand in her path. And years of military marching had given her a masculine gait, with any trace of a feminine hip swish eliminated, leaving a boot-crashing stomp.

I was petrified of SSgt Cox. When whipped into a rage she was as terrifying as a baited bear, and in those first five weeks I gave her plenty of reason to become angered. She ruled our every waking and sleeping hour. In her presence the platoon maintained a fretful watch, desperately not wanting to incur her wrath and avoiding her attentive glare at all times. So like a lightly sleeping monster, we tiptoed carefully around her in the shadows, not wanting to draw attention nor awaken her from her moments of calm to be punished with yet more press-ups.

Even to speak to SSgt Cox you had to successfully get through a pantomime of staged formalities. If she was to be found in her office I would have to march up to the office doorway, arms straight and outstretched, shoulder high, coming to a halt exactly at the office entrance with a 'check, one, two', foot stamp, then freeze to attention. And then request politely, 'Leave to enter, Staff Sergeant, please.' Which sounds all rather straightforward, except it isn't. I simply could not do it. I would muddle my halt, stamp with the wrong foot, gauge the distances wrongly or fluff my lines. Every time. The pressure was unbearable. And each time SSgt Cox would send me back to try again, three, four, five, six times over.

'Go back and try that again, Miss Goodley,' she would say as I did a Michael Flatley hopping skip in her doorway.

'Again, Miss Goodley.' An irate undertone in her voice, as I swung an errant arm into the door frame.

'No, Miss Goodley. Check, one, two.' Her patience would be wearing thinner and her voice pitching higher with each of my attempts. Until finally she popped: 'MISS GOODLEY, GET AWAY FROM ME AND DON'T COME BACK UNTIL YOU CAN SHAGGING WELL DO IT PROPERLY!' she would scream in full falsetto, the veins in her forehead pulsating as she yelled in frustration at me.

Each time my burning question for her became less and less important as the humiliation of not being able to execute the simplest routine shamed me to the point of wanting the ground to swallow me whole. I had a university degree. I had been a City professional. I used to advise on the future of FTSE 100 companies and now I was being belittled and torn to shreds by a small woman from Hull.

And then eventually when the day came that I did get it right, I danced a celebratory jig, which unleashed her fury anyway, getting me into even more trouble. And more press-ups.

A typical day in those first five weeks started with a rude awakening at the deathly early time of 5.15, an hour when only bakers, milkmen and people going on skiing holidays ought sensibly to be awake. I would painfully extricate myself from bed and my first action of the day was to switch on my iron.

Our beds comprised a simple single iron bed frame with plain wooden headboard, firm mattress and army-issued bedlinen of rough white cotton sheets and scratchy woollen blankets. All this had to be carefully ironed and crease free each day, then the bed made with meticulous exactness for the morning inspection. Folding angled 'hospital corners', turning down the sheet and tightly tucking it in, no evidence of the bed having been slept in was to remain, not a stray hair on the pillow nor a crinkle in the sheets. Many people slept on the floor for good reason, but with sleep at such a premium and bed being one of few luxuries, I persisted in ironing my sheets each morning, cutting corners by leaving them still on the bed as I did so. This went disastrously wrong one morning for one of the girls as she sleepily dropped her blistering hot iron onto her bare foot.

At 5.25 we were to be lined up in the main corridor of our Platoon Lines in alphabetical order, me sandwiched between Gill and Gray, with a full litre water bottle for the daily 'water parade'. This would then commence on the arrival of SSgt Cox at 5.30, when we would tunelessly sing the national anthem and then drink the entire litre of water, choking and spluttering it down, so that at a completely inopportune moment later in the morning we would all be bursting for the loo. Over the weeks variety was introduced to this morning service as we were required to learn all six verses of the British national anthem and those too of our foreign cadets (Nepalese before breakfast is especially demanding).

Then, with the Queen sent 'happy and glorious' by our cats' chorus, we were dismissed in a hurried panic of dressing gowns and slippers to shower, dress and race to breakfast. The boys were also required to squeeze the nuisance of shaving into these precious few minutes and those who had once proudly cultivated premature sprigs of stubble at fourteen were cursing as the baby-faced blonds had grace. At Sandhurst the men must be clean-shaven at all times, including even when in the field on exercise, and stringent stubble and sideburn rules are applied. If facial hair is your preference then the Navy is the service for you.

Breakfast was a swift moment at the trough, in which we had to consume as many calories as possible in the allotted four minutes to sustain us through the morning of standing to attention in the freezing cold. Then we all traipsed outside into the darkness for another utterly bizarre Sandhurst ritual: 'Areas'.

Areas involves a litter sweep of an allocated part of the Academy grounds, and Eleven Platoon's area was the western side of Old College Parade Square stretching all the way down to the tennis courts. As a platoon we were required to walk methodically around our area and collect any unsightly litter and dispose of it; except that it was always dark at this ungodly early hour and this was

Sandhurst so in fourteen weeks I never once found anything on the parade square other than a fallen leaf. It was a completely pointless activity and characteristic of many duties we performed at the Academy.

Then after this the cleaning began.

Most mornings were room-inspection mornings and this included the Platoon Lines too. Some highly organized OTC keen-bean had divided up the cleaning tasks in the common areas and created a rota of 'block jobs'. Operating in a three-week rotation, I escaped surprisingly well, being only required to polish the brass on the inside of the main door, the outside of the main door and then sweep the central corridor. To my great relief, my name was not in the rotation to clean the showers of stray hairs nor scrub the toilets. Again I felt the cleaners actually employed to clean Sandhurst got off very lightly.

One morning, as I swept the ruddy red linoleum flooring with a wooden broom, forming small piles of mud and dust before the London stock market had even opened, I thought how drastically different my life had become. I was waking even earlier now than when I had worked in London. I was certainly getting shouted at more. And my appearance had transformed too. My City friends would barely recognize my uniformed self. Former chic shoes had given way to ogreish boots, while City fashions had been replaced with unshapely combats and my hair was now scraped tightly back and wound away. After just a few weeks I realized that the army was already changing me.

*

My room in Old College was a high-ceilinged modest abode, in contrast with the grand opulence of the staterooms to the front of the College. Devoid of character and individuality, it was simply furnished with a wardrobe, a bare desk, a chest of drawers and bookshelves empty except for a Bible. A heavy white porcelain sink hung from the wall below a mirror and a single tall window filled the room with winter light. The floor was covered with dark-red bristly carpet tiles and the cream walls remained unfurnished apart from a small grey lockable safe in which I hid the contraband chocolate my grandmother sent me.

Prison cells contain more.

For an inspection, the room's contents had to be displayed according to a prescribed layout. Everything hung in the wardrobe in a specific order, shoes aligned exactly and drawers were progressively pulled out in a stepped manner, revealing a cascading sequence of T-shirts, jumpers and 'smiling socks' (folded with the bundle-fold facing up in a smile rather than sadly downwards, as I felt). We were allowed a few basic personal belongings: a radio that had to be tuned to BBC Radio 4, a hairbrush and minimal toiletries. Every item of clothing had to be meticulously ironed, with creases down the sleeves and trouser legs and folded garments were to be precisely to the dimensions of A4 paper. All surfaces had to be clean, polished and dust free, the carpet vacuumed, the mirror shining without blemish and the sink dry and spotless. The crates of cleaning products I had brought with me were soon put to good use.

For an inspection issued items of military kit were displayed on the shelves including mess tins, cutlery, water bottles and magazines;[11] along with a set of unused 'show home' toiletries as a squeezed toothpaste tube or used toothbrush were fallible offences. On the bed would be the white Number One 'Blues' Dress[12] belt with its polished brass buckle, navy-blue and red Blues forage cap (a magnet for dust) and shiny black Blues shoes. All displayed for scrutiny.

Hours of preparation were required for the inspection, causing us to work late into the night ironing and folding each item of clothing with great care, polishing mess tins, brass buckles, shoes and anything else that could be forced to shine, while the room was cleansed of dust. The following morning after breakfast there would then be a frenzy of activity in the moments before the inspection began, adding final touches and titivating to perfection. A quick blast of furniture polish and flurry with a yellow duster, a wipe down and dry of the sink, fix the window open to the specified four-inch gap and plump pillows: it was like preparing a potential medal-winning garden for the Judges' Committee at the Chelsea Flower Show.

---

11 Sadly not *Cosmopolitan* or *Marie Claire*, these are the slim metal canisters which hold rifle ammunition and fix onto the rifle. They consist of a metal container, spring mechanism and metal holding plate, all readily disposed to rusting and quite tricky to clean. We were issued with eight of them and for an inspection they all had to be broken down into their component parts and displayed, lightly oiled and rust free.

12 Number One 'Blues' Dress, or Blues was our super smart tailored uniform, worn on special occasions, which usually involved lots of marching.

Then, like a lion spotted on the prairie, we'd all stop what we were doing and scurry into position at SSgt Cox's arrival, standing 'at ease' outside our rooms. The whole inspection was carefully stage-managed and as she burst into the corridor we all 'braced up', springing to attention as she approached our individual rooms and announcing name, rank and army number (which I was still learning and would become terribly tongue-tied with under the pressure of her glare).

'Whiskey, one, zero, six, one, four, five, one, Officer Cadet Goodley. Room ready for your inspection.'

I then stood outside in the corridor facing away and holding my breath as she prowled around my room finding fault: litter in the bin, laundry in the linen basket, water in the sink, a speck of toothpaste on the mirror, a trace of mud on the sole of a running shoe. As I stood outside in the corridor I was unable to see what was going on inside and would look to the face of the person standing opposite me for an expression to indicate how the inspection was going, waiting for a little nod or sideways eye movement. Was SSgt Cox looking in the wardrobe or simply out of the window? The longer the silence, the greater the tension as I awaited her verdict; which was always a fail.

Misdemeanours were slight but the punishments severe as all my hard work would come crashing out into the corridor, pulled down off shelves, flung out of drawers or hauled out of the window into the puddles below, leaving me to pick up the pieces and start the ironing, folding and cleaning all over again in time for the following morning's inspection.

The mercurial moods of SSgt Cox made every morning a gamble to see what she would fail you for, as she hunted through drawers and cupboards looking for imperfections. Then when she found something she would gleefully pounce at it and tear you apart, like a terrier with a rat.

'Miss Goodley, what do you shagging call this?' she barked at me one morning, brandishing my water bottle under my nose.

'Er, it's my water bottle, Staff Sergeant.'

'No, you idiot, this, here inside your water bottle.' She pointed at a tiny drop of water near the rim where my water bottle hadn't yet dried out following that morning's water parade.

'Erm, it's water from this morning, Staff Sergeant.'

'I don't want your shagging excuses, Miss Goodley,' she said, scolding me like a young child. 'It's gopping.[13] If you don't clean out your water bottle, it'll breed germs, you'll go down in the field with scurvy and die. And it'll be your own fault for being so f-ing gopping,' she screeched, tossing the offending water bottle on the floor of my room and spinning on her heel to storm off and attack her next victim, leaving me relieved another inspection was over, but questioning my understanding of the causes and infective severity of scurvy.

The worst inspections were on the occasions when SSgt Cox was accompanied by our platoon commander, Captain Trunchbull.

---

13 'Gopping' isn't in the Oxford English Dictionary yet, but my understanding is that SSgt Cox meant its use to convey something that was contemptible, soiled and disgusted her.

Captain Trunchbull was a bulky, angry lady, with a most vicious tongue and flaky temperament. As strong as an ox, she towered over each member of Eleven Platoon in a frightening manner. On duty she wore her ill-fitting uniform stretched taut over her plump backside and constricted in tightly at her waist with a belt, like a knotted sack of spuds. Like SSgt Cox she too, scraped and gelled her hair back into a small bun fixed smartly to the back of her head like a button none of us would ever dare press. Across her lips she maintained a permanent disapproving pout as she scowled and prowled around the Academy, poised like a jack-in-the-box ready to spring with menacing terror at anything she disapproved of.

SSgt Cox and Captain Trunchbull made a terrible twosome, working in tandem as they scrutinized each room, goading one another like a pair of Roald Dahl's witches.

'SSgt Cox, would you say you could see your face in this mess tin? It doesn't look very shiny to me.'

'Nah, ma'am, it's gopping.'

And then smashing out into the corridor would come the offending mess tin.

'Oh dear, SSgt Cox, this looks like rust on here to me. Here on this magazine.'

'Certainly is, ma'am.'

And another clatter as rifle magazines, springs and metal came smashing out into the corridor as the cackling couple would move on, revelling perversely in the moment. This charade would go on from room to room until the corridor was full of an assortment of clothes, shoes, rifle magazines, mess tins, spilled washing powder and other military paraphernalia.

Not all of us saw the seriousness in this whole charade. The more experienced, the Welbexians and ex-rankers, had been through the rigmarole of a room inspection countless times before. For years they had stood to attention at the end of their beds in basic training or the army Sixth-Form College, as the contents of their lockers and bed space were vandalized, their effort and hard work strewn across the floor and trampled over. They knew it was all a game. They didn't seek logic in the strange false drama as I did. They knew we would all fail and were blasé about it.

One was Officer Cadet Van der Merwe (Merv). She occupied the room at the furthest end of my corridor and had been to Welbeck and Shrivenham, the military university. She was completely unfazed by SSgt Cox and Captain Trunchbull. She didn't get tongue-tied in the pressure of their glare, she didn't stumble when reciting her Army number, she could march and halt in the doorway of SSgt Cox's office. She knew how to fold hospital corners and smiling socks. For her the ironing and folding was effortless, her shoes shone the brightest, and there was never a hair on her head out of place. Because at twenty-three, she was already a veteran of the institution.

As I sprang to attention outside my room and SSgt Cox and Captain Trunchbull disappeared inside scoffing to one another, Merv would play the fool in the corridor outside. She would leap up and down performing an elaborate dance routine, she would lie prostrate on the floor and wiggle like a worm, or tiptoe up the corridor as far as she dared before dashing back, to stand to attention outside her own room again. My blood would race each time she did this, my heart pounding at the wrath she would incur if caught. The brazen risk. Her foolhardy guts. Merv wasn't bothered.

Before long the rest of us realized room inspections were indeed all a game too and after a few further inspections eventually learned some of the rules which allowed us to play along. The trick, we discovered, was to leave an obvious fault: a hair on a pillow, dust on the windowsill, or frowning pair of socks, thus allowing the achievement of the real purpose, which was to find flaw in our work no matter what. The army upholds impeccably high standards, and these inspections imbue that at an early stage, encouraging recruits to have pride in themselves and what they do. Poor personal hygiene and slack discipline in the field would be far more costly than in barracks, whilst picking up the pieces each morning and starting all over again also instil a fighting resolve and determination to keep carrying on. Obviously at the time I didn't recognize any of this and found it all tediously pointless, struggling to appreciate how it was preparing me to command and lead soldiers.

If the turmoil of a pre-dawn start and drama of the room inspection hadn't yet broken me, then the two hours of merciless drill until lunch would defeat any remaining will I had to continue.

Drill is military marching, in rank and file, and is a seriously big deal at Sandhurst, occupying an inordinate amount of our time. Hours of our lives were wasted pacing around the Parade Square to barked drill commands.

Historically, drill was used as an organized way of moving troops around the battlefield, preventing individuals from becoming mixed up with other units. Drill formed the foundations of discipline in battle, making armies more effective to command. It was all about instilling attention to detail and responding to orders. But at Sandhurst it felt as though it was used as a perverse form of punishment.

Anyone who has watched the Changing of the Guard at Buckingham Palace will understand the resplendence of a polished drill performance. The soldiers perfectly coordinated and disciplined, marching tall and proud, their movements in unison. Cameras flashing through the iron Palace railings, as guardsmen call out the commands in immaculate ceremonial uniforms, red tunics with bearskins balanced on their heads, drawing in the tourist dollar. Unfortunately drill during our early days at the Academy was more chaotic car crash than protection of the Queen, as we were shockingly bad at it.

You would think walking along in step with the person next to you would be a fairly undemanding activity, but it isn't. I had safely got myself through school and university but suddenly on Old College Parade Square my brain couldn't compute the difference between left and right. My arms and legs fell out of my control, operating independently to the utter horror of SSgt Cox. For drill is when SSgt Cox became her angriest and shoutiest, as our incompetence whipped her into a frustrated frenzy.

Because on the parade square Eleven Platoon had the disorganization of an Italian ski lift queue, and the smooth cadence of marching troops became a staccato machine gun clatter when we traipsed up and down in front of Old College. Metal tips on the soles of our shoes were intended to create the melodic earthy rhythm of troops in unison, a satisfying clomp, clomp, clomp, but instead they simply exaggerated our disharmony.

Outside in the shivering cold the platoon would form up as an orderly squad, with the tallest girls at the ends and shortest sandwiched in the middle. SSgt Cox would strut to the front from where she barked the commands.

'Platoon!'

Grabbing our attention, we stiffened and smartened up ready to go.

'Platoooooon-shun!'

And we snapped to the position of attention, stamping our feet into the ground, chins lifted up and arms locked straight at our sides.

Then, 'By the right in threes, kweeeeek nah!' (quick march).

And off we went, guided by SSgt Cox shrieking behind us, 'Dufft, dite, dufft, dite, dufft, dite.' (As 'left, right' became in her Hull accent.)

This may all seem fairly straightforward but there was ample room for error: you could stamp with the incorrect foot, set off with the wrong leading leg, have bent arms or, most ghastly of all, tick-tock. Tick-tocking is when arms and legs on the same side of the body move forwards together rather than oppositely. The left leg and left arm swing out mutually in a ridiculous comedy walk that is impossible to correct once entered upon. And on my third day at Sandhurst, in a moment of artless naivety, I was caught in the most horrifying of tick-tocking incidents. Alone in my green coveralls, I was meekly searching for a toilet, bursting from the morning's water parade. I marched around a corner and, with frightful shock, confronted the Academy and Old College sergeant majors on an inspection, two of the most important men at Sandhurst, both guardsmen and drill masters. My heart instantly doubled its beat as terror set in. I tried to appear confident in what I was doing, but my tick-tocking had diverted their scrutiny and I was treated to an unforgettable lesson.

I was especially dreadful at drill. It all went against the natural grain of my wayward limbs and I moved like an ill-disciplined robot. And, unfortunately, awareness of this insanity did not save me from the disease either, as my intractable legs singled me out, drawing attention, wrath and raillery on the parade square. And to stand out on the drill square was most ill advised. Hiding in anonymity was the tactic for much of Sandhurst in those first few months but my droll drill moves thrust me into the corrective glare and I hated it.

Drill sessions began with the dreaded warm-up. Marching at an accelerated breakneck speed to loosen our limbs, hurtling up and down the parade square in double time, arms and legs swinging madly to maintain the percussive rapidity of SSgt Cox's 'dufft, dites'.

'Dufft, dite, dufft, dite, dufft, dite.' And then the shrill: 'ABOUT TURN.'

And we all turned around in a crashing melee.

Left, right. Left, right. Left, right.

Then the complexities of a salute on the march: 'SALUTE.'

Up, two, three, four, down, swing. Poking out eyes and slapping the person next to you as your right arm shot up to your forehead.

Followed by a hopping: 'CHANGE STEP.'

And another. 'CHANGE STEP.'

And another. 'CHANGE STEP.'

And another. Until we were strewn across the parade square, sweating in the frigid January air, legs sore and heels bloodied from the rasping of leather boots, begging for the relief of 'HALT'.

The most feared of drill paces however was the 'mark time'. This was an entirely pointless punishment, which had us all marching on the spot. Thighs raised parallel to the ground, going up, down, up, down, up, down, legs burning with pain as the lactic acid built up. Expending energy yet going nowhere. Stamp, stamp, stamp. On the spot. Eyes forward, chin up, mouth shut. Stamp, stamp, stamp. Steam would rise from us in the chilly January air as we willed it to stop.

As we were put through our paces, SSgt Cox would strut up and down shouting commands and picking out errors: a dipped chin, bent arms, crooked legs, someone out of step, or someone out of time. With the eyes of a hawk she could spot them all and then would dive in and humiliate the offender. Which far too often was me.

'Head up, Miss Goodley. Eyes front. You don't need to look at your feet, they're still there. Get the back of your neck touching your collar.'

'What are you doing, Miss Goodley? You lunatic. Get in step with the rest of the platoon.'

'Come on, Miss Goodley. Left. I said left. All those qualifications and university degree and you can't tell left from right.'

On the drill square SSgt Cox wasn't the only demon in our lives. With the entire Imjin Company being ragged around changing step and marking time, the company sergeant major (CSM) would join the madness and make his presence felt. Company Sergeant Major Porter was a pocket-sized pugilist. A soldier at the top of his game, he was intensely proficient and had years of experience of training clumsy-footed soldiers to march. Shrouded in a long heavy overcoat, pace stick swinging in hand he would peacock around the fringes of the squad scouting for errors and leaping in to correct them.

One morning, as I unwittingly performed a Prussian goosestep, at the halt he swooped in, darting across the parade square as if he owned it, halting sharply in front of me. He swung his pace stick into a hover, a hair's breadth from the tip of my nose, and forced his scrotum through a mangle as he released the most high-pitched squeal.

'What the fuck was that, Miss Goodley? If you can't sort out your shagging legs, I'm going break them both. Then I'll ram this pace stick up your fucking nose and use it to flick you into the lake. You useless idiot.'

I hated being this useless. As the spittle of his anger landed on my cheeks I felt my bottom lip curl. I wanted to cry. I wanted to run away from it all. I wanted to be anywhere but this godforsaken miserable wet parade square. I wanted my easy London life back.

With drill over it was non-stop to lunch.

Each meal time at Sandhurst involved a mass stampede to the dining hall to get to the front of the 270-man queue in order to make the most of the preciously brief time allocated for feeding. Manners and chivalry were forgotten, as people tore along the corridor to queue impatiently boot to boot, craning their necks to see what was available on the hotplate.

The dining hall, known in the army as a 'cookhouse', was the largest room in the College and could comfortably accommodate over 300 people at the long dark oak tables, seated on tall-backed chairs worn smooth from years of bottoms. Around the room, the walls were covered with deep scarlet glazed tiles and adorned with plates of armour, swords and portraits of royalty. Chandeliers hung from the elevated arched ceiling, where lofty narrow stained-glass windows allowed thin shafts of light to reach the diners below. And, for a reason I never quite understood, a glass cabinet took pride of place in the centre of the room containing a large sprawled tiger skin.

Mealtimes were short and there wasn't time to be fussy about dietary needs, as people grabbed whatever was available and wildly wolfed it down as the sergeants stood by the entrance counting down the seconds to summon you back to the servitude. Unfortunately for me, I am a very slow eater and could barely manage a few mouthfuls before SSgt Cox would call us all back out on parade. And at this blistering pace I struggled to consume enough calories to get me through the long days, leaving me perpetually hungry until my grandmother's contraband chocolate parcels arrived. The food was generally good, but quantity was the priority with carbohydrates in abundance and potatoes with everything: new potatoes, roast potatoes, mashed potatoes, sautéed potatoes, boiled potatoes, potato croquettes and chips, chips, chips.

The frantic tempo of training meant we burned up calories fast and the normal three meals a day were simply not enough sustenance so an additional fourth evening meal was provided to get us through the late nights of ironing and polishing.

After lunch there was no let-up. Having already been on the go for eight hours we would gather outside in Chapel Square to be marched off to another lesson in our crash course introduction to the military; there were classes in fieldcraft, map reading, first aid, foot care and weapon training, which was called 'skill at arms'.

In Old College the armoury was tucked away in the basement, and here we would queue in alphabetical order again, me again sandwiched between Gill and Gray, under the hot water pipes in a dimly lit neglected corridor with peeling blue paint, waiting for the armourer to appear with his bunch of keys to unlock and hand out our personal weapons. I clearly remember the first time I was issued my rifle; I held it with great care, like a new parent with a baby, unsure what to make of it. It was designed to kill people and I wasn't especially keen on being part of that. In the army everyone is a trained soldier first, from chefs to doctors, pilots to postmen, and all are required to learn skill at arms in training and pass mandatory weapon handling and firing tests, as anyone could be required to fire their weapon when at war.[14] And standing there awkwardly holding my rifle in my arms brought the reality of this threat a little closer. But first I would need to learn how to use it.

These impossibly important, potentially life-saving skill-at-arms lessons populated much of those early weeks at the Academy, but with cadets working twenty-hour days we were all far too exhausted to comprehend or absorb them. Heads would loll and nod as people battled hopelessly to keep their eyes open and minds focused in the warmth and comfort of the classroom, zoning out as sleep deprivation won over.

When it comes to skill at arms, safety is paramount. I stood awkwardly in the classroom going through the motions of handling the weapon as our instructor barked out commands until the weapon safety drills became ingrained in my muscle memory, like David Beckham taking a penalty kick. I had no deep comprehension of what I was doing: cocking the weapon, peering inside, releasing the working parts forward, firing off the action. I didn't understand the motions but this technique has

---

14 There is one small exception to this: the army's padres are permitted to conduct their work unarmed, protected instead by God.

successfully taught generations of soldier and an understanding of how the rifle actually goes bang is not necessary to safely use it.

We would line up in the classroom dressed for war, helmets and combat webbing on, rifles slung across our chests waiting for the colour sergeant[15] to shout out the command: 'For inspection port arms!'

Safety catch, change lever, sights, cock the weapon, conduct the three-point check.

'Clear ease springs.'

Release the working parts forward, fire off the action, apply safety catch and close the dust cover.

It was all the basic rudimentary stuff of an OTC drill night or cadets' weekend, practised in TA Centres up and down the country weekly. Around me all the girls confidently carried out the movements; they knew where the safety catch was, how to cock the weapon and what they were looking for when peering inside. I took a little more tuition.

'Come on, Miss Goodley,' the colour sergeant would chivvy to me as the rest of the class waited while I fumbled helplessly with the cocking handle. 'We don't have all day for you to work out your arse from your elbow.'

We also learned what to do when firing it on a windy day and how to strip the rifle apart and clean it. We learned how to 'bomb up' a magazine with thirty rounds of

---

15 Colour sergeant (CSgt) is the equivalent rank of staff sergeant but applies only to the infantry. So called because colour sergeants marched into battle carrying the battalion's colours (regimental flag) and staff sergeants carried staffs. Both are one promotion rank above a sergeant.

ammunition in sixty seconds and practised aiming shots at posters of screaming Wehrmacht storm troopers in the dry indoor warmth. It was all clinical and surreal. Lying on the cold hard floor of the classroom, elbows uncomfortably pressed onto concrete, didn't bear any proximity to the rifle's purpose of killing. Danger and death were removed and that suited me just fine.

I liked skill at arms. I liked feeling slightly wary in the clean comforts of a classroom. I liked being separated from the drill square and my ironing board. I liked lying on the floor and looking through the weapon's sights while closing both eyelids instead of one for a nano-sleep. And I liked that Colour sergeant Bicknell, our instructor, was a great big softie and would sneak chocolate biscuits in for us and provide updates on *Celebrity Big Brother* (Jade Goody and Shilpa Shetty were apparently having as bad a time as us).

In those very early days at the Academy we were all strangers. Some of the cadets knew each other from university or school, but on the whole we were on our own. For those first few nights I would get into my bed and stare into the unfamiliar darkness around me, feeling quite alone in the strange surroundings. A strange room, strange people, a strange way of life. It wasn't like starting any other new job and harder than the first days at a new school. At the end of the day, there could be no retreat back to the domestic comforts and relaxed surrounds of home; I was trapped here, along with everyone else. But as the days progressed we soon got to know each other, as numbers became names and faces became characters.

There was Merv, the institutional veteran who knew it was all a game. There was Evans who had already served as a soldier in Iraq, and showed me how to fold hospital corners. There were Gill and Gray who flanked me on parade, and Rhodes who was an ironing-folding whizz and the room inspection queen. Allinson was in my skill-at-arms class and would whisper helpfully to me as I fumbled through the drills and Lea was the naughty one in our number, always being punished with press-ups for her misdemeanours. So despite starting out on my own, I wasn't alone for long as we were lumped together in the thick of it and friendships began to form.

The average age was around twenty-three, as most people typically arrived following university, or after serving some time in the ranks as a soldier. And at twenty-seven I was the oldest in Eleven Platoon, though not the oldest in CC071, as a couple of the boys neared their thirtieth birthdays. At the opposite end of the age spectrum, there was young pup Peters, who was just eighteen, having joined straight from school. While at times I found her schoolgirl naivety frustrating as she still flirted with the new excitement of alcohol and boys, the large age gap between us didn't matter. We were both in it together and indeed in those first few weeks Peters was a better and more experienced cadet than me, as she was already a hardy Army Cadet Force veteran. I found my older age to be irrelevant at Sandhurst and its anomaly was not as unusual as you may first think, since more and more people like myself are making the career U-turn and joining the army. Barristers, bankers, teachers, lawyers – plenty jump ship to enlist. In the boys' platoons there was even a former professional surfer and Singapore nightclub stripper.

One lesson we quickly learned in those first few weeks was that our skills were varied, and in order to get through the commissioning course we were going to have to work together as a team. Those who could fold folded, those who could iron ironed and those who could do drill showed the rest of us, as the platoon clubbed together realizing that collectively we were greater than the sum of our parts. The fostering of this team spirit is one of the marvels of the training process we were in. Sandhurst forced us to build a team, otherwise we would never be able to reach our goal. We were all in it together and all had to muck along. Unfortunately for me I was still searching for my talent to share; I couldn't do any of the things that mattered in those first few weeks and became reliant on the others to help me out, leaving me feeling like the platoon's handicap.

Among my many ineptitudes was shoe shining.

As you might imagine, the military is big on shiny shoes. The sergeants who ran Sandhurst were like magpies drawn to glint and shine. Brass glistened, buttons twinkled, metal shone and floors were polished. And shiny shoes were an especial favourite. Hours were spent on it. And the bane of achieving and maintaining a glistening mirrored surface that SSgt Cox could see her face in was continuous, as we scuffed it away each day on the drill square. We were all issued with two pairs of lace-up brogues, one black and one brown, which were made of dull leather; our task was to convert this into a sparkling patent shine. So each evening when the marching and shouting had stopped, we spent hours in 'bulling parades' trying to perfect it. The entire platoon sat on the floor in the corridor outside our rooms, passing around contraband sweets, patiently applying layers of shoe polish and making gently sweeping circles with a damp cloth in an effort to achieve the smooth glassy surface required to pass SSgt Cox's scrutinizing eye. My shoes spent precious more time on my hands than feet as they assumed almost religious properties. But shoe polishing is a black art and proved to be something else I was incapable of, Merv and Allinson taking it in turns to make the magic happen for me.

Even Sunday wasn't a day of rest at Sandhurst.

We were given the luxury of a brief lie-in until 7 a.m., but straight after breakfast were lined up on parade for a service in the Academy Chapel and, this being Sandhurst, the occasion still involved ironing, polishing, marching and an inspection, this time of us.

Inspections of our turnout were regular and, as well as perfectly pressed clothes and shiny shoes, our hair came in for scrutiny too. Large quantities of hairspray and hair gel, not seen since the eighties, were used to glue each stray strand to our heads in a slicked-back bun like those of SSgt Cox and Captain Trunchbull, which were held tightly with a hairnet. For church a forage cap was perched atop, which refused to sit squarely on my head, insisting on drifting askew.

Captain Trunchbull would arrive smartly in her Blues, sword clinking by her side, to take the inspection, as we all stood stiffly to attention in the freezing cold. She would slowly move along the ranks, picking fluffs of dust, strands of hair and adjusting forage caps, as we all stood chattering with cold until the purpose of messing us around on a Sunday morning had been achieved and we were gratefully dismissed inside the Chapel. Once inside the men had to remove their hats but we ladies wore ours, to great advantage. When tipped slightly forwards on our heads the forage cap peak masked your eyes, so with head bowed in prayer no one need know that I was having a sneaky sleep. God knew I was in need of it.

Sunday didn't stop there either and after lunch we put on our most restrictive uncomfortable clothes for running in and went orienteering. Thick cardboard cotton rugby shirts were tucked into olive, high-waisted trousers that held water when wet, clinging to the skin, and were called 'light-weights' with irony. And so, with compass and map in hand, and dressed like Enid Blyton's Famous Five we trotted off into the woods in search of checkpoints. In the first few weeks, the orienteering courses were run around the grounds of the Academy, but they later progressed to outside in the surrounding area and this involved something of great excitement – leaving the Academy.

All 270 cadets boarded a convoy of coaches that snaked its way out of the Academy gates. We peered out of the window with wonderment at normal life, like shrouded East German communists crossing Checkpoint Charlie. Everyday people walking the dog, shopping at Tesco, holding hands and talking on mobile phones. No one was marching, men had beards, people wore denim and clothes without creases. I gazed longingly at them, deeply jealous of their ordinary freedom.

Sundays also brought a small slice of faux-freedom to look forward to each week, as in the evenings we were afforded the opportunity to run our car engines over, to prevent the batteries from being as dead as we would be at the end of week five. Every Sunday night, in the darkness, for half an hour the Academy roads became gridlocked as cars cruised slowly around camp adhering to the twenty miles per hour speed limit. Each week I would savour this moment, turning up the volume on the Girls Aloud CD, singing loudly and biting the heads off the jelly babies Deborah had left in the glovebox. There, behind the wheel of my car, I felt normal again: no ironing, no polishing, no marching, no one shouting at me. For just a short while I was cocooned in a blissful bubble.

The crippling routine in these first five weeks was endless and incessant. Days fused together as January became February and I lost track of time, falling out of touch with the outside world. Our days seemed filled with the most inane brainless activities: hospital corners, smiling socks, shining shoes, hairspray and fluff. I couldn't see how any of this was readying me for the challenges of war, or what exactly it was teaching me about command and leadership. It all felt so meaningless and required zero intellectual concentration; inside my head my brain was shrivelling to an obedient, saluting, nodding nothing as we were becoming institutionalized. We all slept in identical bedrooms, wore identical clothing, behaved in an identical manner and were being prescribed an identical way to live our lives. To stand out was a dangerous heresy. Independent free thought was discouraged, as we were being turned into submissive orders-obeying clones. I began to question what I was doing here. Had I made the right decision giving up a well-paid City career for this? I wasn't even good at any of it.

As a military virgin I was struggling too, everything was new to me, and I was pretty terrible at all the important stuff: marching, saluting, shoe shining, weapon handling. At least the others had the prescience of OTC or Cadets so their learning curve wasn't as steep and they already knew how to play the game, but I was floundering like a fish on a line and it was draining my self-confidence. I couldn't adjust. I craved some individual freedom and, having been accustomed to vague successes in life, I found it particularly difficult being placed firmly at the bottom of the class. I began to sense that I wasn't quite cut out for life in the army after all and maybe years of Excel boredom were my destiny.

One evening after another pointless day of marching and being shouted at, I came back to my room utterly deflated. Physically and mentally exhausted, my self-confidence was at an all-time low, shattered to pieces. I began to despair. I closed the door behind me, sat on the edge of my bed and wept. Life was thoroughly miserable. Sniffling into a tissue I considered how demeaning it all was. I was being treated like a badly behaved child: pocket money stopped and banished to tidy my room. My liberty and privilege were denied. I did as I was told and there was no apparent reward. As I sat on my bed with my head in my hands, I realized that I'd made a huge mistake in joining the army. I was wretchedly unhappy here, and couldn't comprehend a whole eleven months of this unrelenting drudgery. More tears welled as I seriously contemplated leaving. It was obvious that Sandhurst simply wasn't for me. I leaned over and plucked another fresh tissue, and blew my nose. As I fumbled with the wrinkled white tissue between my fingers I decided that I would persist until the first leave weekend. Then, as I relaxed in abstract freedom away from the intensity of the Academy, I could make my decision on whether to return or drop out. Until then I would grin and bear what they threw at me.

And unfortunately it was all about to get worse as this proved not even to be my nadir.

On the Friday of the third week I woke clammy with sweat and inside my head was foggy and befuddled. My limbs were weak and aching. I felt dreadful. I struggled to stand to attention outside the sergeant major's office for the morning 'sick parade' (the army even make the frail and feverish parade) before traipsing to the Academy Medical Centre. I barely had the energy to sit and lay on the floor of the waiting room until a nurse thrust a thermometer in my mouth. Forty degrees. I had a high fever. Nauseous and pallid, I was 'bedded down' in the ward upstairs above the doctors' surgery, where I was to lie for three days sweating it out of my body.

With sickness came a break from the training that I should have been grateful for. I should have appreciated the respite and valued time away from the room inspections and drill square. I should have lain there taking comfort from the fluffy duvet and a bed I wasn't required to get out of, let alone iron and make. I should have enjoyed my days in bed with toast and Jeremy Kyle, but flashing hot and cold, surrounded by sickness, was even more depressing than the martinet regime. Being in the Army is all about virility, health and fitness. It's about strong young men and women bounding with energy and vigour, society's peak of physical prowess, not high temperatures and feverish sweats. Being ill doesn't fit the army image. It looks weak, and I felt like an outcast separated from my platoon. I lay in bed woefully bored, wallowing in self-pity, fighting the flu, my desolation spiralling, until I was well enough to be discharged and rejoin the training.

And then just when I thought it couldn't get any worse, when I thought I'd hit my absolute rock bottom, someone handed me a spade.

4

EEYORE'S GLOOMY PLACE, RATHER BOGGY AND SAD

Sandhurst isn't meant to be easy. A Queen's commission can no longer simply be bought if Daddy has enough money and knows the right people.[16] At Sandhurst the training is tough and uncomfortable because the reality is even more unpleasant. The commissioning course is about physical and mental robustness; it's about toughening up floppy-haired students and pampered civilians for the realities of war. It's about learning how to live and function in discomfort, about overcoming how cold, tired, wet and hungry you feel and getting on with the job. Eventually, at some point it may even be about enjoying it.

But I was not tough, I was dysfunctional in adversity and I was not at any point enjoying it.

---

16 Until 1870 officers in the cavalry and infantry obtained their commission by buying it under the Parliamentary endorsed 'purchase system'. Hopeful candidates had to obtain the approval of their regimental colonel by presenting evidence of having had 'the education of a gentleman' and produce a substantial sum of money, approx £25,000 in today's money, as proof of their standing in society and as a bond for good behaviour. Subsequent promotion all the way to colonel was by purchase.

So far I thought life at Sandhurst had been pretty harsh and uncomfortable. Death o'clock starts in the morning followed by room inspections and parade square humiliation made my days fairly unpleasant. But then as CC071 deployed out into the field on our first 'exercise', the comforts of fresh food, running water and sprung mattresses quickly came into perspective. For life in the field was the real test of continuing to function in adversity and would take my misery to a whole new level.

Like so much of Sandhurst, I had no idea what to expect of a field exercise. Initially I thought some time away from my ironing board and broomstick was to be welcomed, a break in the countryside, taking in lungfuls of fresh air miles from Old College. I was wrong. As D-Day approached Exercise Self-Reliance was spoken of with sore foreboding, and fearful anticipation pervaded as preparations got underway. We were given maps of the training area to fablon,[17] boxes of foil-wrapped boil-in-the-bag rations to pack and a long list of issued equipment and clothing we'd need. Keenly prepared, I packed the prescribed kit list into waterproof freezer bags and the freezer bags into watertight canoe bags and the canoe bag into my weather-treated rucksack, as reports of the week's weather forecast reached us. And then, having struggled to close the straps on my bulging rucksack lid (which in the military is called a

---

17 Fabloning is an army obsession. It involves sticking *Blue Peter*-style, clear sticky-back plastic over maps and any other paperwork or card to keep them waterproofed. Fablon comes in large rolls and there is a fine art to peeling it off and sticking it down without trapping bubbles and ripples of air over all the important grid references.

'bergen' and I came to rename my 'burden'), I tried to lift it off the ground and onto my back.

I couldn't.

It weighed almost as much as me.

I rolled it over, lay with my back on it and wiggled my arms through the straps, then tried to stand from there with it on, flailing instead like an upturned beetle.

I released myself and manoeuvred to try sitting on the floor and standing up with it on my back from that position.

I still couldn't.

In the end Officer Cadet Wheeler came to my rescue and lifted the bergen burden onto my back and I stumbled precariously top-heavy downstairs, fearful at the prospect of walking any great distance with it on.

Officer Cadet Wheeler was the platoon darling and my polar opposite: intelligent, highly capable and taking everything at Sandhurst in her unfazed stride, she was Eleven Platoon's poster girl. A Cambridge graduate and OTC veteran, she had far too much God-given compassion to be in the army, and watched out for each one of us like a guardian angel. She was strong, both mentally and physically, and always went out of her way to come to the aid of someone who needed it.

Eventually with 'burdens' packed, maps fabloned and rain forecast we were ready to deploy into the field.

Much like my father, the organizers of the training programme at Sandhurst like to avoid the traffic and, with this planning parameter in mind, we were dragged from our beds at 3 a.m. to parade in the dark at the back of Old College, ready to board the coaches.

It was already raining.

Exercise Self-Reliance, or Self-Abuse as it soon became dubbed, was to take place amidst the quaint wealth of the Sussex green belt. And it is here, tucked away where expensive Range Rovers cruise leafy lanes, the idyllic beauty of Winnie-the-Pooh's Hundred Acre Wood can be found, whose childhood innocence was about to be shattered. As the coaches wound their way along the forest track from the main road, I caught glances of gentle rolling woodland, deer skipping through the trees and picnic clearings; how bad could this place be? This wasn't the wilds of Brecon or an inhospitable Scottish training area. Normal sane-minded members of the public came here to walk the dog, for Sunday strolls and to throw Poohsticks from the bridge. But then normal sane-minded members of the public wouldn't choose to spend five days here, sleeping in a woodblock exposed to the cutting midwinter weather.

Exercise Self-Abuse was all about introducing us to the baby basics of field survival and infantry tactics: Boy Scout survival lessons followed by running around with guns playing soldiers. The boys beamed with excitement; this is what they were here for. I was never enough of a tomboy to have tried either, but I had once enjoyed a camping trip to Devon so while my ironing board and parade shoes were a safe distance back at Sandhurst, life looked good.

SSgt Cox started by giving us an introduction to field hygiene: how to keep clean by washing with water boiled in a mess tin and using a scrap of soap; avoiding trench rot and, for the girls, what to do with the indignity of having your period while living rough in the field (frequent trips to the Portaloos or an injection from the Medical Centre nurse). Colour Sergeant Rattray then gathered us in for a cooking lesson and introduction to army twenty-four-hour ration packs.

CSgt Rattray, or 'the Rat' as he was known out of earshot, was Ten Platoon's CSgt. A broad Scot, originally from somewhere near Glasgow, he was thickly accented and proud to hail from north of the border. Through his 'achs' and 'ayes' I rarely understood what he was saying but that didn't matter because he was devilishly good-looking and knew it. A flashy playboy, he would show off in his red convertible sports car, screeching through the Academy, slowing to wink at the girls' platoon with handsome charm.

On Exercise Self-Abuse we all sat on our day-sacks in the wet field adoringly around him, as he produced champagne, caviar, Gentleman's Relish and a copy of the *Telegraph* from the small cardboard box on the ground, like Mary Poppins, chuckling that this was a wondrous 'officer's ration pack'. If only that were reality, because no amount of mesmeric swooning over the Rat could excite us about the contents of our real ration packed meals. That night, huddled over a small hexamine stove tired and hungry, I found the sight and consistency of chicken stew and fruit dumplings in custard gag-inducing. I prodded the brown congealed gloop with my spork[18] and realized the

---

18 A spoon-fork, essentially a spoon with small fork prongs at the end (camping shops think of everything).

boil-in-the-bag horrors would have to be eaten in the dark when too tired and ravenous to care. The alternative Lancashire hotpot, corned beef hash and treacle pudding may have been appetizing recipes for eating in Cold War trenches, but in the heat of Iraq and Afghanistan they are less palatable. What we really wanted in Iraq and Afghanistan, the Rat told us, was to get our hands on American MREs (Meals Ready-to-Eat). With fajitas and buffalo chicken on the menu, complete with squeezy cheese, peanut butter cookies, M&Ms and HOOAH! bars, they provide a whopping 4,000 calories a day so camp-bound Americans can continue to conform to international stereotypes.[19]

It wasn't all inedible. Having lived under SSgt Cox's chocolate ban for three weeks, the ration-pack chocolate bar was most welcome. I peeled back the silver-blue wrapper from the Nestlé Yorkie bar, rebranded for the military as NOT FOR CIVIS with disproportionate excitement and savoured the short-lived sugar rush. An even bigger sugar fix could be found in the small foil packet of boiled sweets, which proved a useful distraction when struggling to stay awake through the night. British rations would also be incomplete without tea bags; an army might march on its stomach but the British Army would come to a grinding halt without tea. After field cookery, we gathered in the forest for a Ray Mears-style shelter-building lesson.

---

19 Conversely, until the eighties, French ration packs contained cigarettes and with each meal in the field red wine was served among the troops.

I'm not really sure what I expected the sleeping arrangements on exercise to be – a tent maybe, or perhaps some sort of wooden shed or tin hut – but somehow through abject naivety I never actually expected to be sleeping in the field, in the open, on the cold hard ground, exposed to the unforgiving English climate. And as the reality sank in, I suddenly realized this was going to be nothing like my week of camping in Devon.

Using a large plastic-coated camouflage sheet called a poncho (not the sort tequila-slamming Mexicans wear) we erected a primitive shelter by tying the corners to nearby trees with elastic bungee chords and propping a stick up in the middle. The shelter had to be as low to the ground as possible, preventing the enemy from discovering it, leaving just enough room to lie down and watch the rain pool in sumps above my nose and think how pitiful a night's sleep under there was going to be. I did wonder what you would do if there were no trees to tie the poncho to, say in the desert perhaps, somewhere maybe like Iraq or Afghanistan, but then I wasn't being paid to think and piping up with stupid questions like that was baiting fate. The poncho shelter promised no protection from the piercing wintry weather whatsoever; its purpose more about hiding us from the enemy than affording a comfortable night's rest. Not that there was going to be any rest anyway.

The heavy grey sky rained pathetically on us all morning and the dampness seeped through every seam of clothing and stitch of fabric straight to the bone. And on day one of five there was no early promise of drying out. The test of our resolve under adversity had begun and already I wished to be back at the Academy ironing and polishing with dry pants on.

And so, with this conditioning in place, it was time for us to play soldiers.

Daubing thick smears of waxy green and brown camouflage cream across our faces and sticking leaves and twigs to the helmets on our heads, we began to look more plausibly like soldiers, albeit more *Dad's Army* than gritty professional warriors. The pouches on our webbing[20] contained magazines filled with ammunition for the first time and we were excited at the prospect of finally using it.

But then out came 'Willy-the-whistle' and the crawling began.

On each blast from Willy we had to throw ourselves down in the mud and nettles and start to crawl. With rifle cradled and webbing on, we crawled. And crawled and crawled. SSgt Cox and Captain Trunchbull screamed murderously at us to stay down and move faster. We crawled across woods, along tracks, over fields and through bracken until our lungs were bursting and limbs bleeding. This wasn't crawling like babies on hands and knees but lower, more stealthily, with belt buckles to the ground, like leopards stalking on the Serengeti. We dragged our tired defeated bodies through muddy puddles and undergrowth, over stones and to the summit of hills, until our limbs couldn't ache any more.

---

20 Webbing is the name for the army assault vest, in which a soldier carries all his essentials: ammunition, twenty-four hours' worth of rations, water, maps etc.

Elbow-ripping, kneecap-grinding, lung-busting crawling.

One blast from Willy and we jumped up and ran forwards, another and we threw ourselves down in the dirt and started to crawl. Up, down, crawl, up, down, crawl; because through pain and Willy we were learning the most fundamental of infantry tactics – 'fire and manoeuvre'.

Partnered up, one of us fired blank rounds of ammunition at an imaginary enemy while the other scurried forwards, dived down and crawled forwards to start shooting, then the other half of the pair did the same. Each running dash covered and protected by shooting fire from the other. A so foolproof simple technique, fire and manoeuvre is at the crux of what the infantry do. A soldier's bread and butter, his gravy and potatoes, the daily grind of a section, platoon and company; two years later in Afghanistan I would watch images from a helicopter of Royal Marines doing exactly this when assaulting a Taliban compound. Their movements were no more complicated than ours were that afternoon as we dashed forth, dropped down, crawled forwards and fired. Dash-down-crawl-dash-down-crawl. Again and again, throwing ourselves down onto the soggy wet ground, panting, breathless and exhausted. Except we were in Sussex in January not Helmand in July and we weren't wearing 35 lb of body armour like the Marines, nor carrying radios, counter-IED equipment, ammunition and all the other gubbins an infantryman is loaded up with. If I hadn't been suffering so much personal pain at this point I may have even been humbled with appreciation for what it is infantry soldiers do.

As darkness fell, battered, bruised and exhausted, we moved into the woods to set up a platoon harbour. Here, tucked away in the thick of the forest, we would be spending the night, cooking up our gag-inducing boil-in-the-bag meals, changing socks and pants, and notionally rolling out our sleeping bags. The harbour was to be triangular, each of the three sides facing outwards ready to spot and fight the enemy. A thread of twine marking each edge of the triangle was meticulously tied around the trees, forcing military straight lines onto the beech and birch of Hundred Acre Wood. Around our triangle home ran a track for us to move along in the dark which had to be delicately cleared of leaves and twigs that could crackle and snap when walked on, alerting the enemy to our location. Perversely this was contrived to involve yet more crawling through mud, as we swept away branches and foliage until we were all thoroughly pissed off with scraping our knees and elbows along the ground.

The flimsy poncho shelters we'd learned to construct earlier were erected between the trees over shallow trenches as we basha'd[21] up. Hollow 'shell-scrapes' were dug beneath these basha, each long enough for the tallest person to lie down and wide enough for two to lie side by side. With my limbs already fatigued from crawling, an entrenching tool (a spade: for some reason the army don't call a spade a spade) was thrust into my hands and I started to scratch away at the dense soil, digging my own coffin hole. By

---

21 Basha comes from the Malay word for shelter and entered the military lexicon in the fifties during the Malaya Campaign.

now I was dead on my feet. All I wanted to do was stop, curl up on the cold, hard forest floor and let sleep take me away. My stomach was empty, my legs were weary, and I couldn't care less if the enemy found us, if it brought an end to the agonizing crawling.

Then finally, as midnight approached, I rolled out my sleeping bag and wriggled in.

Once the crawling and digging stopped I became painfully cold. My damp clothing and sodden boots chilled my body to the core. People don't realize quite how deadly the British climate is. That night, as the January air dipped below freezing, the day's drizzle turned to snow and I shivered despairingly in my sleeping bag, worried that if I fell asleep I might wake up dead, frozen in my self-dug grave. But I need not have worried because someone had come up with a ridiculously complex sentry rota that ensured none of us would be getting any sleep that night anyway. And after less than an hour of trembling in my sleep, I was shaken awake by Allinson for my turn to lie in the numbing cold on stag.[22] I lay shaking with cold on the sentry position next to Wheeler, our breath forming little clouds in the cold air, watching the snow settle around us, as the forest floor got whiter. With my head in my helmet propped against my rifle I stifled yawns and wriggled my legs back and forth, trying to keep as little of my body from touching the painfully frozen ground. From her pocket Wheeler produced a packet of ration-pack boiled sweets and we talked of food fantasies in a hushed

---

22 STAG – Soldier Trained Armed Guard, a military sentry.

whisper to keep ourselves awake (her dreaming of a home-made lasagne, me a Sunday roast with all the trimmings). After an hour of staring into the darkness like this our duty came to an end and we stood to reveal a clear untouched patch of brown earth in the snow for the next two to lie in, creeping back along the track plan to our shell-scrape and climbing back into our sleeping bags for another allotted ninety minutes' rest.

On our second stag I saw two figures approach us through the blackness. I blinked to check, hoping that my eyes were deceiving me, wishing for an uneventful, peaceful hour watching the snow fall. But they were there and coming closer, walking straight towards us.

'Stop. Who goes there?' Wheeler called out the challenge to them.

'SSgt Cox and Captain Trunchbull.'

'Advance one and be recognized.'

The unmistakable misshapen onion-seller's beret of Captain Trunchbull stepped forwards into view.

'Evening, ma'am, staff sergeant,' Wheeler greeted them.

They walked straight past us, disappearing off into the harbour area, emerging a few minutes later with two rifles and heading back in the direction from which they had come. They dissolved into the night.

'Oh dear,' Wheeler exclaimed.

'What?'

We were supposed to sleep with our rifles uncomfortably inside our sleeping bags, so should the enemy creep up on us while we slept they couldn't be stolen, which is exactly what Captain Trunchbull and SSgt Cox had meanly done, plucking them from beside our sleeping comrades. Indeed as morning arrived two of the platoon were missing weapons, and we all knew what was coming.

More from Willy.

With the first light of dawn, I forced down another boil-in-the-bag breakfast (burgers and beans) and had a wet-wipe shower, then joined the Platoon lining up in a forest clearing to await the arrival of SSgt Cox and Captain Trunchbull. One of the benefits of being in the field was supposed to be a separation from the theatre of morning room inspections; freedom from the ceaseless ironing, polishing and cleaning crap. So as dawn arrived we were all rather perturbed to be standing with mess tins, boots and those weapons remaining laid out on the ground ready for inspection. And were even more pissed off to subsequently be running up and down a hill, knees to chest, doing press-ups in the mud because we hadn't passed. Captain Trunchbull and SSgt Cox screamed at our rancid 'gopping' ill-disciplined selves, teaching us another brutally delivered lesson. The lax discipline of a few had brought collective punishment to us all. Those who had failed to clean their mess tins, polish their boots or sleep with their rifle saw us all suffering, hounding home the need for us to stick together, if one person failed we all did. It didn't matter if you couldn't bear the person you were basha'd up with, you still had to work together to get through the hell of Self-Abuse.

Commanding soldiers under fire, in the heat of battle, is arguably the greatest leadership challenge. While the infantry accounts for less than a third of the army, the primary role of the remaining two-thirds is to support them. Whether it be providing radio communications, artillery fire, defusing bombs or flying helicopters, everyone in the army requires a basic understanding of what it is infantry soldiers on the ground do, and for this reason Sandhurst uses the infantry model to teach leadership.

Each of the three annual intakes to the Academy are split into three infantry-style rifle companies, each of these sub-divided into three platoons of around thirty and each of these platoons subsequently split into three infantry sections, consistent with real infantry rifle platoons.

In the army three really is the magic number.

On completion of their training the cadets from Sandhurst commissioning into the infantry would take command of a platoon. Though the army isn't foolish enough to grant custody of thirty soldiers to a young man in his early twenties, who only a year earlier had most likely been a jaunty, carefree student, so a young second-lieutenant's enthusiasm and naivety are reined in by a war-hardened platoon sergeant. Sergeants are hard-bitten experienced senior soldiers who have been promoted through the ranks from private to lance-corporal to corporal and then sergeant, toughened at each stage by arduous NCO[23] leadership courses in Brecon. Although the second-lieutenant is officially in charge the sergeant can hold greater true authority, especially in the early months

---

23 Non-commissioned officer. Includes all soldiers above the lowest rank of private who are not officers and who consequently don't hold the Queen's commission.

while the baby Platoon Commander is still wide-eyed and wet behind the ears. Sticking to the infantry model at Sandhurst we cadets made up the platoon's number with Captain Trunchbull as the notional and uninspiring platoon commander while our real respect was for SSgt Cox. Over the year as we deployed on more horrific weeks like Self-Abuse and the exercises progressed we would each take it in turn to act as platoon commander and sergeant, being assessed for leadership ability in trying to command our friends and peers.

The manpower in an infantry section is further split into two four-man fire teams. At the lowest level these are the most basic building blocks in the British infantry. And on the second day of Self-Abuse we grouped into our own little fire teams, to build on the previous day's fire and manoeuvre training. This time four of us would do the dash, down, crawl routine together. We practised all morning, a team at a time, firing rounds at imaginary enemy in the copse beyond an open field. The snow and rain had finally stopped and, as I sat on my daysack waiting my turn, the sun broke through the clouds to warm my tired muddy face. As the sky cleared the picture-perfect rolling hills of Winnie-the-Pooh country unfurled in front of me, the open heathland brightened by splashes of yellow gorse and purple moor grass.

There was something restful in that physical landscape that gave me a small moment to extract and ponder, a brief peaceful interlude in the shouting-shooting-crawling exercise melee. I smiled inwardly to myself. It was my birthday, and I would rather have been here on this hillside, with newfound friends in the fresh open air, feeling the warmth of the sun on my cheeks than cooped up behind a computer screen like a battery hen in an office. Next to me Wheeler leaned over and snapped off a chunk of her Yorkie bar and handed it to me. And in that brief moment, with the sun on my face, looking at open fields, I felt content and, for the first time, that I wanted to be here.

*

That night after sundown we were sent out on a navigation patrol to put our orienteering skills to the test and prove that the compasses we had been issued could be used as more than just a short ruler. So with map in hand, I stumbled around Christopher Robin's playground in the dark on my own, finding my way from checkpoint to checkpoint through the night. For two hours, I crossed over forest streams, clambered stone walls, waded through tall deer grass and considered stopping for a snooze in an empty barn. By now the tiredness was dragging me down. It was only the second night of the exercise and I felt wretched. We would be getting minimal sleep again that night and I wondered how long my body could cope with the sleep deprivation until it packed up and I started to fall asleep on the march. Inside my head my brain had already slowed to mush and all I could think of was succumbing to the relief of sleep. My head grew heavy as I battled with my eyelids, forcing them open. I obsessed with thoughts of climbing into bed and surrendering to slumber. I fantasized about slipping between crisp clean sheets, laying my head on a plump pillow, inhaling Lenor Summer Meadows and letting the duvet envelop my drained body, taking it away to be renewed. But none of this could become a near reality, as the release of sleep was a long way off.

Two hours later, with all the checkpoints found, I eventually staggered to the finish point cold, wet and pissed off, then returned to the harbour area for another night of stag and half-sleep, shivering in my sleeping bag, desperately willing the ordeal of Self-Abuse to end. An hour later Wheeler and I were back at our sentry post together, sharing boiled sweets and discussing plans for our first weekend of freedom (she had a student party back in Cambridge to attend, I was going to Twickenham for Six Nations' rugby). Strong friendships are quickly formed in these situations of adversity. People I had never met four weeks earlier now knew me better than lifelong friends. Thrown together on the first Sunday in January, we were all enduring the same bad dream together and were bonding through the misery and hardship of it all.

Some of us suffered more than others during those long cold wintry nights, and none more so than the overseas cadets. The overseas cadets had been plucked from the comfort and familiarity of their native lands and thrust into the British weather at its most raw and unwelcoming. Each year about fifty foreign cadets from all over the world attend Sandhurst, integrating fully with the commissioning course. Sandhurst is hard enough if English is your indigenous tongue, but deciphering the excited shouting of an apoplectic Glaswegian colour sergeant when your brain works in Dari, or understanding drill when orderly queuing isn't even in your culture set additional challenges for the overseas cadets.

For some overseas cadets Sandhurst has become a rite of passage; a prestigious finishing school for Arab princes and future world leaders sent to learn the secrets of British leadership. All modern-day heirs to the Jordanian throne have attended Sandhurst, including the current King as well as the reigning Sultans of Oman and Brunei. Former Kings of Spain, Tonga and Thailand are all also among Sandhurst's alumni. Others represent the cream of their home armies, chosen through vigorous selection while an unfortunate few, like Mahmoud, had just been in the wrong place at the wrong time.

Mahmoud had left a wife and three children in Yemen to join Ten Platoon; chosen because he was simply in the room when his commanding officer was tasked with selecting someone. He wouldn't return home to his family for the entire year. And not only did Mahmoud have to contend with the inclement climate and strictures of British military authoritarianism, but he was also a devout Muslim and had to match his prayer timings, halal beliefs and Ramadan customs to the training programme as well; orientating to Mecca in the middle of a fire fight in Brecon brings a whole new dimension to covering your arcs and praying.

In Eleven Platoon we were joined by Officer Cadet Black from Jamaica, whose chilled, laid-back totally tropical Caribbean ways were in for a cruel car crash collision with the strict Sandhurst regimen. Her Creole drawl brought a Malibu gloss to our little army and she shivered continually for the entire eleven months. We also had Khadka, our own bantam Nepali warrior, whose English was impeccable (I once heard her use the word 'monocotyledon' in casual conversation) and despite coming from Kathmandu she too suffered terribly with the British weather. Although, in spite of the air miles, Khadka wasn't as far from home as you might expect in Surrey since Sandhurst and its neighbouring Camberley have a large army Gurkha population who kept her company.

Twelve Platoon were enriched by Maganizo from Malawi who had never seen snow and Karumba who was actually from south-west London but routinely mistaken for another external import.

With uncharacteristic humanity, Sandhurst did bestow small pity on these legal aliens (and Karumba), issuing them with extra-warm cold-weather clothing: thick down jackets, arctic gloves, socks and Gortex boots, all of which Black and Khadka wore religiously.

Eventually after four horrendous days and sleepless nights our angry camping ordeal came to its painful conclusion. In the darkness before the arrival of dawn, as the platoon innocently slept, the harbour got 'bumped'.

The enemy had finally found us.

Panicked shouting and crackling gunfire suddenly shattered the early morning calm of Hundred Acre Wood. Through the darkness around us, pandemonium broke. Bawling and hollering, the enemy came, crashing through the forest to storm our position.

Rat-a-tat-tat.

Firing at us through the trees, they came thundering towards us.

Startled into consciousness, I was still wrapped up in my sleeping bag, rifle tucked at my side and sodden boots on. I tried to dismiss the noises around me as a bad dream. I just wanted to sleep and pretend it wasn't happening. Beside me, Wheeler was already awake and galvanized into action, thrusting her sleeping bag into her bergen and tearing down our poncho shelter.

She shone the light of her torch at my face, rousing me out of my dream into the nightmare. 'Come on, we've got to go,' she urged.

Behind her, I could see Allinson and Merv up and ready to go, lifting their bergens onto their backs. Reluctantly I left the relative warmth of my sleeping bag and joined the flustered confusion. By now the harbour area was a flurry of activity. The platoon were hurriedly gathering up possessions in the dark, stuffing them into bergens and webbing while Captain Trunchbull and SSgt Cox had arrived to add to the mayhem.

We were fleeing, clearing out of our woodblock home in a blind blustering panic to the ERV (emergency rendezvous). With bergens packed and hoisted onto our backs, we stampeded out of the copse and down a forest track, with someone at the front clutching a map and compass that would point us to safety. Ahead lay a five-mile forced march in fighting order across the Sussex Weald to showers and breakfast. The pace was brisk and demanding. Captain Trunchbull ran along beside us, unhindered by kit, shouting threatening words of abusive encouragement, which we allowed to wash over our ears. The bergens and webbing on our backs weighed us down as we trudged along the muddy tracks, stumbling over stones and tree roots, our legs lazy with exhaustion. Straight from the lines of a Wilfred Owen poem, we staggered, bent double and coughing like hags in the moist winter air, rifles cradled in our arms. It was a battle of wills to keep going. My back ached and legs groaned. My years in London had trained me to handle pounds sterling and a calculator, not pounds of kit and a weapon. I tried to focus my mind elsewhere, thinking thoughts of the reward, of bacon, eggs, toast and beans, the elation of being clean and warm back at the Academy.

And that was it, the magic of Self-Abuse. After four days exposed to the uncomfortable realities of soldiering I viewed the confines of Old College and the endless ironing-cleaning-boot-polishing insanity as relief. I wanted five uninterrupted hours of sleep and I was content to iron my bed in the morning in order to have it. I could tolerate the national anthem dawn chorus if it meant hot showers and clean clothes. The melodrama of room inspections were a worthy exchange for a roof and four walls, because Exercise Self-Abuse had broken me and forced me to acquiesce.

That morning five miles felt like twenty. It was hard going. I still felt weak from my fever and the pain must have been clearly visible on my face, as Wheeler reached out her hand and gave my arm a reassuring squeeze.

'Come on, Héloïse, not much further to go.'

Eventually we reached the safety of camp, beaten, broken shadows of our former selves. Finally it was over. I felt every muscle in my body relax with joyous relief as I loosened my webbing and bergen and dropped them to the floor, happy to leave them lying where they fell. I stretched out my back, feeling the muscles release and unwind, vertebrae slotting back into place. I felt almost emotional; I had survived the most unpleasant week of my entire life and was still in one piece, and I had war stories to boast exaggeratedly about to friends in London on my first leave weekend. Inside I had a quiet feeling of pride, of having achieved. Though only trivial and minor by army standards, I knew my civilian self-exacting brain would never have completed it. My tolerance of cold, pain and discomfort had never been so violated. The conversion from civilian to soldier was far from complete, but I had overcome my first true test of grittiness and headed triumphantly for the showers.

It is truly horrifying how bad the body can smell after a week of war games. Mud mixes with dried sweat, flaking camouflage cream and damp clothing to create a toxic whiff, which can overwhelm the freshly bathed, and which after a time I worryingly got used to. As I finally got to the camp showers, my stomach satiated with sausage and beans, I caught a glimpse of my reflection in a bathroom mirror and recoiled. I looked like an aged rock star at the end of a hedonistic weekend: hair bedraggled, make-up smudged, clothing dishevelled, eyes narrow and puffy. I had turned feral. Peeling off my filthy clothing and stepping into the steaming shower was like being reborn. I scrubbed at my skin trying to discern bruising from dirt, as water and soap washed away five days of caked mud, bringing my body back to life. I watched the frothy brown water swirl around the plughole mingling with blades of grass, leaves and filth. Looking at the soggy pile of muddy kit on the changing room floor, I groaned, thinking about the toil involved in washing and ironing it all when I got back, ready in time for the following morning's room inspection.

The cycle was tireless.

That night back at the Academy, I finally climbed into bed, fresh, clean and smooth, crushed with exhaustion. I lay back and was asleep in moments, plunging into a deep blissful slumber. I slept like I had never slept before, a velvety smothering sleep, too tired to even dream as my battered body was restored. The eventual release of mind and limb felt like arrival at Valhalla, like succumbing to an opiate, like pressing pause on life and taking time out. I was grateful that the Exercise Self-Abuse bad dream was finally over, but fearful that there would be more field exercises in the coming months, and they would only get harder.

Having survived Self-Abuse we returned to the Gulag with a mere week now separating us from the outside freedoms of our first leave weekend. A week of room inspections, polishing and drill, lots and lots of drill. The usual inane dross continued as Sandhurst persisted to test our leadership and resolve. For a few days SSgt Cox confiscated all of the platoon's watches, leaving the unlucky cadet in charge herding cats as the only person with the time. Regular and rushed uniform changes were called, seeing us parade hurriedly in barrack order, then combats, then blues, orienteering kit and back to combats or barrack dress, then Blues or running kit. Too little time was given for each costume change and all my clothes became strewn across the bedroom like a messy teenager, leaving me to later pick it all up, wash it, iron it, fold it and put it back in its correct location for the morning's room inspection. My favourite of these senseless mess-arounds involved the entire platoon standing still for an hour, in stony silence on an empty parade square being taught a 'lesson in waiting'.

And it wasn't just Eleven Platoon who got this treatment. Early one morning I ran down the stairs from my room in Old College to line up outside for the morning parade, and as I burst through the double doors into Chapel Square, I was confronted by the whole of Ten Platoon on the ground doing press-ups in front of the Rat.

'Come on. Ye'll keep doin' this until ya can get them all,' the Rat shouted at them, as they raised and lowered with each press-up motion. I walked discreetly behind them to where Eleven Platoon lined up, trying not to draw attention to myself and took up my place in the middle rank, looking over to watch the spectacle. What were they doing?

'Bagpipes,' one of the Ten Platoon boys shouted out as sweaty steam started to rise from their backs in the cold winter's air.

'Yes,' the Rat shouted. 'Well done. Tha's one of me five favourite things. Ya got two more ta get. Come on, men, think.' In front of him they continued to do press-ups, a couple of huffing grunts of discomfort now being expressed. The Rat was playing one of his favourite games. He would get the boys of Ten Platoon to do press-ups like this until they could name each of his five favourite things: a transient list that changed with each iteration of the game. This always included Irn-Bru and porridge, and usually his wife, but the rest was anyone's guess, depending on his mood and whim, and they could be stuck doing press-ups like this for long protracted periods until they finally landed on whatever obscure pleasure took his Scottish fancy that day.

I had now been at Sandhurst for nearly five weeks but had barely spoken to any of the boys. I recognized some of their faces and we all wore name badges but I didn't know anything about any of them. There was a forced separation between us and we rarely risked the wrath of SSgt Cox by speaking to any of them. They were not allowed to enter our accommodation and during those first five weeks we ate, worked and marched everywhere as a platoon of just girls.

That particular morning as Ten Platoon finished their press-ups for the Rat, SSgt Cox emerged. Stepping serenely through the doors into Chapel Square, her head held high as if sniffing for prey, she walked coolly past the captivating charm of the Rat with a quick gleeful gibe in his direction, and came to take her place at the front of Eleven Platoon. In Chapel Square we lined up in numerical order, with Eleven Platoon sandwiched between the two boys' platoons of Ten and Twelve, neither of which we were allowed to speak to, even though one of the girls, Holmström, had her boyfriend in Twelve Platoon. Earlier as SSgt Cox had been absent outside, Holmström had seized the moment to sidle up to her boyfriend, Officer Cadet Browne, and have an innocent little chat with him. There was no opportunity for intimacy in Old College, but a quick exchange of smiles and brief squeeze of the hand made all the difference. And as SSgt Cox joined us outside she instantly locked eyes on them.

'Holmström,' she shrieked. 'What are you doing talking to that boy?'

'Nothing, staff sergeant,' Holmström replied, quickly leaping away from Browne, stung by SSgt Cox's arrival.

'Don't lie to me, Miss Holmström, I saw you. Perhaps Mr Browne might like to explain,' she said as she came to a stop in front of us, her eyes firmly fixed on Officer Cadet Browne. 'Mr Browne, would you like to come over here and explain to me what you were doing talking to one of my cadets,' SSgt Cox goaded, putting her hands on her hips and lifting her head aloft in his direction. He had no choice. Bravely he stepped forwards, leaving the comfort of Twelve Platoon and marched over to SSgt Cox's bait. Smartly he came to attention in front of her, keeping his head held high, his eyes never meeting hers.

'I'm sorry, staff sergeant. I was talking to my girlfriend,' he said in a low meek voice. Around him the rest of Imjin Company remained silent, intently watching and listening, to see what drama would unfold.

'Your girlfriend,' SSgt Cox shouted in a high-pitched shriek. 'Girlfriend.' She spat out the word. Her eyes widened and a sly temper began to build, fuelled by her distaste that there could be a cosy couple in Imjin's midst.

'We'll see about that.' She stamped her feet together and took a pace towards him, meeting his gaze with a challenging eye. 'You know you are not allowed to speak to my girls, Mr Browne,' she snapped, her finger waving at him in disapproval. 'But perhaps this morning I might permit you to sing to them instead.'

What?

We all looked at Browne. A perplexed frown formed across his face. Did she seriously expect him to stand there and sing to Holmström, in front of the whole company? What could he possibly sing in this situation?

'Go on then, Mr Browne,' she provoked.

Silence.

He said nothing. His mouth remained firmly shut, his brain working in overdrive to think of a suitable way out of this awkward situation.

'I'm waiting,' she said, as the seconds ticked on.

In Officer Cadet Browne she had picked on the wrong person. He was a quiet personal man, not a confident exhibitionist. He wasn't going to make a fool of himself in front of everyone as she wanted. But what was he going to do?

The seconds ticked on.

'Come on. We haven't got all day, Mr Browne.' She sighed. 'You better hurry up before I think of a more severe alternative punishment for you.'

The whole company stared at him, waiting in anticipation. How the hell was he going to get out of this one? Then he lowered his head, briefly closed his eyes and exhaled. He looked over to Holmström, opened his mouth and began to sing in a low croaky voice: 'You never close your eyes any more when I kiss your lips.' He glanced at the rest of Twelve Platoon for encouragement and they joined in with him, their voices building as they sang.

It wasn't quite Maverick and Goose in *Top Gun*, but he'd pulled it off, putting a smile on all our faces, and getting a curt dismissal from SSgt Cox.

Holmström and Browne were the love story of Imjin Company. They had met as young University Officer Cadets in Newcastle and decided to join the army together. As they arrived with each other on that first Sunday in January they had no control over which company they would be allocated to, but with pure luck they were both united in Imjin Company. Their romance survived the trauma of Sandhurst, sustaining them through the low points in the course, giving them a crutch on which to lean when times were bad. And they are now happily married, both as serving officers.

Despite my glimmer of contentment as the sun broke through over the rolling hills of Winnie-the-Pooh country, I was still bitterly unhappy at the Academy. I was still sitting firmly at the bottom of the class and knew that I was unlikely to survive another ordeal like Self-Abuse. I was perpetually tired and my patience was wearing thin and I couldn't see how any of this would get better. I was pondering this one evening at dinner, pushing a lone potato around my plate, as I stared into the distance at a hanging portrait of the Queen, my mind elsewhere. I had been quiet for some time and my eyes were glassy. Merv and Wheeler were with me and picked up on it instantly.

'Are you all right, hun?' Merv asked, putting her hand consolingly over mine.

I didn't want to answer her. I knew if I did I would start to crack up in front of them. Crying would be seen as weak and pathetic. I wanted to avoid it so looked at them and pulled a false smile.

'No, it's not,' Merv said, not fooled.

'Are you sure, Héloïse? What's bothering you?' Wheeler prodded further.

Their concern was heartening. I'd known them for just four weeks but they cared about me.

'I don't think I can carry on,' I said, opening up and choking on the lump in my throat. 'I can't do it. I'm useless and I just don't think the army is for me.'

'Don't be silly, Héloïse, you'll be fine. Of course this is more difficult for you, we've all done it before, but you'll catch us up in no time,' Wheeler cooed, soothing my fears.

'I'm thinking about leaving at the end of week five,' I said, expressing my rational conclusion.

'No. Don't do that, hun. Give it more time. You'll make a fantastic officer when you get the hang of things,' Merv interjected, trying to save the situation. 'You can do it, so don't be put off by the struggle of these first few weeks, you'll find your feet. And trust me it gets better. Honestly. Plus, we'll miss you if you go, won't we, Wheelie?'

'Of course. Héloïse, don't give up yet. The platoon would be lost without you.'

Their compassion was heartfelt but it didn't help allay my fears. I had no talent for any of it and was floundering terribly. I'd had enough and was ready to tuck tail and run, rather than continue with the fight. But there was something sweet in their sympathy. In their eyes I was one of them now, a part of the Platoon and they genuinely didn't want to see me leave. In just four weeks I'd made stronger friendships than I had in more than four years in the City and that wasn't something to forget.

With life in those first five weeks galloping at breakneck pace, there were few opportunities for us to sit back and reflect, take a deep breath and appreciate the significance of it all. The hours of pointless running around (and standing still 'waiting') detracted from what was supposed to be the privilege of our circumstance; and when there were slim breaks in the fribbling tedium I tended to switch my brain off rather than engage it.

One moment for brief contemplation did come at our Attestation ceremony.

Smartly uniformed in our Sunday best, the 270 newest cadets squeezed together shoulder to shoulder in the Indian Army Memorial room to pledge allegiance to obediently serve Queen and country. Entered from the hall of the Grand Entrance, the Indian Army Memorial room is a spectacularly stately venue. With its high ceiling and coats of armour, it was here only weeks earlier the General had wooed parents with biscuits and tea. Originally the Academy chapel, the room now commemorates those who served in the British Indian Army during ninety years of Crown rule, fighting bloody and brutal British battles in Asia and northern Africa. Around the room light radiates in through brightly coloured stained-glass windows that pay tribute to muddy, bloody battles in Burma, Afghanistan, Eritrea, Waziristan and Shanghai.

We marched in stiffly, me sandwiched between Gill and Gray again, shuffling along to take up our positions, then standing at ease while we waited for the General, our hands clasped behind our backs. As I stood patiently, in those quiet, still moments I glanced up at the window directly in front of me. It portrayed a Second World War Tommy in tin helmet, wading through jungle, while behind paratroopers fell through a flush and purple sky. At the base centre of the window was a small simple red crest, a white stripe running across its middle, and in its centre a sword with three tiny black letters 'XIV'. The Fourteenth Army. I had seen it before, embroidered onto cloth, lying in an old drawer at my grandparents' house in North Wales. My grandfather had fought with the Fourteenth Army in Burma alongside units from the Indian Army in what became the longest campaign of the Second World War. I thought about what joining the army had meant back then. What would have been going through the minds of officers attesting in 1939? I hadn't joined the army thinking of the intrinsic death and sacrifice. Today's new officer generation are too far removed from the tragedy and life loss of the World Wars to recognize the distresses of war. It may have been grossly naive but hardly anyone in that room had considered the full seriousness of what they were potentially pledging to in their new careers; the proximity to danger and death were not outwardly published during recruitment and the connection between coffins stopping traffic in Wootton Bassett and our morning room inspections was too tenuous. In Afghanistan and Iraq, soldiers weren't dying in the catastrophic numbers seen in the World Wars but paying the ultimate sacrifice is still a veritable reality, and only three years later two people attesting with me in the Indian Army Memorial room that day would have done so.

With the trauma of weeks one to five nearly over, only one thing now remained between me and a long weekend of unrestrained freedom, one sizable hurdle, at which I stood every chance of falling – a drill exam. The exam was designed to demonstrate that we had achieved the basic level of soldiering and could march in an orderly obedient fashion. Except I still couldn't. My two left feet and intractable legs continued to persist on the parade square, and my nerves whipped me around in a vicious circle of blundering balls-ups and agitated angst. To make matters worse an unnecessary amount of fuss was being made over the importance of 'passing off the square' and SSgt Cox coldly issued threats that those who failed would be staying behind for the weekend.

'Passing off the square' was also to be our first small taste of military pomp and ceremony, of marching to a brass band, smart in our Blues. In the preceding days an inordinate amount of our time was spent on practising and preening. We rehearsed by marching up and down the

Academy corridors, saluting framed paintings and halting in doorways. Late into the night, we polished and shone, ironed and spruced, ready for the pre-parade College Commander's inspection. When Friday morning arrived the platoon marched into the Indian Army Memorial room again to stand painfully to attention as he and the College Adjutant perused the ranks inspecting our efforts. Staring up at Granddad's window thinking excitedly of the weekend ahead I felt a little light-headed in the suffocating heavy wool uniform and central heating. As moments passed people around the room started to wilt and eventually there was a gentle thump from the back rank as Allinson passed out under the bright lights and choking tightness of her shirt collar. Ruse or not it worked, the inspection phase was complete and we passed.

Outside, the parade square was characteristically wet and uninviting. The Academy band stood huddled under the cover of the Grand Entrance, snuggled in their heavy overcoats, the brass instruments catching what little light sparkled through the grey skies. Now all that separated us from the relaxed joys of the civilian world was just a bit of left-right-left. It was tense. We formed up. Straightened our skirts, adjusted the forage caps on our heads and gave little whispered words of good luck. Then a deep bellowing drumbeat resonated across the square and SSgt Cox barked out the commands as thirty-one[24] left feet shot forwards: 'Dufft, dite, dufft, dite, dufft, dite.'

---

24 After five weeks we had already lost one member of the platoon. The girl who had dropped the iron on her foot whilst ironing her bed was out with the burns injury.

We were off. Quick march, slow march, salutes and an about turn. Round and around the parade square, executed with deft finesse; then with one final 'HALT' we came to a standstill and it was all over, five weeks of unadulterated hell finishing on a drizzly parade square. Back inside Old College glasses of port were handed around as people rushed to packed bags and parked cars in a mad dash to the M3. Wriggling out of suits and into denim jeans (the Devil's cloth) in the corner of Tesco's car park outside the Academy gates.

We were free at last.

'It is true that liberty is precious – so precious that it must be rationed';[25] and with this maxim in mind, respites from the control and captivity of Sandhurst were rationed to small heady slices of freedom. Escape from the Academy during Juniors was confined to just three 'leave weekends' in a fourteen-week term, each short enough to prevent the ill discipline of 'Civvy Street' from undoing our Sandhurst indoctrination. Like corks popping from champagne bottles, cadets raced to bars and pubs to catch up with friends still living laid-back student lives; sprinted to join new graduates in London, adjusting to their unfathomable City wages and equally unfathomable rents; dashed home to mothers' cooking; hurried into loved ones' embraces; lounged on friends' sofas catching up on mindless television; and enjoyed two deliciously long nights in a bed that didn't have to be ironed, tucked up each night

25 Vladimir Lenin.

barely before the ring of last orders, weary, worn out and exhausted.

I ate lots, slept lots, got drunk far too easily and struggled to walk along the street without being in step with the person next to me. I also found that Sandhurst had distorted my perception of public reality too. Having spent five weeks sheltered in a narrow enclave of society I realized that I hadn't seen children, old people, any homeless or many women. I hadn't heard a child cry, or busker play and overweight people had become an intriguing oddity after the svelte fit world of the forces in training.

For my first weekend of freedom, I retreated to Deborah's flat in Putney, folding out the sofa bed and uncorking a bottle of wine. At dinner, I ate my first home cooking for five weeks, savouring each mouthful of Deborah's lasagne, while she poked around for news of how I was finding Sandhurst.

'So, tell me all about it. I haven't heard from you for weeks. I'm guessing you've been busy. What's it like? Are there any nice men?'

'Debs, it's manic,' I said between mouthfuls. 'My feet haven't touched the ground since I got there. I've been surviving on just five hours' sleep a night and get shouted at all day long. It's horrendous.'

I explained the room inspections, the drill, the water parades, Sunday orienteering and the trauma of Exercise Self-Abuse. Having finished my plate of food with impolite speed, I picked up my glass of wine and curled my feet up under me on the sofa.

'Oh, oh, and yes,' I said, flapping my hand with excitement. 'And I've fired a rifle. You don't get to do that every day in London.'

'Oh, wow. That's pretty cool. So you're a trained killer now, are you?'

'Well, not quite yet, Debs.'

'But are you actually enjoying it? It sounds like it's pretty hard work, but is it worth it?'

'No, I'm not,' I confessed. 'And that's the problem. It's been an interesting venture, but I don't think it's for me long term. I'm not good at any of it for starters. If my marching and shoe shining are anything to go by, I'll make a useless officer.'

'So what are you going to do?' Deborah asked, a little concerned at the prospect of my failure.

'Well, drop out, I suppose. I'm free to leave at any time.'

'I think you should at least stick it out a little longer. Give it a bit more of a chance to see if things might improve. When does first term end? Perhaps you can make your decision then.'

'I'm not sure I can carry on for that long,' I said. 'There are another nine weeks until the end of Juniors.'

'I think you should,' Deborah said sagely. 'Because if you don't, you'll live to regret it, and will be forever left wondering, "what if".'

It was easy for Deborah to say. She wasn't stuck in the nightmare as I was, hating every single miserable minute of it. Our actions at Sandhurst felt so pointless, our priorities were distorted and I still couldn't understand how executing a perfect drill move was going to help me out on the battlefields of Helmand or why smiling socks and hospital corners would improve my command of soldiers. Self-Abuse had nearly broken me and I was dreading the prospect of sleeping in a cold, muddy hole once again. I was hanging on by a thread, only stubbornness and self-pride keeping me going. But I knew I would snap soon. For now I was too embarrassed to admit my failure, and ashamed to put my hands up admitting I was unsuitable and it was all a little bit too hard for me. Sandhurst had brought me close to my breaking point. I couldn't face another forced march in fighting order, but I couldn't face returning to Underground delays and a flickering computer screen even more. I needed to find my place in the platoon and discover where I belonged. I needed a skill to bring to the party, but there wasn't much promise of me finding it on my return. Because back at the Academy we would be boarding coaches again, and this time the obstacles set down in front of us would be far more challenging than Christopher Robin's playground.

5

AIN'T NO MOUNTAIN HIGH ENOUGH

Snuggled into a cosy cleft at the base of the Black Mountains, outside the coverage of 3G and DAB, beyond the reaches of high-speed internet and high-speed trains and over thirty miles from the nearest Starbucks lies the quiet Welsh market town of Crickhowell, a sleepy farmersville. Here, dour grey stone buildings with purple slate roofs house doilied tearooms, family butchers' and shops selling love spoons and bara brith. In Crickhowell, allotments and home-run chickens are not a suburban trend for the new yuppie generation, but a countryside practicality. Range Rovers speeding along the country lanes here actually have muddy wheels and Presbyterian ways reign strong.

I was standing in a small car park behind the village post office, beyond Crickhowell Castle, where a coach from Sandhurst had just deposited me, along with my team of six others. We were sitting on our bergens in the empty parking bays, dipping processed white bread into paper bowls of steaming stew, filling up on our last hot fresh meal. It was nearly 6 p.m. and I had dozed well on the three-hour journey along the M4, stocking up on crucial sleep. Above, day had just become night as the sky turned black and the orange-neon street lights flickered on, illuminating the paper and glass recycling banks in the car park's far corner. This was our starting point. Around the edges of the Black Mountains in four further car parks at village schools, pubs and community centres more cadets were also tucking into their last hot dinner because at six o'clock precisely the first teams would be setting off.

We were gathered in the Black Mountains for Exercise Long Reach; one of the toughest endurance tests in the army. A real test of men and the stuff of Sandhurst legend, every officer in the British Army can recall for you the tale of their Long Reach experience. The exercise covers seventy kilometres over tightly packed contours taking in five summits and over 3,000 metres of climb and descent with bergens on and the clock ticking. In the preceding days we had pored over maps, planning our route, plotting on checkpoints, making complex speed-distance-time calculations, and trying to remember what Naismith's Rule was all about.

At 18.30 it was our turn to start.

Merv, Rhodes, Thomas, Khadka, Evans, the Platoon Donkey (who was as inept as me, but without the excuse of never having done any of it before) and myself.

We helped each other hoist the bergens onto our backs, checked the straps were sitting comfortably and that we weren't wearing too many layers (as soon as we started walking we'd get hot). Map cases dangled around our necks and at the front I set my compass as we exited the car park. We turned left up the hill and passed the church (place of worship with spire, minaret or dome) where the gentle soothing sounds of a male voice choir drifted hymns from the warm light inside. Then right at the crossroads towards Llanbedr. We followed the road as it wound steeply north, past a phone box, 'PH' and farm on the right, out of the village, leaving the relative security of houses and civilization behind us.

After about an hour we arrived at our first checkpoint, where Captain Trunchbull and SSgt Cox were waiting for us on the opposite bank of a swollen river, grinning with anticipation. On the muddy near bank lay an assortment of empty oil drums, ropes and wooden planks; it was unfortunately obvious that we were going to be required to undertake some sort of *Krypton Factor*-style river crossing. Looking at the broiling river waters circling in high flood, none of us were much enthused to join the other bank, falling into the freezing waters at the beginning of our seventy-kilometre ordeal was definitely not a good idea.

Merv and Rhodes quickly took charge, lifting planks of wood onto the barrels and delegating me to do something with the rope. Khadka was a ninja at rope climbing and I tied a knot ready for her to scale a tree and walk the tightrope. We worked busily together as a team moving the barrels and planks of wood, but despite all our feigned concerted efforts none of us actually wanted to risk the freezing waters and attempt the river crossing, happy instead to let the clock timeout and forgo the Brucey

Bonus. Because after five weeks in the Sandhurst machine we'd now learned how to play the game and here we played a strategic fail.

So with boots still dry and morale intact, we moved on up the valley to our next checkpoint three hours' trekking away and more ridiculous blindfolded-rope-tying-plank-balancing-bridge-building nonsense. Nine of the fourteen checkpoints dotted around the Black Mountains had these absurd tasks awaiting us, and early on we met them with reasonable enthusiasm but after *forty* hours, and having watched the sun rise twice I couldn't care less where the number nine needed to go in the giant Sudoku laid out in the field in front of me, I just wanted to stop stumbling around these unforgiving Welsh mountains and go home to bed. Because Long Reach was not just about physical endurance, it was about testing mental endurance too. It was about challenging our ability to make sensible decisions when our minds had become an exhausted mush. And as the knot in a rope failed, releasing a steel drum of 'toxic chemicals' bouncing 300 metres down the hillside into the woods below I realized our mushy brains could make little sense of decisions.

Worse than the checkpoints with these *Krypton Factor* challenges were the ones without. Each was pitched at the absolute summit of a towering mountain top which we had to scale our way up, creeping along ridge paths as gale-force winds tried to knock us off our feet. At the top, snow nestled in sheltered hollows, reminding us that it was still winter and we shouldn't be there. We trudged along tracks, gloves on and hoods lowered, through muddy quagmires, our heels stinging from hours of rubbing in sweaty leather boots.

And then there was Checkpoint X-ray, lofting high up in the clouds, 500 metres vertically above us.

To get to the summit we zigzagged our way along a steep, precipice dirt track, tripping over stones, our legs now clumsy with exhaustion as the bergens on our backs dragged us down. This was Wales at its most unforgiving and the climb to the top took over an hour. We bowed our heads into the driving rain and shuffled our feet slowly to the peak in silence, too tired to even speak. Peering out from my shrouding hood, I watched the neon glow of Crickhowell village as it disappeared into the grey mist below and I felt surprisingly content. Here we were in the middle of one of the most arduous challenges we'd do at Sandhurst, if not our entire military careers, but as I trudged to the summit in search of Checkpoint X-ray, I could see my circumstance broaden into perspective. I wasn't crawling. I wasn't digging. I wasn't ironing or marching. I wasn't being shouted at and I wasn't polishing my shoes. I was walking in the hills with friends, albeit in the freezing darkness of midwinter, but this was tangibly normal and it put a small smile on my face.

As dawn approached on the first morning we descended west from the summit of Checkpoint X-ray into the tiny hamlet of Cwmdu. Climbing down I could see a tiny speck of light shining from the village pub below drawing us in, radiating the rich malty warmth of real ales and farming men with their dogs. We prayed that through the darkness next to the pub there stood a village church (place of worship with tower), not so as to hear our prayers but because if the church wasn't there then this wasn't Cwmdu but Pengenffordd and we were too far north. A church alone however wasn't confirmation enough; if a church was present but without a tower (place of worship without such additions) then this was Tretower and we had stumbled too far south and had more unwelcome walking ahead. Every cluster of houses here seemed to have a church. We checked our compasses, hoped and prayed.

As we neared the village, stepping down onto the gentle flattening river plain, we joined a meandering footpath with tall thick bramble hedges on either side. We were all tired now and walked in silence, the grumble of our tummies the only sound, as we had agreed to stop for breakfast after our next checkpoint. On the track ahead of us, I could vividly see a lady approaching. She was dressed beautifully in old Victorian fashions, her bustle and flouncing petticoat trailing in the mud. An open parasol rested on her shoulder and there was a genteel frilly bonnet on her head. I stared at her for quite some time as we moved closer. She looked completely out of place on a boggy wet path in a National Park. I wondered if the others had noticed her, but I was too tired to speak out, and glad that I hadn't because of course she was out of place. As we got nearer she disappeared, replaced by a signpost and overhanging tree. I had begun hallucinating. In the early morning half-light, tiredness was winning and playing havoc with my brain. Later, as we walked up a steep slope on our way to another towering summit Merv swore she saw a drove of pigs, rosy pink and incongruous on the

Welsh mountainside; she was adamant that they were there, but the rest of us saw nothing. Then at dusk my eyes deceived me once more as a looming farm building morphed into a singing ice cream van.

The tiredness frayed tempers too.

As the hours clocked by there were tantrums and tears as the Platoon Donkey stubbornly refused to continue. Sitting down on a slippery wet rock in a tight river gully, she refused to take another step. Not a budge. The agony and exhaustion had pushed her past her breaking point.

'I can't do this any more,' she blubbered between gasps of tears. 'This is fucking killing me, I can't go on.'

'Come on, don't cry. Look, you can do this,' Rhodes soothed. 'Just think, it'll all be over soon and you can rest. It's nearly the weekend, and you'll be back at home with your boyfriend in no time,' Rhodes reasoned. 'So let's keep going, shall we?'

'No, no. I can't,' she wailed as she put her head in her hands and started to sob loudly. 'Honestly, this is the end for me. I can't go any further.' She was broken. Mentally, she had given up, as the Long Reach challenge had taken its first victim.

I looked over at her. Crying here was going to achieve nothing. We were nowhere near a road or access track and Mountain Rescue would hardly scramble to save an able-bodied adult having a petulant strop. There was only one way off the mountain and that was to continue walking. But what exactly were we supposed to do with her?

'Here, have one of these,' Evans said, walking over to her and offering an open packet of Haribo sweets. 'A couple of these and you'll get your energy back. You just need a little boost, that's all.'

The Platoon Donkey looked up, her eyes wet and puffy, a little bulb of snot at her nose. 'Thanks,' she said quietly, taking one with a sniff and popping it in her mouth. She chewed on it as we all held our breath, waiting for her to snap out of this malaise and get back on track. But she just sat there, staring into space and feeling sorry for herself. Now I just wanted to walk over and throttle her. This was so selfish. No matter what, we still had to get to the next checkpoint and all she was doing was slowing us all down. But I bit my tongue and kept quiet. This was not the time for a temper tantrum.

'Do you think you're ready to try and carry on?' Rhodes tentatively quizzed. 'We can take it slowly if you like.'

Slowly! Slowly was not going to get us there by our six o'clock deadline, but I knew Rhodes was right, the Platoon Donkey was being stubborn and needed gentle coaxing. I looked down at the map and moved slowly to lead the way. I knew it was going to take us at least two hours to reach the next checkpoint, even more if she continued to be precious about it.

'We don't have much further to go,' I said, pointing at the map and trying to encourage her to her feet. 'It's no more than an hour to the next checkpoint.' It was a lie. My grandfather used to use this trick on me for years before I realized what he was doing. As my brother and I would sit in the back of his blue Ford Fiesta on long car journeys he'd always promise us that we were nearly there. When we pressed him for a specific time, he'd always half it, turning forty minutes into twenty, twenty into ten, psychologically making it seem more bearable.

'Here, do you want to take some of the load from your bergen and put it in mine,' Merv offered. 'It'll make things easier.'

And at that she saw her window of opportunity. 'Oh, if you don't mind. That would help,' she said, lifting her head to look at us.

And so as the tears dried on her cheeks, Merv squeezed the Platoon Donkey's sleeping bag and half of the contents from her bergen into her own. I was grateful that we would finally be moving again but incensed that she had given up so readily. It felt wrong. Alone she would have failed, but for us to pass as a team, some of us would have to work harder than others. However, in the army that is just the way it is sometimes.

By six o'clock on the second evening we had been walking for twenty-four hours without rest. We were shattered with exhaustion and ravenously hungry. Ahead lay one more checkpoint challenge before an enforced four-hour rest. As we staggered along a stretch of quiet country road separating checkpoints seven and eight CSgt Gleeson suddenly jumped out of a field beside us. CSgt Gleeson was a bit of an unknown to Eleven Platoon. He was a Physical Training Instructor (PTI) in the Academy gym and we saw him occasionally strutting around Sandhurst in his tight red and white PTI vest tucked neatly into a pair of navy bottom-skimming shorts that perfectly framed his toned backside. He was body-beautiful and knew it. As he leaped from the bushes that evening in

Wales he was freshly shaven and undoubtedly freshly fed, and looked far perkier than our lack of sleep would allow. Behind him a mud-splattered green Land Rover chugged noisily, the engine ticking away keeping the heating on and inside enviably warm.

'Ladies,' he grinned as he eagerly greeted us. 'How are you all this fine evening?'

'Fine thank you, colour sergeant,' Thomas piped up chirpily (never let them know you're broken).

'And where are you heading to now?' he asked as he unfolded a map out in front of us on the bonnet of the Land Rover.

I peered in. Looking down at the map as I hovered my right index finger over where I thought we were, jabbing to a point on the map.

'We're walking along this road here, colour sergeant; from checkpoint seven to eight,' I said, tracing my finger along a small yellow B road on the map. A fatigued error on my part because in the Army you never use the inaccuracy of a fat finger to point on a map.

'Oh dear, dear, dear, Miss Goodley. What have you been told about pointing to maps with your finger?' CSgt Gleeson said, reaching behind him into the Land Rover. 'You must always point at a map with something pointy,' he said, bringing out a fresh, warm triangular slice of pizza, oozing with oily cheese and succulent pepperoni. We couldn't believe our eyes. He used the pointy tip of the pizza slice to trace our route on the map and then took a large satisfactory bite as we stood salivating helplessly in front of him.

Exercise Long Reach was emotional. We returned to the Academy scarred, beaten, stumbling wrecks. For the next few days, cadets hobbled around like battery hens on swollen, broken legs and feet. Leg muscles were tight and unwilling, forcing people to walk slowly and deliberately with the precision of a geriatric. Raw, open blister wounds wept and the softer soled limped weakly to the medical centre for sick notes to wear trainers instead of boots, their pain excruciating enough to suffer the mocking ridicule of the rest of us.

But with the pain of Long Reach had come my Sandhurst turning point.

Looking back I now see Long Reach through heavily rose-tinted spectacles. I know I must have hated it at the time, but now all I feel is nostalgia for the Black Mountains: their quaint National Park status, the clearly marked footpaths, enchanting Welsh cottages and Crickhowell's peculiar charm. Today I can't recollect any of the pain or blisters that I must have suffered. I don't remember struggling with my bergen for forty hours. I don't recall getting lost and I don't even think we were that cold. Hindsight is a most dangerous and deluded perspective. Our brains are cleverly wired to forget pain (otherwise women would never give birth a second time). Pain isn't lasting and blisters heal, but it's glory that is laid down in history, to be exaggerated by each generation of story-telling. What I do remember of Long Reach is the euphoria of crossing the finish line, the satisfaction of having achieved something quite special, the coming of age, passing the Sandhurst initiation test, completing a rite of passage and finally, after weeks in the wilderness, finding my talent. Because Long Reach changed my Sandhurst fortunes. For it was on Long Reach I found my place. Finally I could take part, because on Long Reach I discovered my useful skill. I could read a map.

In Australia the Pormparaaw tribe of Aboriginals don't have words for left or right; instead they use the cardinal compass points. A sixth sense means they always know their orientation, even when in an unfamiliar darkened room. I've always been fascinated by this skill and, while nowhere near this talented myself, I can competently use a compass and read a map. I was aware that I could do this before I went to Sandhurst, but I was not aware that so many others couldn't. In the army, officers have a dreadful reputation among soldiers for being incapable of reading a map and routinely getting lost,[26] and conforming to female stereotypes should have further compounded this for me, but instead in this instance two wrongs make a right. And with map in hand I finally became a useful addition to the platoon. My parade square ineptitude and inability to shine shoes became forgivable, because at last I could join the club, no longer standing in the queue outside feeling useless, racked with guilt and incompetence. I could take part. My special skill meant I could contribute after all. I could hold up my side of the bargain. While the other members of the platoon helped me shine my shoes, dig

---

26 One of my male Sandhurst contemporaries was later awarded a Military Cross for his heroics during a fire-fight in Helmand. If he had not been lost in the first place, he would never have found himself in that battle with the Taliban.

holes and disguise my two left feet on the parade square, I became indispensable with a map.

I desperately hadn't wanted to return to Sandhurst after that first long leave weekend. And as Sunday night arrived I slipped into a deeply depressive 'Sunday blues', moping around Deborah's flat, like a child reluctant to return to school at the end of the long summer holidays. I dragged my heels to the car, wishing for any excuse to escape: lightning strike, alien abduction, natural disaster: anything to get out of going back to boot camp. My first weekend of freedom had brought a taste of the free world and I so much wanted to be part of it again, and the thought of returning to the oppressive Sandhurst regime filled me with dread. The endless cycle of cleaning, polishing, marching, meals on the run, incessant shouting and the feeling of continually being on edge, trapped under a fear of misdemeaning and recrimination, filled me with anxiety.

As I had left the Academy at lunchtime the previous Friday, screaming my way up the M3 motorway as fast as my VW Polo would carry me, Deborah's jelly babies long demolished, I made a personal promise: if things didn't improve, if I didn't improve, on my return I would jack it all in and return to the City to ask for my old job back,[27] the itch scratched. There seemed no point in flogging the dead horse. If I was going to suffer the slashing pay cut, the

---

27 In fact, had I done so I would have found myself redundant within the year, another 'victim' of the recession as the Northern Rock house of cards came crashing down, dragging everyone else along with it.

demeaning indignities and back-breaking, blister-giving, muscle-snapping training, I should at least be competent at it, and right now I wasn't.

But that was until Long Reach.

Long Reach changed my fortunes and, with it, it changed my Sandhurst experience. With Long Reach the course of my fate jibed around the buoy and onto the right tack, as I had my lucky break. Back at the Academy, while cadets limped around on languid limbs I had a small spring in my step, because finally I got it. I understood something. Just because I could read a map, it didn't suddenly overnight mean that I could shine shoes and march, but it did give me a tiny little break. A modicum of skill with which I could play the game, like everyone else.

Those early days of the commissioning course were all about weeding out the unsuitable. Identifying those who wouldn't last the course, whose absenting potential may have been missed by the filtering sift at Westbury. If you were struggling, as I was, you found yourself under greater staff scrutiny. The magnifying glare honed in, focusing unnecessary additional heat to the pressure cooker we were already in. The only way out of this was to excel at something. Getting top marks in a map-reading exam allowed you to bask in the glow of being top of the class for long enough to overshadow other inadequacies. Having an immaculate room bought more time to practise the slow march, the shiniest shoes provided a smoke screen under which to improve press-ups and being fast at running protected you from everything. The Sandhurst vultures circled for the weak and the lame, the ones who universally struggled, and then they hounded them.

So for now I was safe.

Just.

After the rigours of the first five weeks, we returned to an ever so slightly relaxed regime at the Academy after our first leave weekend. From now on our days would begin with a generous lie-in to half past six, the national anthem dawn chorus stopped, the chocolate ban was lifted, our mobile phones were released from SSgt Cox's office, but only to be used in our rooms, and meal times were extended by a lengthy five minutes (although by now my eating habits had adapted to the breakneck pace of feeding, much to my mother's disapproval). Our rooms became our own space, as we no longer had to adhere to the prescribed layout. Kettles, photographs, personal effects and homely touches were allowed, as the farcicality of room inspections relaxed, but unfortunately didn't stop. In my room, I added a pot plant and a rug, and replaced the army-issue quilt with a brightly coloured duvet-cover set. On the bare shelves, I placed books and photographs, while at the back of my underwear drawer I squirrelled away bottles of wine to get me through the late evenings of polishing and shining. Alcohol was strictly banned in our rooms, and being caught with it would have been a serious offence, but as I was now twenty-eight years old I felt responsible enough to control my own consumption so hid it away at the back of the drawer behind my bras and pants.

So with the shock of capture over, we began to grasp the essentials and Academy life got fractionally easier. Occasionally we would get too comfortable and a healthy dose of maddening nonsense would be dealt our way: a late-night parade, early-morning inspection, guard duty or threat of return to 'weeks one to five', but on the whole we settled into the routine and started to play the game, as the remainder of the Junior term subsequently passed in a forgotten blur. The cycle of drill, inspections and parades persisted, interjected occasionally with glimmers of academic lectures to awaken our brains.

*

In keeping with the ideals of sound Christian leadership, religious ceremony was a weekly fixture in our new world. Each Sunday during weeks one to five, we paraded in Chapel Square dressed smartly for inspection and then took our pick from the faith options on offer. There was the choice of joining either the large Anglican congregation in the Academy Chapel where the service was lengthy but provided plenty of scope to fall asleep unnoticed in prayer, or the shorter, smaller Roman Catholic ceremony where the slumber potential was much reduced. The overseas cadets were all excused to the 'multi-faith room' where none of them ever went, instead sloping off to their rooms for an extra hour in bed. I like to think that everyone's God understood our unanimous pan-faith requirement for sleep.

And at some point I do recall my parents coming to one of the twice-termly Chapel Sundays when the whole of Sandhurst, all of the cadets and staff, marched to church to a brass band and filled every seat in the cathedral-like Chapel. On these occasions the euphony of 1,000 people belting out 'I Vow to Thee my Country' to resounding organ pipes, made proud shoulders bristle and spines stiffen, as the music echoed around the eaves and pews.

On my parents' visit my mother fussed terribly over how tired and gaunt she thought I looked, shocked by the dark circles under my eyes and pallor of my skin. My father belted out the hymns and couldn't resist the urge to execute some Nazi-style marching, demonstrating for SSgt Cox and Company Sergeant Major Porter that my drill ineptitude was not due to personal ignorance but the fault of my unfortunate genetics.

But the Chapel was more than just a place to sleep and worship, it also bears memorial to Sandhurst officers who had died in service. Every pillar, pew, stained window and spare inch of wall is inscribed with the names of the fallen. Over 3,000 Sandhurst graduates lost their lives in the First World War alone, most painfully young and their names and teenage years can be found carved into the marble and oak all around the chapel. At the front, before the choir stalls, a raised glass and wooden cabinet sits, inside which lies the Book of Remembrance, a thick tome listing all the names of Academy alumni who have died in active service. Each day a page is turned. And in the arch above the altar are etched the words spoken by the Chaplain in his sermon on the last Sunday of term in July 1914: '*Dulce et decorum est pro patria mori'*: 'It is sweet and right to die for one's country', the 'old lie' there for each new generation to decide.

With the thrashing of the first five weeks over, our Sandhurst world started to expand too as we broadened out into the classroom and lecture hall. We used the firing ranges and sports facilities, gymnasium, assault course and were now also permitted to venture to the NAAFI (Navy, Army, Air Force Institute). The NAAFI was a café cum local convenience shop, selling everything from Mars bars to hairnets, and provided us with rare slivers of normality on the brief occasions we sought refuge there. Like driving around in my car on Sunday evenings eating jelly babies, the NAAFI became a sanctum from which to escape the prying eyes of the Sandhurst machine. A place to hide and forget, because for now we were still largely confined to camp. Ten o'clock curfews meant that there was no scope to vanish into London to catch up with friends, and we were still too tired to do so. Occasionally there would be a trip to Camberley Tesco just outside the Academy gates to stock up on jelly babies and freezer bags, but otherwise the only feasible means of escape was to play a suitable sport.

As you might expect, sport is a big deal in the army and at Sandhurst it was compulsory. After week five, sport became a mandatory fixture every Wednesday and Saturday afternoon. To select your mode of glory or escape, a university 'Freshers' Fair' style event was held at which each cadet had to register with sporting options from an exhaustive menu. There were two philosophies of approach to this: one, to choose a sport that you loved but that might turn into a twice-weekly additional physical thrashing and see you confined within the Academy gates; or two, choose a sport with benefits such as rowing or sailing which involved trips to one of Surrey's local lakes with a shopping stop at Sainsbury's en route. I chose to swim, which had double benefits. I could swim in the Academy pool where the far too kind-hearted retired Colonel took pity and allowed us to paddle around serenely, propped up on a float while gossiping in the shallow end and then go back early to our rooms for a siesta. Or I could travel to Aldershot to use the Olympic-sized garrison swimming pool, where, once I'd got my hair wet, I could slope off into Guildford for a few stolen moments in Caffé Nero, savouring a coffee and warm chocolate brownie while smelling of chlorine.

But where physical exertion was concerned sport was definitely the soft option because physical training, or PT as it is known, was when our bodies were truly pushed to exhaustion at Sandhurst.

Now I'm no slouch but Sandhurst PT involved serious amounts of pain because PT hurts. Each gruelling session involved parading at the gymnasium in immaculately ironed clothing ready for whatever horrendous form of physical torture the instructors had prepared for us: a boot run, circuits, loaded march, hill reps, combat drowning (army swimming) or a visit to the assault course. Then the physical training instructors (PTIs) would emerge grinning, jostling and joking with excitement at the prospect of another masochistic session. They strutted up and down in tight white vests which framed their carefully sculpted biceps, inspecting the platoon, checking bergen straps, clothing creases, shoe laces and socks for whiteness. Because even PT couldn't start without an inspection.

Any activity inside the gym was a bonus; at least sheltered inside it wasn't wet, cold or muddy. But draconian Sandhurst rules extended within the gym too. There was to be no walking, only running; no standing still, just jogging on the spot; no talking and no fun. All infringements of these rules were punishable with yet more press-ups or, worse, the maintenance of some ridiculous stress position. A tiny little natter would see the whole platoon down on the floor hovering and quivering in a down press-up stance, muscles crying out to be released, beads of sweat dripping onto the varnished parquet floor. And pity the fool who forgot to remove their watch.

Our dedicated platoon PTI was a small chippy female sergeant, called Sgt Walker, who was a freak of female nature. Superhumanly fit, she unfortunately expected the same of each one of us and used physical training sessions to thrash us to within an inch of our lives. She would scream red-faced at us as we clambered over one another trying to find a way over the assault course twelve-foot wall or wriggled hopelessly at the bottom of a rope climb. And as the only female instructor, she felt she had a point to prove too and would insist we matched the male platoons at everything. In the machismo army world there is some value in her dictum, but a great deal of pain was suffered in its delivery. The physical ability of females in the army is a much-mooted issue. There are many who strongly believe that because women are not as physically able as men, they should not serve alongside them, and in the infantry this is the case. In this instance, I agree, but in planning roles, desk jobs, chefs, even pilots, I don't believe this distinction is necessary. I recognize that women are not physiologically comparable to their male counterparts – we can't throw, catch or bench-press twice our body weight – but most of the roles in today's army don't require this level of physical prowess either. I would rather a bright enthusiastic female soldier than a lazy witless male one who can run fast. I accept that in the Army it is important to be physically fit, but matching the men I feel is narcissistic vanity. Although this didn't stop Sgt Walker from flogging us, and her favourite method of achieving this was on a loaded march.

These unfortunately regular sessions involved a high-speed endurance march with a packed bergen on our backs and rifle cradled in our arms. For hours we would speed-walk around the sandy tracks and one-sided Escher-like hills of Barossa, the wooded training area behind the Academy, notching up miles and blisters. We panted up never-ending hills, in neatly organized rank and file, our hearts pounding inside our chests as we tried to keep to the punchy pace. A rehearsal of soldiers getting to the battlefield, this 'tactical advance to battle' (TAB) was to become a staple of our training along with room inspections and drill. Starting by carrying no greater weight than a small bag of sugar, they ramped up progressively over the year until we could comfortably spend hours covering long distances with over half our body weight strapped to our backs, battling more with the boredom than discomfort. Wheeler and Merv were awesome at this. Both strong and mentally stubborn, they would simply put their heads down and slog forwards. But I found it more of a challenge. None of my pre-Sandhurst physical training had prepared me for these marches and at first I struggled to adjust to carrying the additional weight. My back ached terribly and my legs quickly grew weary as I suffered under the extra load. But at Sandhurst the initial training built up in a slow progression, giving me time to adapt and catch up, and before long I was comfortably slogging along with the rest of the platoon, bored and waiting for it to finish.

And I was motivated further when I discovered the benefits of all these endurance marches as my legs and bum began to tone up. Years of sitting static at a desk all day long in the City had brought on a premature sagging, soggy peach effect, but within weeks of being at Sandhurst this had firmed up nicely. The daily gym sessions and hours of standing to attention also honed my core stomach muscles and the endless press-ups had finally obliterated my bingo wings; for all the pain and suffering, Sandhurst proved to be the most effective 'bikini diet' I've ever been on.

PT was also unfortunately one of few occasions on which we had to endure Captain Trunchbull. She would turn up at the gym with her bergen already on her back. Then as we set off she would stay at the back of the platoon, trotting along with SSgt Cox shouting 'encouraging' abuse at us, as if we cared for her truculent criticism. She picked off those suffering at the back and demoralized them further, like a nasty school prefect picking on hapless fourth-formers. Her words might have had meaning if only we'd thought she could do the same herself, but one grey morning as we hauled ourselves up a hill through the rain we found out she couldn't. As our boots were sinking deep into the mud, Officer Cadet Thomas stumbled over a protruding tree root and the weight of her bergen forced her off balance. She grappled forward for something to steady herself and, reaching out to Captain Trunchbull's bergen, she discovered it provided little resistance, proving squishy, yielding and feather light, compared with the heavy ones we were carrying. She had stuffed it with a pillow and with its discovery any residual respect we may have had for her instantly evaporated in the sweaty mist.

These bergen PT thrashings were a painful necessity in the training. Without them we would never have been able to carry the heavy load of all our equipment around on exercise with us. So gradually, with sadistic joy, Sgt Walker was actually building up our strength, so that by the end of Juniors we were ready for our first significant military exercise, and this time my map-reading skills alone were not going to be enough to get me through.

6

IN THE LINE OF FIRE

As the end of Junior Term neared, one substantial hurdle
still loomed large on the murky horizon; one remaining
encumbrance separated us from the reward of three blissful
weeks of freedom on Academy leave before we came back
for the Intermediate Term. It was our big final end-of-term
exam. Another back-breaking, whimpering week in South
Wales. Five long days and four sleepless nights on exercise
again. I had survived twice. Barely. But this time things
were going to be very different, as Exercise Crychan's
Challenge would offer none of the cosy Home Counties
security of Winnie-the-Pooh's Self-Abuse, because
Crychan's was taking us to Brecon. An altogether different
place. And for good reason, there are fewer words in the
military lexicon that strike with greater dread than Brecon.

Far from the gentle leafy lanes and rolling hills of the
South Downs, Brecon is raw, gritty and non-commissioned.
Brecon is about infantry tactics and bloody combat; about
'FIND', 'FIX' and 'STRIKE'. Brecon is about serious
professional soldiering on the doorstep of the Infantry
Battle School and selection ground for the Special Forces.

Brecon is Wales at its most inhospitable and promised to be cold, wet, miserable and thoroughly shit.

Of course we had already been exposed to the foul climate and hostile Welsh hills on Exercise Long Reach, but on Long Reach there was no enemy. On Long Reach we didn't worry about tactics and doctrine, or principles of war. And on Long Reach we left our weapons behind in the Academy armoury. Long Reach had been an amble in the comforting security of a National Park, with its well-marked footpaths and glimmers of civilian inhabitancy. Crychan's was on Sennybridge training area, on the other, darker side of the Black Mountains, trapped beneath its rain shadow.

Our Crychan's ordeal started early – at half past four on a Monday morning. The platoon gathered outside in the pitched blackness of Chapel Square, busying around by the lights of the waiting coaches, packing food, ammunition and radios into already bulging bergens. Two days of rations, 200 rounds of ammunition, the latest Bowman radios, binoculars, medical kit, right-angle torches, weapon night-sights and absurdly a brown paper bag containing lunch, which included, with no forethought, a pot of yoghurt. All this was squeezed into pouches and pockets until zips and straps would no longer close. Our weapons had been drawn from the armoury and helmets and body armour were coming too.

Ahead lay a week of serious austere infanteering.

Packed and war-ready, we clambered onto the coaches for the depressing drive to Wales, settling down to sleep as we sped west along the M4, the last unmitigated rest we'd get until Friday. I quickly nodded off, my lolling head intermittently banging against the windowpane, awakening me at Reading, Bristol, the Severn Bridge and eventually Crickhowell where spots of rain started to fall. The clouds thickened and the sky greyed with brewing showers. As the coach wound its way around the mountain road, I caught a glimpse of Checkpoint X-ray, its peak lost ominously in the mist. At Sennybridge, we left the main road behind and crept up a steep track to the training area, the coaches' low gears growling in protest as each hillcrest disguised another. Finally at the top, we rattled over a cattle grid that announced our arrival and the heavens promptly opened. Heavy raindrops started to splatter against the windscreen while, outside, sheep huddled in hollows for shelter. It was stark and bleak. The patchwork of bare open grazing was windswept and exposed, broken only by tight forest blocks and icy cold streams. As we disembarked the coaches at Dixies Corner, my boots squelched into the sodden ground, water pooling around them like a squeezing sponge.

I knew then the week was going to be insufferable.

The point of Crychan's was to test us. To test our understanding of the basic soldiering fundamentals we had been taught so far in the Junior Term. Those that failed would stay behind in Old College to repeat the term, while the rest progressed from shorts to trousers, entering New College and Inters.

The exercise would be fully tactical, deploying under a realistic scenario, with an actual enemy to fight and objectives to take during four days of conventional war fighting. Our mission: to seek out the baddies and kill them. Simple. And this would be done using our most recently rehearsed tactic, the 'advance to contact'. On Exercise Self-Abuse we had already learned what to do when shot at – the agonizing dash-down-crawl routine of fire and manoeuvre – and advance to contact took this further, in looking for the enemy in the first place, then killing him. But to my civilian brain the whole concept of this high-risk game of hide and seek seemed utterly absurd.

As we went through the motions my internal monologue was baffled:

'So let me get this straight: you think there's a baddy hiding somewhere in the bushes on that hillside?'

'Yes, that's right. He's camouflaged so you can't see him and he's got a gun.'

'Erm, OK. And what you want me to do is walk slowly towards him?'

'Yes, that's it.'

'But he'll shoot me.'

'Yes, that's what we want. Then you'll know where he is.'

'You're fucking right I will.'

The concept was bananas. Walk blindly up to the enemy and wait for the bang as he takes a potshot at you. Then if I survived the initial attempt on my life, I had to hurl myself on the ground and do the whole fire and manoeuvre routine to get to him and kill him. And to add insult to gunshot wound, I had been appointed the platoon 'point man', out at the front like a sacrificial lamb, because I could read the sodding map. I had not chosen my specialist skill wisely.

As soon as we got off the bus and gathered our belongings, the war started. We strapped our helmets and body armour on, oiled weapons, smeared on waxy warpaint and camouflaged with grass and moss. We'd been given a grid reference to get to and set off across the boggy ground following a compass bearing, Captain Trunchbull and SSgt Cox trailing at the back observing. Feeling exposed and alone at the front, I scanned the horizon through the rain, scrutinizing every bush and clump of grass, waiting in anticipation for the inevitable. After a mile, we neared a babbling stream when the crackling sound of gunfire rang out from a tree line to the left. I dived onto the ground, desperately looking through my weapon sights for the enemy.

Nothing.

I wriggled forwards a bit to get a better look.

Still nothing.

A further crackle and pop rattled out from the trees and then from behind a scrubby bush I saw him. A Gurkha dressed in brown desert uniform stepped forwards and gave me a little wave (the Gurkhas play enemy for all Sandhurst exercises, usually dying in highly dramatized Oscar-winning death displays). I started to fire at him. The weapon recoiled into my shoulder, as the rounds were released, sending hot empty brass steaming out onto the wet grass beside me. Behind me, Captain Trunchbull came charging up to the front to oversee the action screaming at us to 'get into cover'. I looked around me – One Section had flattened forwards into a defensive line, Allinson, Lea, Gill, Khadka, Rhodes, Thomas and me, all of us lying on our stomachs pinging off rounds at the waving Gurkha.

'Get into fucking cover!' Captain Trunchbull screeched at us.

Looking up and down I didn't understand what she meant. We were already lying on the ground and there was nothing more for us to shelter behind. Then I looked across to my right, at our far flank.

No, no, no, no. She wouldn't. Not on the morning of the first day.

Thirty metres or so to my right was a narrow ditch along which flowed the frozen waters of a whispering stream. Captain Trunchbull wanted us to get in it. The cow. We had no choice. So, while back in London my friends and former colleagues were probably standing on station platforms battling Monday morning Tube delays, I found myself crawling along a freezing muddy riverbed. The chilling waters seeped into my boots, soaking through my woolly socks and quickly numbing my toes. As I clambered forwards through the sludge, I was forced lower in the waters, until my trousers and jacket were sodden too. The icy water trickled through fabric and stitch, stinging my skin as it reached my body. The cold shock made me gasp and knocked the breath from my lungs.

All of One Section flanked right, through the glacial stream waters, each one of us crawling over stones and squelching along the muddy riverbank, while Captain Trunchbull continued her screaming tirade from the safety of the dry embankment, yelling out every filthy expletive she could lay her tongue on. She hopped up and down in anger, because it was in Brecon that Captain Trunchbull became her apoplectic best. As red as Lenin, she screamed uncontrolled blue murder at us, spinning into a fulminating rage like a caged Tasmanian devil. Her torrent of expletives provided us with little teaching guidance, serving more as an irritating distraction. And she didn't know what she was instructing anyway because the last time she had conducted an advance to contact was more than ten years ago, when she herself had been in our position as an officer cadet.

We crawled for what felt like miles, through the muddy stream and spongy field to assault the enemy position. Until eventually, panting and wheezing, with lungs croaking like broken organ bellows, we got to within reach of the enemy. Next to me Officer Cadet Gill dug into one of her webbing pouches and fiddled with the safety clasp around a grenade, pulled the pin and launched it towards the Gurkha. We waited, crouching and tense for the explosive bang before leaping forwards, weapons to automatic, blazing into the enemy hide. The Gurkha let out a mournful wail, dramatizing his final death throes and jerked in comic spasms on the forest floor.

Then a silent pause.

Had we finished?

I was knackered.

In my ear I could hear a broken radio message, asking if there were any more enemy.

By now I was hungry and wondering about the state of the yoghurt pot in my crushed daysack, when another crackle of rounds came from deep inside the trees. This time it was Two Section's turn to get their feet wet and bust a gut crawling. So as the shouting melee moved forwards, One Section could relax and recoup in reserve and conduct our own intelligence gathering operation, because in One Section we had the platoon's best weapon, our own Gurkha spy, Officer Cadet Khadka. After each slogging assault, Khadka would chat away in Nepali to the Gurkha dead, getting handouts of vanilla fudge and finding out where the next enemy were, how many more positions we had to assault, what was in store for us that night and, most importantly, what time the coaches were coming back for us on Friday. These little snippets provided a much needed morale boost in an otherwise miserable week.

We spent three continuous days walking around Brecon in 'arrowhead formation' advancing to contact and patrolling towards the enemy on an 'axis of advance', waiting to be shot at. Assaulting up hills and streams, in woodblocks and farms, from Dixies Corner to Gardiner's Track. Position after position. After each iteration, we would regroup and sit on our daysacks in an open square while Captain Trunchbull admonished us all for not trying hard enough, threatening that the reality would be far, far worse and that with real bullets we'd all have been dead. In reality, I'd be tucked up in a rear-echelon desk job, leaving the infantry madness to the insane. As we flogged ourselves at enemy positions again and again I couldn't help thinking of Einstein's maxim on insanity: 'doing the same thing over and over again and expecting different results'.

Perhaps we should have packed straitjackets in our bulging bergens too.

Each night we retreated into a dark, dense woodblock and set up a harbour area as we had done on Self-Abuse. Digging shell-scrape coffins, clearing a track plan, stringing out twine, boiling up horrendous corned-beef hash dinners and taking our turn to stay awake on sentry. This time I was sharing my basha with Cadet Gill; another university OTC veteran, she was joining the army to be a teacher and had a healthy laissez-faire approach to all the irrelevant crawling and digging she had to do to get there. We worked together as a team, me digging our shell-scrape while she fetched drinking water and cooked our dinner, kindly giving me her rice pudding, the only meal option that didn't make me heave. On the first night, we unfurled our roll-mats and sleeping bags under our poncho and wriggled in for what very little sleep we could snatch before our turn on stag. The rain had continued intermittently all day and by now the ground was cold and squelchy beneath us. Pulling the sleeping bag cord tightly over my head, I curled up at the bottom searching for some warmth. I left my wet boots on, trying to dry them out, afraid that if I unlaced and took them off they might freeze solid as the temperature plunged. Forty minutes later, we were shaken awake to start our turn at night watch and I undid my sleeping bag to sit up. As I did so there was a sloshing sound as a bow-wave of water splashed along the bottom of the shell-scrape which had now become a shallow pond as the rainwater trickled in.

Brecon had become unadulterated misery.

On sentry, Gill and I lay shuddering with cold staring into black nothingness, stagnant at the cusp of hell. The temperature dropped further until my numb fingers lacked the dexterity to even unwrap a boiled sweet let alone pull the trigger. I looked at the time on my watch – twenty minutes past midnight. I had been awake for twenty of the last twenty-four hours, which on our £67 a day Officer Cadet wage equated to nearly half the statutory hourly minimum wage. I could be flipping burgers in McDonald's for more, and at least in McDonald's I'd have dry boots on. For the non-graduates like Prince Harry, it was even worse: they earned only £39 a day, which was a paltry £2 an hour to crawl through a river and sleep in a muddy puddle. I thought of all the times I'd battled across a Tube-less London because the greedy Underground train drivers were striking again, demanding more pay and better working conditions. The most basic infantry soldier risking his life in Afghanistan earns just a third of what a Tube driver does for driving a train through a tunnel.[28]

On our second stag of the night we once again lay with our heads propped against our rifles, staring into the inky void waiting for something to happen, but rather hoping it wouldn't.

'God, I'm so cold I can't even move my fingers,' Gill moaned. 'If the enemy suddenly appear in front of us I

---

28 'An officer is much more respected than any other man who has as little money. In a commercial country, money will always purchase respect. But you find an officer who has, properly speaking, no money, is every where well received and treated with attention' Samuel Johnson.

don't think I would actually have the movement to grip the trigger and fire at them.'

'I'm so tired I think I'd offer myself up as a hostage,' I said.

'Only so long as they didn't feed me any more corned-beef hash.'

'Urgh.' I made a gagging noise. 'Where have you put that CWS thing we're supposed to be using?'

We'd been given a 'night-sight' to use and, after fiddling with batteries, knobs and eventually removing the lens cover, we managed to turn the darkness around us into a view of soupy neon green. In the distance I could make out the outline of a ridgeline and forest block on the horizon. I played with the new toy for a while, scanning around the field in front of us, picking out sheep and turning around to investigate the harbour area behind me. Among the lines of thin pine trees the platoon slept, cocooned as little sleeping bag mounds at the bottom of their coffin holes. I switched it off and decided I needed to go for a wee, so, leaving Gill behind on her own to keep sentry, I nipped off into the wood with my rifle in search of a suitable spot.

Away from the platoon harbour the forest floor was marked with shallow ditches where previous exercises had dug their shell-scrapes and I stumbled about in the dark until I selected one, carefully putting my weapon down on the ground beside it. The ditch was only about a foot deep, and I stepped in, unzipped, lowered my trousers and squatted. I was mid-relief when a terrible thought crossed my mind: we were not the only people in this woodblock. The two boys' platoons of Imjin Company were also harboured up in here. I wasn't sure where, but I was sure that they too had night-sights. Suddenly, I was gripped by stage fright. I pulled myself together, zipped up, gathered my rifle and hurriedly made my way back to the sentry spot, hoping the super-keen infantry boys were not keeping a vigilant watch in my direction.

By the third day we were completely exhausted and utterly fed up with flogging ourselves up hills after the enemy. As the day came to a close, we anticipated another night shivering in a woodblock harbour area somewhere, feet frozen to a crust at the bottom of our soggy sleeping bags. But as we plotted and followed the given grid, instead of leading us to another dense forest, we arrived at a farm. A delightfully dry farm. No digging shell-scrapes and lying contorted on the wet forest floor, tonight we would be sleeping in the sheltered warmth of a barn, with the comfort of a roof over our heads and solid floor beneath us. It was basic but total luxury.

When we got there, the Company Quartermaster appeared with big green thermos containers full of steaming stew and we queued eagerly to fill paper bowls with as much as they could hold. I dipped slices of bread into the thick brown gravy and scooped chunks of potato with a clean plastic spoon rather than the dirty one that I had licked, wiped on my trousers and stored in my pocket for the last three days. That night, sheltered in our new sanctuary, we would be rewarded with some sleep too. I stripped off my boots, wriggled my damp toes in the fresh air, changed my clothes and boiled a mess tin of water for a soapy wash. After three horrendous days these were all the luxuries we needed: warm food, a roof over our heads, sleep and clean clothes. Brecon had reduced us to these bare essentials, to the primal needs of man.

The reason for this relative luxury was to give us a well-earned break, to allow us to recoup, recharge our batteries and energize ready for one final big push, our first Company attack. Because the next day, relatively refreshed from the gift of four uninterrupted hours of sleep we began the preparations, plotting, planning, scheming, rehearsing, thinking of every eventuality. Coordinating 100 wannabe officers in the dark with tactical aplomb soon translated into a complex feat of organization. The enemy were holed up in a farm and, with the first light of dawn the next morning, we would be there to bring them the good news. Storming their hide and winning our five-day war.

As Imjin Company consisted of one girls' platoon and two boys' platoons the boys were going to be doing the hard work, while we lay along a ridgeline in fire support. After all, this is what the boys had joined the army for and they didn't want us coming along and ruining their fun.

That night we set off in the dead hours on a torturous long walk across the training area, sneaking along a roundabout route to avoid detection. One long silent line of troops marching quickly through the night. As we trudged along the darkened track, it continued to rain, driving harder as the wind whipped droplets towards us. The drops prickled on exposed skin, making me screw up my eyes and draw the hood of my jacket in closer. I hummed along quietly to myself, needing a distraction to keep me from falling asleep on the march, and after a while the chorus of a James Blunt ballad became stuck on an irritating loop inside my head. James Blunt had been an army officer, he had been through Sandhurst and Brecon, and probably attacked this very barn, probably even trudged along this very track in the rain. And now, amid the misery of exercise, I completely understood his capacity for such self-pitying song writing.

After two hours of head down, sleepy walking, we got to the form-up point and Eleven Platoon separated off into the woods to shuffle into position on the ridgeline overlooking the enemy farm. Below in the farm's yard I could see a group of Gurkhas sitting comfortably around a bonfire, snug and warm, their faces glowing in the firelight. They knew we were coming. Lying in position, we waited, checking watches, waiting for H-hour. Minutes passed, the big hand moving slowing around the clock face. I rested my head against my rifle, watching the view in front of me move up and down with each breath. I was tired and it was a strong battle of wills with my eyelids, as they drooped heavier and heavier. Eventually the inevitable happened, as from the far end of the platoon row came a loud truffling snort as someone drifted into sleep.

At H-hour, flares lit up the purple sky and the air filled with the volley and thunder of gunfire as we started firing, jolting those snoozing awake with a shot of adrenaline. To the left flank the boys' platoons came racing in, charging through the morning mist, across the field and fences, into the farm and clearing through the buildings, killing the enemy as they found them. Moments later, we ran hurriedly down the bank to join them in the farm complex, securing the area and checking the enemy dead. The whole operation was all over rather quickly. Everything had gone smoothly and exactly according to the well-rehearsed plan. Now all we had to do was walk back to Dixies Corner and catch the buses back to Sandhurst. I was almost excited; the sun was coming up, another hellish week on exercise was over and in one week I'd be on Easter leave. Life was good.

Then a loud explosion boomed into my ears and reverberated through my guts.

What the hell was that?

We were being mortared.

Suddenly the perfectly planned, slick operation descended into chaos and mayhem as more explosions bounced around us knocking the wind out of my chest.

And as we started to run, fleeing the farm, the first casualty fell, Captain Trunchbull picking them off, telling them to lie down immobile. Fortunately, Lea was the smallest, lightest member of Eleven Platoon and Wheeler quickly scooped her up and staggered forwards with her slung in a fireman's lift over her shoulders. But a fireman's lift was not going to get her all the way back to safety and more explosive bangs detonated along our escape route. We quickly created a makeshift stretcher using a poncho and took it in turns to haul Lea back up onto the ridge. Halfway up another casualty fell. Picked off in the midst of the melee by Captain Trunchbull. And then just as we tried to establish a method for moving two casualties we were struck with another. And with three the platoon were crippled.

We made two more poncho stretchers and loaded the fresh casualties in, then hauled the three of them up the steep ridge slopes, seeking safety at the top. Dragging the heavy loads was agonizing, back-breaking work. My lungs wailed in pain as I tried to hold up my corner of the poncho as we struggled to the top, bumping the casualty indelicately along the ground. My ears filled with screams of urgency and, with each explosive boom, the pit of my insides resonated. With each step the body hanging in the stretcher cradle got heavier and heavier. Rifles swung into the way and daysacks slipped from our backs. I felt as though I couldn't carry on. We were never going to make it. I had to stop. This was too much. But there was no option to stop or slow down. Dragging those bodies back to Dixies Corner was worse than marking time on the parade square, worse than leopard crawling around Hundred Acre Wood, worse than loaded marches and worse than digging my own coffin hole. Red-faced and shattered, we finally got there, but I felt no elation at the finish line. It wasn't real, nowhere near real, but it was horrendous. And casualty evacuation like this was to become a routine fixture on exercises for good reason.

At Dixies Corner I sat on my bergen awaiting the arrival of the coaches, my head cupped in my raw chapped hands, chest rising slowly to the rhythm of my lungs. Brecon had been as horrid as advertised. The rain had fallen, the ground squelched, the temperature plummeted and the winds stripped and squalled. I wiggled my frozen toes in the bottom of my soggy boots and wondered if they would ever thaw and regain feeling. My fingers were numb, limbs

Smart as a carrot

On Old College Steps

Learning to love Billy the Whistle and the dash-down-crawl routine

The Big Dig

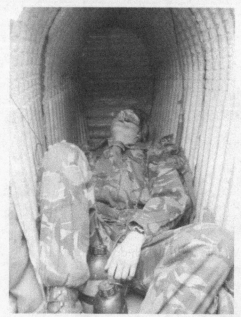

Zzzzzzzz

Camouflaged with Officer Cadet Gill

Officer Cadets Wheeler and Van der Merwe

Breaking and
entering in
Celini Village

Living the
dream as
platoon
sergeant

Gas, Gas, Gas!

Eleven Platoon with CSgt Bicknell in his element

Assault course madness

The End – Final Exercise

Receiving my bling

bruised and my eyes were tired from lack of sleep. On the distant horizon the coaches appeared like a mirage, coming to rescue us, and I looked out beyond them, across the mountains and hilltops, taking in the dramatic setting. Over on a far crest the grey clouds were parting, breaking for beams of sunlight to shine onto the fields of sheep below. It was beautiful, a picture-perfect scene, and one I should have felt privileged to witness, but it was ruined for me. Crychan's Challenge had stripped Wales of its majesty and beauty. I would be going home with no desire to ever return to this stunning corner of Britain, plagued by the memories. Tired and silent, I boarded the coach, asleep before we rattled back over the cattle grid, fleeing to sanctuary in the fields of Elysian.

A few hours later the coaches came to a stop and we stepped off at a motorway service station, walking down the coach steps and entering the strange humdrum of civilization like submariners emerging from a submarine that has been roaming the seabed for months. Dazed, bleary and confused, it felt like being a tourist in a foreign land, gawping at the pleasures of normal life: newspapers, magazines, hot food, fast food, chocolate, freshly ground coffee, people in everyday clothes from all walks of life. I wandered across the car park with Merv and Gill, staggering on weary legs through the throng of commuters and Friday traffic, searching for the relative luxury of a porcelain toilet. Eyes followed and stared as we made our progress, fascinated by what must have looked like 270 scraggy and unwashed tramps flooding the services, stinking of the slime on a sewer rat's belly. Inside everything felt so clean and polished after our feral woodland existence. In the toilets I caught sight of my reflection in a mirror and balked at the hollow mud-smeared face blinking back at me; no wonder people were staring. In W. H. Smith, Gill and I queued for an ice cream and sat outside on the grass with them, soaking up the sunshine, letting the warmth return feeling and form to our broken bodies.

Looking around, I noticed that the service station seemed particularly busy, heaving with families and cars laden with luggage; bikes clung to roof racks and back windows were obscured by bags and bedding. Children ran up and down outside, skipping between benches and picnic tables with an excited holiday spirit. I sensed a feeling of careless freedom in the air.

'It's really busy, isn't it?' I wondered out loud. 'What's going on that we don't know about?' I poked the wooden stick of my now finished ice cream into the grass.

'I don't care as long as it doesn't stop us from getting home, to a shower and my bed,' Gill replied, closing her eyes and tilting her face towards the sun. 'This sunshine is lovely, isn't it? Why couldn't we have had weather like this for the last five days? Brecon would be a totally different place if the sun ever shone there.'

I continued to watch the merry children skipping outside, their smiling parents, wagging dogs' tails and cars packed high with luggage, and then the reason for this convivial scene dawned on me: it was Good Friday, the beginning of the long Easter weekend, and everyone here was on holiday. I was so out of touch I hadn't even known that it was Easter weekend. Stranded in the remote isolation and seclusion of Brecon had completely cut us off, severing my grasp of normal life. I had only been away for five days but it felt like an entire lifetime.

Crychan's was over. It had been hell, but it was over and we were shattered. It had been far more miserable than even Brecon had promised, but we all passed the end-of-term test and now just a mere week separated us from three weeks of gluttonous freedom beyond the Academy gates.

And during that week, while the Intermediate and Senior intakes spent their days pacing the parade square rehearsing for the Sovereign's Parade, we suddenly had relatively little to do. After thirteen weeks in the fast lane, life slowed to walking pace and in Eleven Platoon we found ourselves absurdly bored. Confident that we could now iron and polish, SSgt Cox left us to it, while Captain Trunchbull disappeared into her study to write completely bipolar reports on us all. Without someone shouting and ordering us about we suddenly didn't know how to behave, lost without the regulated guidance we had grown accustomed to. And soon we became bored, bored, bored.

And bored minds have time to think.

There had been one event that took place during our week in Brecon which bothered me, something which struck with an unwelcome jolt and forced me to ponder.

As Gill and I had made our Good Friday toilet and ice-cream stop at the motorway services, the front pages on the newspaper stand brought news of soldiers who had died the previous day in Iraq, killed as a roadside bomb exploded. While not an uncommon occurrence itself, this particular incident had greater significance for us because one of the dead was a new young officer and, of particular concern, she was female. Second-lieutenant Joanna Dyer had been an intelligence officer attached to an infantry unit patrolling in Basra. She had commissioned from Sandhurst only four months earlier along with Prince William. Just a year ago she, like me, had been digging and crawling around Brecon. Like me, she had spent the week shivering on sentry and eating corned-beef hash, hauling casualties and shooting at waving Gurkhas. She was no different from me. As a female in the army I had always felt that somehow the duty of death didn't apply to me, that it was the preserve of the infantry units, the boys on the ground. Women are not allowed to serve on the 'frontline'. Women are prohibited from 'closing with and killing' and this I thought precluded us from danger, but in Iraq there was no 'frontline'. In Iraq there were no columns of advancing tanks or nice trenchlines in the sand marking out where the enemy were. Because in Iraq the enemy were everywhere, because Iraq was not a conventional war like the ones we were learning about. Iraq was a counter-insurgency campaign, like Northern Ireland, Malaya and Afghanistan. At Sandhurst we were still learning about convoys of communist tanks and how to defeat the Russian Shock Army (you can't). And as I thought more about it I couldn't help wondering why we were still working from Cold War tactics if in Iraq they were playing by different rules. And why decision-makers still insist that women don't serve on the 'frontline' when there isn't one and women are already in the line of fire.

That Saturday night as the Company got heavily inebriated in the cricket pavilion, bopping on the dance floor to disco lights and the Killers belting out the lyrics to 'All These Things That I've Done', I noticed the 2006 Academy hockey team photograph framed on the wall by the bar, and Jo Dyer's smiling face in the front row.

Perhaps we would be taught the relevant stuff next term. And at least for now I could march and polish shoes.

Oh, actually no. I couldn't do that either.

7

I'VE GOT SOUL, BUT
I'M NOT A SOLDIER

I'm back in my old stomping ground. Back behind enemy lines in the City and feeling distinctly uncomfortable. Ann, Deborah and I have convened in Coq d'Argent for cocktails, gossip and panoramic views of London. The bar overlooks the Bank of England and is a mere stone's throw from my first London desk at the former offices of HSBC, light years away from my life right now. Ann is at the bar pressing herself forwards, trying to catch the barman's attention – it won't take her long – while Deborah and I are perusing the room, seated on white leather upholstered stools at a low table. It's still early, most City workers are stuck at their desks and the bar is yet to fill up.

Ann and Deborah are both smartly suited and booted, having come straight from work. I've come straight from Sandhurst and am glad to not be booted for the first time in fourteen weeks. Earlier that afternoon, back in a far corner of Tesco's car park in Camberley, I wriggled into my jeans again behind the wheel of my VW Polo, choosing not to show off my bruised legs tonight by wearing a skirt.

Tucking my freedom into my back pocket and unlocking my femininity, I dusted off my make-up bag and delved in, applying a different kind of warpaint. My hair is down, blow-dried and styled, freed from its bun, hairnet and gel. Earrings dangle from my lobes and I feel like a girl again. Although I'm struggling to remember how to act. The raw chapped skin on my hands and boyish short fingernails are the only giveaway that London's cocktail bars are no longer regular haunts.

'You're looking great, Héloïse,' Deborah says.

'Thanks, Debs. I feel good too,' I reply. 'All this time we're spending outdoors running around is doing me some good. I feel so much healthier and alive now than I ever did when I lived here.'

'That's fantastic,' she says. 'And have you lost weight too? You're looking trim. I bet it's a good diet regime in there.'

'No, I haven't actually. It's a completely different kind of fitness. I can't lose weight or I wouldn't be able to do it. We carry so much weight in our bergens on exercise that you need to be strong. I'm actually eating twice what I used to. It's great. Some of the girls have lost loads of weight though. One lost a stone in the first five weeks.'

'Goodness. Can I sign up just for that? Just the five-week weight-loss plan, please.' We laugh at the thought of it. 'So are things better at Sandhurst now then?' she asks, recalling how low I'd been when we last met.

'Absolutely,' I say with enthusiasm. 'I know what I'm doing now and things have relaxed. It's bearable. Don't get me wrong, it's still incredibly hard at times, but I'm enjoying the challenge now and I think I'll make it to the end.'

'That's good to hear,' Deborah says.

Ann returns to our table clutching three extortionately overpriced mojitos and plonks them down on the glass tabletop. I take a sip and my eyes water; not just from the alcohol that springs into my bloodstream but at the heady London price tag and prospect of my round next. I'm still adjusting to my new monthly bank balance and know that tonight will probably cost me the equivalent of a week of crawling and shivering in Brecon. Ripping my knees open in a wet muddy field and sleeping in a soggy hole is in such contrast to London's flash trendy bars, with their highly paid clientele. From the open windswept Welsh hills of Brecon to Bank Tube station, corporate head offices and bright City lights. I've gone from cold, tired and hungry to the glitzy surroundings of material gain and monetary greed: my old world. I can see now why I left it all behind. Why I had an inner urge to burst out and do something else with my days. I can see as clear as a bottle of gin that I don't belong here any more; my drive is in a different direction, my conscience doesn't fit with the City's scruples. I've made the right choice joining the army. Now beyond the bounds of the Sandhurst bubble I can see that.

I take another sip of my mojito and twizzle the straw between my fingers, chasing crushed ice and muddled mint around the glass. Ann and Deborah are discussing recent events in the City: giddy bonuses, mergers, movements and share options; I'm listening but can't keep up. I've only been out of the loop for a few months but the pace of the markets and London life have already left me behind, leaving me happily adrift in its murky wake. For now times in the City are good. Ann and Deborah are both busy and business is booming. My former colleagues have just creamed off the benefits from another round of whopping bonuses and the money markets are sound. The cracks of a global recession are yet to appear. Depositors are still merrily putting their money into Northern Rock and shopping at Woolworths (although clearly not buying enough pick 'n' mix). The braying City tossers filling the Coq d'Argent this evening certainly seem as bullish and cocksure as ever, revelling in Gordon Brown's 'age of irresponsibility'.

Oh how the mighty can fall.

As the bar begins to swell with the arrival of more pinstriped stockbrokers and fat-tied barrow boy traders I find myself on the receiving end of some dreadful chat-up lines. Rounds of champagne cocktails arrive at our table followed by a group of Goldman Sachs boys who sidle up to us, trying inconspicuously to impress by flashing their Coutts gold cards. Without a boyfriend I find myself in the midst of an odd singles world at Sandhurst. When it comes to men, being a girl in the army is like being thirsty at sea: men are everywhere. Good-looking, well groomed, uniformed, eligible men. Daily, I am surrounded by them. Muscular toned sculpted men who have biceps and abs as a matter of course, because of their job, not crafted through hours of vanity in the gym. Real men, who are trained hunters, gatherers and killers. Men with primordial skills that women are tuned to desire. Strong alpha male types who can survive in a real jungle not just the concrete one within the confines of the Square Mile. Men who are not motivated by pecuniary gains. Men who are simply far more attractive than these Goldman boys.

I have caught the attention of Rupert, a Savile Row-suited fund manager with a client-dinner paunch and unhealthy complexion. He is busy leaning into my ear (and peering down my top) telling me about himself, how important he is and how much money he makes. Me, me, me. I feign interest in his egotistical blitherings, thankful that the bar bill is not on my tab, cooing and swooning at appropriate junctures. As the jazz music is turned up he eventually diverts his attention from himself and asks me which bank I work for.

'I don't work for a bank any more,' I tell him. 'I'm in the army.'

His mouth drops to the floor and he suddenly recoils as if I've just spat in his face.

'Really. So are you a lesbian then?' he asks, finally settling on an answer for my rebuttal of his advances.

'No. I just decided to do something different with my life,' I tell him.

I can tell from his perplexed expression that this is most preposterous and utterly beyond his comprehension. 'Why on earth would a pretty little girl like you want to go and do something like that?' he retorts.

*

One of the most soul-destroying activities of my former London life had been the painful daily commute on

London Underground. Standing on a station platform each week morning, queuing four deep with waiting passengers, silent and motionless in the winter darkness, a sea of grey and black woollen coats and umbrellas, watching the rain hammer down onto the track. Praying that as the next carriage drew to a stop in front of me there would be a sliver of space that I could wedge myself into as the doors slid open. The depressing ten-mile journey from Fulham to Canary Wharf each morning and night took a whole hour, stealing two hours of my day. Two hours of being pressed like a sardine in a can. Two hours with some random hungover Australian backpacker breathing hot, heavy alcoholic fumes into my face. Two hours with a sweaty unwashed armpit hovering its damp patch over my nose. Two hours with a total stranger's crotch pressed against my upper thigh, rocking and bumping with the swaying train as it sped along the tunnels between stations. Sadly, if my boyfriend was out of town, my daily Tube journeys were the most intimate I'd find myself with someone else all week.

One particular cold morning as I travelled on my commute to Canary Wharf I was part of a very British incident.

I was on the Jubilee Line racing east, ticking off station stops: Westminster, Waterloo, Southwark, London Bridge, Bermondsey. At Bermondsey, the train doors beeped open and someone stood up and departed, leaving me with the rare pleasure of a seat. I sat down and settled in, unfolding my newspaper, and hiding behind its broadsheets, as the train sped on towards Canary Wharf. At some point, in the blackness between station stops, I sensed something down at my feet. Peering over the top of my newspaper shield, I saw there was a woman kneeling on the floor of the carriage, crouched over her rucksack praying. Wedged between mine, and the other passengers' feet, she was curled on the floor with an open copy of the Koran in her hands, reciting and muttering its verses. She was sweating in the large puffer jacket she had on too. This was before London had experienced its own version of Al Qaeda's terrorism in the 7 July bombings, but September 11 2001 had occurred two years earlier and Londoners were all too aware of the threat to their capital. I leaned forwards and tapped her shoulder, whispering the offer of my seat, but she declined.

If she was planning to detonate a suicide vest of explosives on this Tube train, she'd chosen well: the carriage was packed with London capitalist scum. The suited City types most hated by extremists: Occidentalism, amoral, greedy, materialistic infidels.

I am quite sure that had such a scene occurred on the New York subway it would have been encountered very differently from the London experience I was part of that day. I would guess that New Yorkers would have met this infringement into their day with outspoken American hysteria, with accusing raised voices and confrontation, but certainly not the stony silence that filled that overloaded carriage somewhere deep underground east of Bermondsey. I could feel the uneasy tension filling the stale air around me as I sat with my paper lowered, waiting for events to unfold. Now everyone on the carriage was conscious of her, but no one uttered a single word. A very British stiff upper lip kept what may have been our last moments alive politely quiet. Avoiding the discomfort of a challenge or action we all 'kept calm and carried on', dealing with our last prayers and testament personally in reflective silence.

Whatever it was we witnessed that morning, it wasn't a suicide bomber. She didn't click a trigger to martyrdom, but she did succeed in bringing fear to our morning. A terror and terrorism. She may have simply been a nervous passenger, turning to her faith, but as each one of us alighted at Canary Wharf our hearts were racing as though we'd just stared down the barrel of an Al Qaeda gun.

But the whole experience didn't cause me to have an ideological epiphany. I didn't get to my office, kicking off my high heels to take up arms. The links that day were far too tenuous for any of us to make. The war in Afghanistan and London bombings are too disparate to be linked. But they are, at a political level. The safety of our streets (and Underground) is the reason soldiers board RAF planes bound for Kandahar, it is the reason soldiers return in coffins draped with the Union Jack flag, it is the reason they are fighting in Helmand in the first place, but it is not the reason they fight. War today is not about defending and invading territory. There isn't the obvious patriotism of protecting British soil like the Falklands or defending allied borders as in the World Wars, because the wars in Iraq and Afghanistan are more obtuse. It isn't the threat of Al Qaeda bombs in London that drives a soldier to arms, because today's PlayStation generation are not motivated by religious zeal or political ideals. They don't go to war so

Fat Cat bankers can sit more comfortably on the Tube, and they don't patrol around the villages of Helmand Province concerned with spreading democratic values (not to say this doesn't occupy more senior commanders). They do it because of their friends, their mates and their Army family.

This is one of the incredible successes of the British Army's inherited structure, the regiments and corps that we would have to select from. It is this army family that gives soldiers their motivation in war, because in the army it is left to the politicians to decide the reasons why we go to war, as ours is 'but to do and die'.[29]

It is the esprit de corps that binds army units and makes them so effective. A spirit fostered from the identity and proud traditions that a soldier lives and breathes from the moment he joins his 'cap badge'. The pomp, the ceremony, the centuries of history, honours and battle glories, are what give soldiers and officers their sense of shared community and belonging. Regiments and corps are like tribes, with individual identities, chiefs, ancient customs and battle cries. And it is a soldier's comrades-in-arms who matter far more than the politics that decide their battles.

And it was this camaraderie that I was lacking in my City job. This all-together, together-as-one attitude that existed in Eleven Platoon. The collegiate, the group, the greater sense of purpose. I realized that I had been seeking something more than just commuting to an office; I had a need to be part of something much more than simply

---

29 'Theirs not to reason why, Theirs but to do and die' Alfred Lord Tennyson in the poem 'The Charge of the Light Brigade'.

being an employee on the payroll. The bonds we were forming at Sandhurst would last for ever and be far more meaningful and deep rooted than any normal working relationship, because we had been through the hard times together, staggering up hills in Brecon, digging shell-scrapes in Kent, shivering on stag; we had been through it all together, and were a closer unit because of it. The bonds that form between a soldier and his fellow comrades can be stronger than any family tie, stronger than even the relationship with his wife, because normal everyday life rarely tests you to the extremes of those demanded in the military.

But it wasn't a normal everyday life that I wanted.

At the conclusion of the Junior Term the Commissioning Course went into hiatus, releasing us back into the outside world for three weeks of unbridled freedom away from the inspecting glare. Three weeks freed from the horrors of the parade square, unshackled from our ironing boards. Three weeks without spade and rifle. Three weeks of slouching, putting our hands in our pockets, leaning against walls and wearing the devil's cloth (unironed). Three weeks to kick back, unwind and let the bad habits creep back in.

Except I couldn't.

I'd changed.

On the train out of London, I sat by the window, watching London Bridge and Canary Wharf flicker between gaps in the city. Small raindrops splattered against the glass, forming long stuttering streaks as the train brushed past them. A group of teenagers were in the carriage, enjoying the last of their Easter holiday. They were a co-ed mixture of young boys and girls with all the complex sexual and social interplay that goes with that age of angst. Boisterously showing off, I found myself irritated by their lack of discipline. I tutted with contempt as they put their skateboarding trainers on the train seats and rolled my eyeballs at the loud music they subjected the carriage to from their mobile phones. I'm sure I was oblivious to this sort of out-of-control disorder before Sandhurst, happily shielding myself behind the spread of a *Financial Times*.

At my destination I found my car in the car park and hopped in. I retuned the radio to listen to the news on Radio 4 rather than the latest pop music I was now completely out of touch with on Radio 1. I drove the short distance to my parents' home, where my father greeted me on the doorstep as he always does, coming out with a cheery smile and a peck for each cheek. As he did so I caught myself drawn to his footwear. Glancing down at his feet I was shamed by the scruffy state of his shoes, a scuffed pair of well-worn collapsing brown loafers that would probably have been rejected by a London tramp, but my father can't part with them – had they ever been polished? (I would never have the heart to personally berate my father for his choice in footwear and, unaware of their scruffy inappropriateness, he chose to wear this favoured pair again when visiting me at Sandhurst, where the sole finally gave up and fell off as he crossed the parade square.)

The Sandhurst conditioning was working. I was starting to be re-engineered. My standards and expectations were changing and, as time passed, I found I had developed a low tolerance for dithering and inefficiency. I became intensely frustrated by people who dawdled in the street, irate with 'Sunday drivers' dilly-dallying at traffic lights and roundabouts and irked at the lack of urgency in listless supermarket checkout assistants. The army is all about rapid reaction and urgency, it's about responding quickly and making decisions in a split second. And with the breakneck pace of life at Sandhurst, stepping off the roller-coaster at the end of the ride was a comedown that left me feeling as though everyone else was missing out and just didn't get it.

From the day I started Sandhurst I stopped being late too. Unless someone had died en route I would always arrive five minutes early, whether fashionable or not, because somewhere at the back of my brain the muscle-memory was fearful of the press-up punishment lateness would incur. The London norm to meet friends in a bar an hour after you arranged to now felt plain rude.

As I crossed the threshold into my parents' home, my father was already bombarding me with questions about life at Sandhurst, racing ahead of me into the kitchen to switch on the kettle.

'So what's your room in the Officers' Mess like?' he fussed. 'Do you have someone cooking your meals and cleaning your room for you? Oh how lovely. I bet the food is good. They say an army marches on its stomach you know.'

My father's view of the forces was stuck in a time warp, still back in the day when the Empire was strong and officers could buy their commissions. A time when army officers were stationed in India and the Far East, flitting between cocktail parties and dinner nights, countering malaria by drinking plenty of gin and tonics.

'No Dad, I don't live in an Officers' Mess, it's Sandhurst,' I said. 'I'm just a scrote in training, no one cleans my room for me. In fact it's us who pretty much clean the whole Academy.'

'Oh,' he said, taking two mugs out of a cupboard. 'So what rank are you now then? Are you a Captain yet?'

'No, I haven't even commissioned yet, Dad. I'm only an Officer Cadet. I'm the lowest of the low. A worm. I'm not even an officer yet. I won't be one until I commission in December and then I'll only be a second-lieutenant.'

'Oh,' he said again, a little disappointed. 'It won't take you long though, will it? And then when will you be a major? Major Goodley sounds pretty good.'

I gave up. My parents didn't get it, but bless my father for trying. Major was a decade away, so far off that I couldn't even comprehend it. I couldn't even comprehend what second-lieutenant would be like and the responsibility of soldiers, let alone major.

He handed me a mug of steaming tea.

'And how are you getting on? Are you showing all the other girls how it's done?'

'No, Dad. It's not like that.'

My father had been used to school report cards full of As and prizes on Speech Day. Hearing that his little girl was nothing special to the army was something I didn't have the heart to confess to him. How was I to explain that so far at Sandhurst merit seemed to be based on the shininess of my shoes and the ability to put one foot in front of the other on the parade square? It was all such a different world, and one I was starting to realize people on the outside couldn't comprehend.

If my return to the outside civilian world had felt different, my return to Sandhurst would bring differences too, because having survived the horrors and challenges of Junior Term we had now earned some stripes. We knew how to play the game and were beginning to fit the officer mould. We were no longer bottom feeders languishing at the base of the food chain, no longer the new greenhorns in the herd, wet behind the ears, fearful and naive. As we moved into Inters, we would be treated like four-year-olds rather than three-year-olds, given a little extra pocket money and a later lights out. It was a small but significant step up. We were not quite the playground bullies but comfortable enough to no longer need to hide in the library at break-time. I knew my way around. I still couldn't march and polish but I knew how to disguise it. Unlike my first day of Junior Term I now had friends and coping strategies.

As we progressed from Juniors to Inters, we physically moved too, out of our rooms in Old College and into New College. While not as dreamy and architecturally impressive as its older neighbour, the vast redbrick warren of New College was just as imposing. The college consisted of a collection of outstretched buildings all linked by one long continuous corridor, which boasted to be Europe's longest; something which late at night in my socks was not contested. Downstairs, these corridor walls were covered from floor to ceiling with dark-green glazed tiles giving a Victorian classroom feel to the whole building and its stone floor clacked suitably loudly at the approach of authority. Our accommodation rooms were upstairs above the offices and study rooms, and not much different to the ones we'd left behind in Old College. Part of growing up meant that our rooms were no longer subjected to the same level of scrutinizing inspections as before, and as I unpacked my belongings again, disregarding locker layout and showcasing my toiletries, I recalled the twisted knot of apprehension that had sat in my stomach as I unpacked in Old College just four months earlier. Those first-day nerves, new career nerves, holy-cow-what-have-I-done nerves that I felt just a term ago someone else had now. Because while we set up home in our new rooms in New College the vultures circled again at the Grand Entrance to Old College, welcoming in the latest batch of new recruits, fresh-faced and wide-eyed, nervously carrying their ironing boards and cleaning products up Old College steps.

The next intake in the Sandhurst sausage machine.

Poor sods.

With New College came new people too as we left some of our tormentors behind.

By the time we reached the end of Juniors, SSgt Cox had taught us everything she knew. Her knowledge was all imparted. We could now make our beds, iron our uniforms, polish doorknobs, pick up litter, march (ish) and shine our shoes (well, not me, but everyone else could). And she had reached the end of her useful life because SSgt Cox wasn't actually a real soldier, not of the gun-wielding, bayonet-between-the-teeth, steely-war-fighting kind. What we needed now was a real warrior, someone who had seen the whites of the enemies' eyes, someone who had fired a rifle in anger, someone who had actually done what we needed to be taught. SSgt Cox had successfully delivered us into the military but her midwifery duties were now over and we were untied from her apron strings and deposited into the care of a real infantryman, a guardsman to be precise: CSgt Bicknell – the sympathetic softie who smuggled chocolate biscuits into our skill-at-arms lessons when SSgt Cox had banned them.

CSgt Bicknell's arrival was a revelation in our lives and he soon became the hero of our little world. His approach was less about messing us around with Sandhurst nonsense (though that didn't cease) and more about making sure we knew what we needed to in order to not embarrass ourselves in front of soldiers when we finally commissioned (infantry tactics, not just the latest gossip from *Celebrity Big Brother*). A professional soldier nearing the pinnacle of an impressive career, he had joined the army at the young age of seventeen and made it his life (he would have joined at sixteen if he had not still been wearing fixed braces), and was now in his thirties with the benefit of years of experience behind him. He was a tall, jolly man with rosy cheeks, a great sense of humour and a comic chuckle, which would ripple down the corridor from his office. Always immaculately turned out without flaw, he had served with the Coldstream Guards in Northern Ireland, Bosnia, Iraq and Afghanistan and had a glistening rack of campaign medals and true tales of gritty combat to tell. He had guarded the Queen at Buckingham Palace, taught the Jamaican Army, trekked the Papua New Guinean jungle and topped his peers at every stage of his career ascension. But at no stage in this illustrious army career had he been prepared for the peculiarities of girls. From the day he signed the enlistment forms as a tender schoolboy recruit, to patrolling the streets of Basra and Armagh, to standing outside Buckingham Palace with a bearskin on his head, at no stage, never, for one single moment, had he considered that joining the army would put him in command of girls. Hormonal, emotional, sensitive girls. And after twenty years in a masculine, frontline, war-fighting environment, he wasn't prepared for it, and was soon to receive a crash course introduction to the specific delicacies of female psychology. Forget time-of-the-month, 'does-my-bum-look-big-in-this?' quandaries, Eleven Platoon were thirty girls, living together, under pressure and there was only so much gratitude chocolate biscuits could buy.

CSgt Bicknell wasn't the only new man in our lives as we started the Intermediate Term. While we unpacked boxes in our rooms and tentatively explored the new surroundings, a fresh figure hovered quietly in the shadows. Watching. Silently observing each one of us. And then, with the incisive exactness of a heart surgeon suturing a vein, he accurately sussed each one of us out. This wasn't a man of great physical stature, or many words, but his sheer presence changed the way the world moved around him. A sighting of him on the parade square horizon would stiffen sinew, silence birds in the trees and bring blades of grass to attention on the polo pitch. Utterly professional, with remarkable shrewd sagacity he was the new Imjin Company Sergeant Major, CSM Mockridge. A living legend.

He was a rifleman by heritage (and later left Sandhurst to go on to be the regimental sergeant major of a Rifles Battalion) and his gift for soldiering and clear, incisive mind had seen him rapidly rise through the ranks. He had an angular jawline, with a narrow face and the hair on his head was a thin dirty blond colour. He wasn't tall like CSgt Bicknell and the other guardsmen who populated Sandhurst, but his shoulders were broad and strong and he had earned himself the nickname 'the Lung' for his superhuman physical abilities. He regularly ran the ten miles to work each morning and the ten miles home at night, with boots on his feet and a heavy bergen on his back, bringing his beloved Jack Russell, Trigger, with him, sometimes tucked under one arm as the little dog failed to keep up with his demanding pace.

'He's slacking on me again, Miss Goodley. Slacking,' he'd chortle as he trotted through the Academy gates; Trigger looking sheepish in his grip, longing for the basket under his desk.

A quiet personal man, little was actually known about him by the cadets and this intriguing mystery added to his legendary aura. In the eight months I knew him I never discovered where he was from, whether he had children or was married. Various rumours abounded that he was the millionaire part-owner of a luxury car dealership in London's Mayfair; others said that he had served in the

French Foreign Legion; while some had heard that he had been in the special forces but chose not to wear the badges. Any of these could have been true.

To me he simply became the single most impressive man I have met in the Armed Forces. He was an utter inspiration, and someone whose judgement I trusted implicitly. I would have contentedly followed the man over broken glass and off a cliff if he had told me that was the way to go. He commanded the utmost respect, and had the true gift of being able to give a monumental bollocking without losing it. When enraged, his anger could be a storm to shelter from but when it passed you didn't find yourself walking away filled with contempt thinking he was an unreasonable idiot, but instead ashamed of yourself for having let him down.

But with the *'bonjours'* came *'au revoirs'* and, as we moved into New College not everyone in Imjin Company was there to unpack their bags. Some had enjoyed their taste of freedom outside the Academy too much and chose not to return. The break between Juniors and Inter was the point in the Commissioning Course when most people bolted. In Eleven Platoon one girl left us, quitting the digging-crawling routine to start a life of accountancy exams and Tube strikes in London (I did try to warn her). She was free to go. The army wasn't for her and she'd given it a good shot. Outwardly, we were saddened to say farewell but inside we felt smug. Smug that, as people left, it gave credit to those of us remaining, hacking it out. Bailing when things got tough reinforced that Sandhurst wasn't easy and gave greater credence to those of us left in the game.

As the Junior Term had come to a close, I was left considering the value of what we were being taught at Sandhurst in light of Jo Dyer's death. Aside from all the cleaning, polishing, marching inanity, the tactics felt dated. I wasn't a military tactician but I could tell that the plans we were making to defend the south of England from an invading Russian Motor Rifle Brigade were not the contemporary tactics that would get us around the streets of Basra or Sangin. What did we do if the enemy weren't in tanks advancing in straight lines? What about suicide bombers? And IEDs like the one that had killed Jo Dyer? The British Army was at war, but not the Cold War, not with the Russians, relic Russian weapons yes, but not the hoards of armour in a Russian Vanguard. I thought Russian relations are warmer these days. Over Easter leave I had consoled myself that with Juniors complete the army were now content with my ironing and bed-making skills and could start teaching the really important stuff: hearts-and-minds and counter-insurgency, wars about people and clashing civilizations that would all surely start on our move to New College. And so with this in mind three weeks into the Intermediate Term I packed my bergen once more, ready to deploy into the field again: on a First World War trench-digging exercise in Norfolk.

One standard I had discovered at Sandhurst was that anything you had yet to do was going to be *the* worst experience you'd have at the Academy. And listening to exaggerated war tales from battle-worn cadets in the intake above us, exercise First Encounter was built up into

Operation Near Death; horror stories of cadets collapsing from exhaustion, being hospitalized with trench-foot, or sectioned with sleep-deprived delirium made for effective scaremongering as we stuffed clothing and sleeping bags that wouldn't be used into our bergens.

The exercise plan was simple.

With Norfolk's turkey farmers and mustard makers under threat from advancing enemy we would find a suitable spot on Thetford training area and dig a line of trench defences, just like those dug by our great-grandfathers along the Western Front. Extra spades and picks were packed along with plenty of Redbull and Pro-Plus, because in reality the exercise was actually less about our ability to dig a hole in the ground and more a painful experiment in sleep deprivation.

The excitement about exercise First Encounter (which soon became renamed Worst Encounter) was that it was taking us somewhere new; this time we weren't going back to the hideousness of Wales or the misery of Eeyore's Gloomy Place, because Worst Encounter was in Norfolk, an area of the British Isles renowned for one especially gracious quality: it is flat. As a pancake. No horrendous hills, no seemingly insurmountable mountains. The maps we were given barely even had contours drawn on them. There was not a knoll, mound nor pimple in sight, just field upon field of arable sugar beet and brewers' barley, growing in a nice diggable sandy loam. And it was now May, so having cried with cold on my previous two excursions into the field I was looking forward to the promise of more balmy conditions; the prospect of being able to feel my toes and not cracking an icy crust from my sleeping bag as I woke for stag.

So despite the scaremongering things were looking up for Worst Encounter.

And really, how difficult can digging a hole be?

I'm not sure if the coach driver got lost, but the exercise started on the hard shoulder of a main road, while Monday morning rush-hour traffic sped past. As we got off the bus, Captain Trunchbull, who unfortunately we hadn't left behind in Old College, was busy shouting at us in her usual nettling manner while CSgt Bicknell tentatively chivvied us along, still finding his feet with his new brood. Once again we hauled all our heavy kit onto our backs, shovels and picks poking from the top of our bergens like prospecting miners, and steadied ourselves for the evil bergen carry onto the area.

Once we arrived at the pre-agreed 'X' on the map, our trenches were marked out on the grass with white tape and we began mentally preparing ourselves for the 'big dig'. Except digging a trench isn't as straightforward as simply putting spade to soil; first a demoralizing de-turfing process has to be completed, which involved ripping innocuous clumps of grass from the topsoil around the planned hole. There were two trenches per section and with me I had Allinson, Rhodes and Lea. The four of us worked uninterrupted, fuelled by beginning-of-exercise zeal, but this disheartening de-turfing still took us twelve hours. Twelve whole plucking hours. We started at lunchtime on day one and it was deep into the first night before we were even ready to scrape the surface and put shovel to ground.

And the exercise was covert too, so we now found ourselves digging in complete darkness, unable to switch on our head torches in case the enemy were alerted. It was a particularly calm night on the first night. The air around us felt heavy and still, damp with the smell of the day's rain. Trees stood motionless on the horizon, not a rustle from their branches. Occasionally I could hear the hoot of an owl, but otherwise there were just the gentle sounds of spades tucking into the earth and the odd whisper. With the grass removed, we made good progress and after an hour were a foot deep. In our trench we developed an efficient routine in which I swung a pick to loosen the soil and Allinson and Rhodes cleared it away with their shovels, forming small piles of earth around the trench. As I dug, we found the sandy ground was pocked with sporadic flinty stones that we discarded as they were dug up, continuing on with our mission to get six feet down. In the early hours of what was now the second day, sparks began to fly as I brandished my pick and it struck hard against a particularly large flint rock. A couple more arches of the pick and I began to think it unusual. It was certainly larger than those we'd been finding and not loosening in the ground as I hit it. I stopped and reached down to feel with my hands, hoping to find a corner to lever it out with, but the moment my bare hand I touched it I realized straight away that it wasn't a rock. It was clearly metallic and man-made. As I explored with my hands, groping at the dirt, I could discern the obvious fluke of a tail at the top, leading into a rusty body. A rusty unexploded body. I quickly fumbled in my pocket for a torch and shone a small light at it, unmindful of the light discipline we were supposed to be digging by. There unmistakably before me was an unexploded bomb. A rusty Second World War relic, now with a couple of clean scratches along the metal shell where I had chipped away with my pick. If I hadn't previously given much consideration to the dangers of war, I had certainly given no consideration to the dangers of training. I would have preferred a pot of gold.

Despite the distraction of unearthing a bomb, we continued to work straight through that first night and into the following morning, slowly deepening the trench (which was relocated two metres west until the bomb could be destroyed), and by dawn word reached us that the first of the boys' platoons were complete. The sooner you finished the sooner you could rest and we weren't even halfway there. As the sun rose and burned off the morning mist, tiredness started to take its toll. With helmet and body armour on, it was exhausting work. We had had no sleep. Not a wink. The big swinging arches of my pick had become small scrabbling hiccups, while the spades full of excavated earth dwindled to tiny handfuls. As time wore on, our pace slowed further, and the slower we worked the longer it was going to take us to complete and the more time wore on. But fatigue wasn't our only problem, because back at Sandhurst 'rations-gate' was unfolding and CSgt Bicknell was about to get an important insight into the female psyche.

While at Sandhurst strict rules are applied to using only the military-issued kit and equipment. While not the best money can buy, it does the job and we had to learn how to live with it, if only to be able to sympathize with the private soldiers' whose salaries couldn't supplement them in Millets or Blacks. For example, the army-issued sleeping bags we had all been given were just as effective as expensively bought non-issued ones from camping shops, except they took up three times as much space in our bergens and added precious more weight. On our feet we had to wear only the issued leather boots despite their blister-giving properties and through the freezing cold nights we were limited to just the issued thermal clothing. On Worst Encounter we had all stuck religiously to these rules and our bergens were conformingly packed with issued sleeping bags and clothing that we were barely even going to get to use over the course of the week. But where we had bastardized the rulebook was in its application to food. On the Sunday before deployment, after Chapel, we had enterprisingly driven to Tesco and stocked up, stacking the trolley full of more appealing alternatives to corned-beef hash. Then that night, before departing for Thetford, we had opened up our ration packs and emptied them into the bin, stuffing our bergens instead with Pot Noodles ('Fuel of Britain'), peperamis, malt loaf, Haribo and lots and lots of chocolate.

Remembering that an army marches on its stomach.

Our error in this deceit was that the following morning as we boarded the coaches to Norfolk, these bins remained unemptied. The evidence of our crime left us exposed.

Laid bare and waiting. Waiting for the Academy commandant, a major general, accompanied by a delegation of foreign dignitaries touring the Academy, to happen upon them, like parents finding a squirrelled stash of pornography as they came into our rooms. Landing us in a whole mountain of trouble that would see us grounded for the rest of our lives.

Rations-gate was something that simply wouldn't have occurred in a boys' platoon. Boys are not precious or fussy about food. CSgt Bicknell had contentedly eaten boil-in-the-bag horrors for his entire military career and would never have contemplated our rejection of them. So when our actions surfaced he was livid. Livid because we'd cheated. Livid because he hadn't thought to check. And livid because he'd received a monumental bollocking for it, so we were going to get an even bigger one. He called us all in, gathering us together under a tree, lined up to attention, leaving shovels and picks in our half-trenches. He paced back and forth in front of us, pulling his hair out. He raged at us: 'You fucking idiots, what did you think you were doing? You will bloody well eat what you are given to eat. If you are issued ration packs, then you bloody well pack them and eat them. I don't care if you don't like them. In war you don't get Pot Noodles and sweets. Do you think I had Haribo in Iraq? Do you? No, I didn't. I spent six months in the desert eating fucking ration packs and I'm telling you that the shitters there were not a place to spend more time than necessary. But I ate them. I didn't go into downtown Basra to buy peperami and Mars bars. You lot need to learn to stop being so fucking pampered.'

He stopped and took a deep breath, putting his hands on his hips, his face now red with fury.

'You've made yourselves look like fucking fools, you have. Not just to me, not just to the commandant but the whole fucking Academy. I don't ever want to have to remind you of this again. You are a fucking disgrace. The lot of you. When I've finished with you here,' he said, his rant nearing a febrile crescendo, 'I want you to go back to your fucking trenches and dig as though your lives depend on it. Because I'm going to make sure this is a lesson you never fucking forget.'

He was angry, very, very angry, but anger was not the answer. And with this ranting rage he had got it hugely wrong, because girls do not respond to maddened shouting. As he finished with piqued conclusion, he looked to us for some sort of confirmation, a reassurance that we'd heard and understood. Instead he received a blank response as we flounced off in a girly huff, heading back to our trenches to bitch about him, metaphorically stomping upstairs and slamming the bedroom door. We walked away from him and brooded, turning our backs to avoid him. Some cried. His words had upset us, but not taught us a lesson.

That was the one and only time CSgt Bicknell bollocked us. With this one incident he realized that girls required a different, more measured approach. Girls respond to a 'you've-let-me-down' emotional message not the rage of men. And eventually with Eleven Platoon CSgt Bicknell embraced the new angle to army life girls brought. After twenty testosterone-filled years, he relished his role as the guiding father figure in our lives. He took us under his wing and became defender of our honour, agony aunt and opener-of-jars.

The trench-digging continued through Tuesday and into the second night, bringing with it extreme tiredness. There had been no let-up. We hadn't stopped to rest or sleep since arriving and, now suffering from chronic fatigue, everything we did became slow and measured like the movements of a drunken tramp. We stumbled about in our trenches, breaking occasionally to join the growing queue of people outside the Portaloos, where inside people had fallen asleep. My bloodshot eyes stung as I battled hopelessly to keep them open; my head lolled heavy on my neck. As my consciousness waned my awareness clouded. That night, in the cathedral calm of darkness, I became hazy and confused, having an almost out-of-body experience I was so tired. I felt nearer death than life. And my capacity for clear coherent thought became lost in the piles of excavated dirt. I have never been more tired than I was at 5 a.m. on that Wednesday morning, when finally my will to sleep was consented. I had been awake for over 48 hours. We eventually downed tools and I unfurled my sleeping bag on the bare grass and climbed straight in, as I was, sandy boots still on, sleeping on the damp earth under the night stars, catatonic with the eventual release of sleep.

And then a miracle happened.

As I lay unconscious in the grass an angel appeared, haloed by the dawn sun. The angel shook me from my slumber and guided me to a Land Rover, its waiting engine growling in the morning mist. Blundering blearily, I was too tired to comprehend what was happening and blindly followed the angel's lead. On the hard seats in the back of the Land Rover I slept again as we bounced through the fields and along muddy tracks. Eventually, behind the barbed wire of a military camp, I was transferred into a white minibus and onto the main road. We sped south, along A roads to the motorway. Intermittently in my sleep I got a sense of traffic slowing with rush hour, stopping at traffic lights or the bus swinging around a roundabout, but I remained oblivious to my surroundings, wrapped in the soporific sounds of the engine. All my body could do was sleep, my brain had shut down, my eyelids clamped firmly shut.

Eventually we reached our destination – Aldershot in Surrey, 135 miles from my unfinished trench. The minibus parked in a car park and as the engine was switched off I stirred, waking in civilization. Still wearing the same clothes I had been in for more than two days, I was unwashed; the sweat of digging had dried to my body, sand and mud clung to my boots and I stank. A foul putrid unforgiving stench, that lingered in the nostrils of the freshly bathed like a ripe French cheese. My hands were blistered raw and clenched from wielding the pick and my eyes had withdrawn to dark pinpricks in my skull, like an addict at the end of a high. Ours wasn't the only minibus in the Aldershot car park that morning. Around us others were disgorging groups of people in coordinated team tracksuits and trainers, with sports bags slung over their shoulders looking fit and competitive. We were all gathering here for the Army Swimming Championships. My race preparation could have been a little better.

Before I joined the army, a sage infantry officer had given me much valued advice on the emotional extremes of military life. He had warned me that in the army 'the highs are higher but the lows are lower too'. And there, in Aldershot, standing stiff in the car park this maxim could not have been truer. Hours earlier I had been scrabbling around at the bottom of a hole, sick with fatigue, blistered, sore and stinking a rotting stench. But now my swimming had saved me. While the rest of Eleven Platoon was still trapped in the Worst Encounter nightmare, I was living a dream. I headed straight for the shower, plugging the drain with matted hair, filth and grass. I slept. I showered again and then slept. I curled up on the poolside and slept between races, oblivious to the rowdy competition goings-on, shaken awake for each of my races. I hauled myself up from under my towel, put on my hat and goggles and made my way to the starting blocks, and stood there gazing at the fifty metres of crystal clear water ahead of me, as the other competitors limbered up. Stretching their limbs and standing tall, while my shoulders hung. I was knackered. The last thing I wanted to do now was thrash myself in a swimming pool in front of a large crowd. But as the starter buzzer bleeped, I was in and it felt incredible. The cool water rushed over me, the crowd cheered and the adrenaline kicked in to power me through the water.

As lunchtime arrived, I ordered Domino's pizza to the poolside, gorging on the fatty cheesy slices, and even sought out somewhere to launder the mud from my crusty combats. All the while back in Norfolk the big dig continued. Guilt did pass over me. As I bit into another slice of pizza, savouring the salami juiciness, I was forced to consider the boil-in-a-bag alternatives. As I stood under a hot shower for the fourth time, soaping away ingrained grime, I spared a thought for the grubby less fortunate. It was intensely selfish, but I challenge anyone to behave differently in the circumstances.

Back in Thetford, the rest of Eleven Platoon was suffering in the deep throes of serious sleep deprivation, and knowledge of my privilege would not have been greeted warmly. So that night, when I finally returned, clean, rested and fed, a gold medal tucked into my pocket, I kept my mouth shut. I paraded a sullen face, trying not to give away traces of the adultery I had committed. Not that anyone would have noticed. Because as I arrived back at my trench, smelling of shampoo and fabric softener, total lunacy had taken hold.

In my absence the platoon had been given just one more hour of sleep and were now delirious with fatigue. I became the only sober person at the party as hallucinations and disorientated mumblings set in. People were falling asleep standing up, mid-sentence and while eating. Someone had even conducted their own assault on an invisible enemy. But somehow through this mental imbalance the trenches had now been finished, complete with corrugated-iron reinforcement and the grassy turf replaced around them. But at six-foot deep, they proved difficult to get in and out of, especially when laden with kit, in the dark. That night our position came under a brief enemy mortar attack and my section were dispatched to investigate. Over the radio I was ordered to get One Section out and conduct a clearance patrol to our east. I roused everyone in our two trenches to get ready and looked carefully at my map. I was still adjusting the helmet on my head when the Platoon Donkey declared she was ready to go. Already out of the trench, she whispered down to me, 'Which way are we going, Héloïse?'

Goodness, maybe people weren't as unhinged as I had estimated, if the Platoon Donkey was still compos mentis. The rest of us got ready and clambered awkwardly out of the trench. I adjusted the settings on my radio and sent a message through to Platoon HQ to let them know we were departing. As I closed the cover on the radio pouch, I looked down at the Platoon Donkey's feet. They were bare. She wasn't wearing any boots. I looked up and realized she didn't have her body armour or helmet on either and her rifle was missing from the picture too. She seemed completely oblivious to these deficiencies. We didn't have time to now start doing up her shoelaces. We couldn't leave her behind either, she had to come with us. This was going to have to be quick.

So we hurried out of the trenched harbour, the Platoon Donkey following at the back in her socks. We disappeared off into the darkness between the trees and out of sight, hoping not to bump into any real enemy. Conducting the bare minimum patrol, we returned twenty minutes later, eager to get back into our trench and the Platoon Donkey out of potential sight. I set the bearing on my compass and headed through the darkness to where our trench should be, except when I got there it wasn't there. I paced left and then right but couldn't find it. I whispered out loudly hoping to catch the attention of someone in another trench. Then suddenly behind me the Platoon Donkey disappeared. I heard a muffled yelp and small crumpled commotion as she tumbled headlong into our trench, collapsing in a dishevelled heap at the bottom.

We grew quite attached to our trenches. They briefly became home. We cooked, ate, slept and lived our lives in them, like scenes out of *Blackadder*, with Baldrick making tea and cunning plans. It was saddening on the final day to have to rip them apart and fill them back in. We stripped out the corrugated iron and sandbags, collapsed in the carefully cut walls and bulldozed all the dirt back over, leaving just a small scar on the surface as evidence of our occupation. On the final day, we clambered onto the magic bus, which whisked us back to Sandhurst, skeletons of the cadets we had been five days earlier. I was a mess. My hair had matted into a thick sandy knot with sweat and ground around my head by my helmet. My palms were blistered and chafed, my nails brittle and cracked. There was nothing whatsoever feminine about the way I looked, but in just twenty-four hours I had to become a girl again. I had to wash the war away because in just twenty-four hours Imjin Company were throwing a party.

8

WOMEN AT WAR

There are times as a woman in the army when you have to sadly let go of your femininity, cast it to one side, and forget it. When you're shoulder deep, digging a trench, salty sweat trickling down your spine; when you're puffing up a hill with your bergen strapped to your back, dragging you down; when you're on your stomach, crawling through the mud, your rifle cradled in your arms, waxy combat facepaint smeared across your face – in these situations any urge to be a girl gets lost in the rough, because sometimes being a lady in the army is just not possible. French manicures and beauty regimes have no place on military training areas. And on exercise there were no mirrors, no hair straighteners, no tweezers or shine control. After four days of living in a woodblock, you have to ignore the dirt tucked deep beneath your fingernails, forget about the windswept frizzy hair matted to your head, and ignore the absence of make-up and dignity, because joining the army means sacrificing girliness. To the army girl, perfume, lip gloss, mascara and style become abandoned relics. And on exercise, standards can't help but slip, as there are no showers, no razors, no waxing strips nor mirrors. As you wash with a flannel from a mess tin of tepid water there is no cleanse, tone and moisturize routine, because 'you're not worth it'.

The appalling reality of how horrific this had become was then unceremoniously revealed to me when the Gurkha enemy started firing and I would leap to the ground, my body armour crushing to my chest, squeezing out a warm puff of noxious air from the depths of my clothing. On exercise I smelled and looked like a tramp. And at the end of each exercise, the evidence of how far girly standards had declined, swirled around the plughole, as dirt and grass mingled in a soapy whirl, draining away my lost femininity.

When men put on an army uniform they become more attractive, women swoon after them, and even the most average Joe Bloggs develops something about him when wearing uniform. A bit of Richard Gere from *An Officer and a Gentleman*. A sexy masculine authority. But when women put on the uniform it has the opposite effect. Even Cheryl Cole struggles to make combat trousers sexy. They're baggy, shapeless and unflattering; they obliterate feminine curves, because the military uniform is cut for the male form. Despite 10 per cent of the army now being female (that's approximately 10,000 girls) we still all wear the same clothes as the boys. Clothes not designed for hips and breasts.

On our feet the footwear was equally graceless. No soft, calfskin Italian style, because army boots are big, thumpy,

Doc Marten clodhoppers, which rub mercilessly, leaving weeping blisters and then dry calloused heels. And after six months of wearing them, I could no longer stand in my former towering City high heels, as my toes had been allowed to comfortably spread and they now protested at being squeezed back into a tight leather point. And although this may have been saving me from Victoria Beckham's bunions, it was another nail in the coffin of my femininity.

There is nothing attractive about being a girl in the army. Nothing sexy about the uniform. No class or elegance. With my hair gelled and scraped back on my head, baggy combat pyjamas hiding my feminine curves and clumpy boots on my feet, the girl had gone. Banished. Her loss mourned. Which is why any rare occasion there was for us to dress as girls was grasped with overstated excitement. Nights out, dinners, parties, balls, our girliness would fight to the fore, and the masculine military environment at Sandhurst actually exaggerated my femininity. Out of uniform, I embraced florals and pastels like never before. Pretty dresses and jewellery. Reds, pinks, silk and lace. I honed in on them. I lapped up copies of fashion magazines and luxuriated in the pleasure of 'dressing up'. This bid for girliness was at its most extreme after I returned from Afghanistan, when, for a month, I would barely leave the house without perfect hair and make-up, having been deprived of a single girly day for four uninterrupted months in the desert.

So while on exercise girly standards slipped, out of uniform they became flawlessly upheld, with great effort going into the preparation for a night out, because it became a treasured treat; like a lazy Sunday lie-in or the taste of home cooking, it was something we yearned for and missed. I wanted to be a girl again and break from the army mould, express a bit of my individuality and feel feminine. So, as we returned from Exercise Worst Encounter, I scrubbed the war away. I rinsed the Norfolk sands from my hair and scoured Thetford's dirt from under my nails. Lip balm was smeared over cracked lips and intensive moisturizer soothed onto dried skin. I selected an outfit to conceal the patterns of bruising on my limbs and applied make-up to mask the darkened circles under my tired eyes. Transformation complete, the tramp had been converted into a lady again. Ready to party.

And Sandhurst knows how to throw a party.

The commissioning ball held at the end of the course is rated by *Tatler* magazine in the top ten events in the social calendar. And during the course of the year, there are plenty of other smaller parties, formal dinners and charity fund-raising events, providing a balancing yin to the hard-working muddy yang of the rest of the commissioning course. All of these required us to morph back into ladies for the night, as officerly social decorum at these functions called for the girls of Eleven Platoon to be girls, to look pretty, act with grace, beguile, charm and forget that only hours earlier we may have been shooting to kill on the rifle range or thrusting the cold metal tip of a bayonet into a bloodied sandbag. So with a ball gown on, we converted easily from Mr Hyde to Dr Jekyll.

When it came to organizing these parties, boy-girl stereotypes were adhered to fiercely, with the girls of

Imjin Company typically tasked with arranging the decor, food and party theme, while the boys were responsible for the provision of alcohol. So on the last Saturday of term, as I carefully strung up bunting and helped lay out plates of nibbles in the cricket pavilion, the boys had gone on a gin binge in the nearest Camberley off-licence. Using one litre of spirits per person as their provisioning metric, they were loading trolleys with value vodka and never-heard-of branded Belgian beers, aiming to maximize quantity with no regard for quality in ensuring a fairly toxic and eventful evening.

Officer Cadet Peters was with me inflating balloons and flirting outrageously with one of the boys from Twelve Platoon in her young, naive and unsubtle manner.

'Urgh,' she said, stretching up to pin a balloon to the ceiling. 'I can't quite reach, can someone lift me?' The Twelve Platoon object of her desire instantly took the bait, putting down the beer cans that he was loading into the fridge and coming to her aid. 'Can you just lift me up so I can attach this balloon?' she asked, touching his arm and looking doe eyed at him.

'Of course,' he said, putting his hands around her waist. 'You just tell me when you're ready.'

'You'll have to be very strong,' she playfully teased, flicking her hair over her shoulder. 'Let me know if you can't handle me.'

I cringed as I listened to them.

They carried on like this for a few minutes. Him lifting her up, she coquetting in his arms, getting closer and closer to him. Nothing more intimate was going to happen between them with me there in the room like a lemon, but she was lining him up, ready to pounce later that night as the benefits of the boys' alcohol ratio kicked in under the disco lights. He had a girlfriend at home of course, and he wasn't going to leave her for Peters, but the boys did strange things at Sandhurst and Peters would be an innocent victim. Filling in for those lonely nights he spent away from his real girlfriend.

In the all-boy companies these parties could be a bit Band of Thebes man-heavy, but in Imjin we had a ready-made mixed party crowd. The boys would then supplement this by inviting every girl they'd ever met, using the Academy backdrop as a means to impress the ladies, plenty of whom would have shunned their advances in the past, but now couldn't resist the opportunity to be on the Sandhurst guest list. As well as the uniform, actually being at Sandhurst also enormously elevated the boys' kudos and 'pulling power'. Dating an army officer still holds considerable cachet among the fillies of a certain social set.

My jealousy would simmer slightly at the sight of these 'civvy' girls, with their freshly highlighted hair and salon blow-dries, their unblemished, smooth skin and florid complexions. At a party these spectres at the feast would teeter at the bar in heels my feet now rejected, flicking manes of rich thick hair with polished, manicured nails. I envied them. I envied their femininity. I envied that on Monday morning they wouldn't have to be on parade. That on Monday no one would be inspecting their boots. That on Monday they wouldn't even be wearing boots. I was jealous because on Monday morning as I scraped and gelled my hair back into a bun and put my uniform on, they would still be girls, retaining their femininity. Because unlike them, for me, being a girl had now become just the preserve of my weekends; it was a hobby like the weekend dress habits of a cross-dressing transvestite.

Now we were in New College there was more interaction with the other platoons too, and more mixing with the male officer cadets. In the first five weeks of Juniors, it had been a punishable offence to be seen talking to one of the boys. A press-up-enforced gender apartheid was imposed. I was once severely chastised by Captain Trunchbull for accepting the hand of a male cadet who offered to assist me to my feet when sitting on the ground in an outdoor map-reading lesson. Rebuked not only for holding his hand as he helped me to stand up, but also for accepting the help of a man. And for the first five weeks the only people I actually spoke to were female: SSgt Cox, Captain Trunchbull, Sgt Walker and the thirty-two other girls of Eleven Platoon. In a bizarre twist I'd joined one of the most masculine organizations in the world and found there to be only women in it. Sandhurst had become the most female-dominant environment I'd ever been in; my school days had been mostly boys, at prep school I was the only girl in my class, I'd read a science degree at university and worked in the male-dominated field of banking in the City. I was used to being a woman in a man's world and it never bothered me. Suffragettes chained themselves to railings so gender would be irrelevant in my life decisions. So when I joined the army, I wasn't fazed about being a female in the minority.

Indeed I believe I had previously benefited from positive sexual discrimination in the City. Having a girl on the team in a bank brought a welcomed dilution to the testosterone and egos. My boss at HSBC found that bringing a girl along to the meeting table diffused tensions when the men began to lock horns. With a girl present, the ugly head of male bravado was less likely to surface and real business could be discussed (and my bottom patted patronizingly in the lift). Indeed this downplaying of testosterone worked in the army too. The effect of the girls' platoon in Imjin Company was to reduce the competition between the two male platoons, and they became mutually supporting rather than trying to outdo each other, unlike the rivalry that existed between platoons in the all male companies.

Tellingly, I have never experienced sexism in the military, despite the machismo nature of the army. For an old and traditional organization, the army is actually quite progressive in its attitude to women and I genuinely believe that it recognizes the benefits of women in its ranks. If you are a competent, capable female you will have as equal and fulfilling a career as a military man, because despite the infantry frontline ban, doors in the military are wide open for women and there is far less of a glass ceiling than I ever felt in the City. And if motherhood is on your agenda then the MoD is definitely a sympathetic employer, offering an unrivalled maternity package that my City friends balk green-eyed at.

Anyway, much of what they were trying to teach us at Sandhurst is already innate to women. Cleaning and ironing are traditionally women's chores, while women are naturally more organized and tidy than men. Attention to detail, subtlety, organization, multi-tasking, smartness of dress: in all these, women have the advantage.

But finding your identity as a woman in the army, as in any male-dominated environment, can be a complicated and thorny process of trial and error, and, as I commissioned from Sandhurst, I still hadn't found the balance I am now comfortable with. Conducting yourself as a female in a man's world, you run the risk of being either too girly and not taken seriously, or too blokey and being seen as a fool. Many girls try to be 'one of the lads', attempting to match the boys at their own game, competing with them in the gym and then the bar. I unfortunately have the biceps and alcohol tolerance of a gnat so this tack would never have worked for me. When I first started working in the City I considered taking up football, not because I had any interest in the sport, but so that I could take part in 90 per cent of the conversations of my colleagues, but then I realized that it wasn't my place to try to compete with them, because I was not one of the boys and there was no requirement for me to be so.

Being able to be comfortable and successful in a man's world is down to the individual and for this precious girls need not apply. There is no space for marshmallow pink, fluffy softness among the hairy chests and belching. With men, crying, blubbering and stamping-of-feet have no currency, because for a job in a man's world it is only puddle-jumpers who will be accepted, girls who are happy to jump straight in, feet first, mindless of the mud.

*

So there is no sexism in the military, but what about the sex?

Well, there were couples at Sandhurst. Three of the girls in Eleven Platoon arrived at Sandhurst with their boyfriends and all three completed the commissioning course with relationships intact (and strong press-up muscles). Others arrived with boyfriends outside the Academy but with the pressures and demands of the course these relationships soon fizzled out. Gill was different. Her boyfriend wasn't at Sandhurst and wasn't even in the military, a rarity for an army girl. She and Rich had met at university and went on to marry after Sandhurst and start a family together soon after (so she isn't even Gill any more but New).

Other, more transient, relationships also blossomed and withered inside the Sandhurst pressure-cooker, as Cupid blithely fired arrows, fuelling the rumours that the army thrives on. Indeed the number of girls applying to Sandhurst increased markedly when Princes William and Harry attended the Academy. Presumably as some thought they could catch a prince's eye somewhere between the assault course and parade square.

If it could be found that someone still thought you attractive when you hadn't washed for a week and had mud, sweat and facepaint smeared across your cheeks then there were powerful grounds on which to start a romance. The boys saw the girls at their absolute low; forget bed-head and morning breath, at Sandhurst the sex kitten was stripped back and exposed, no make-up or styled locks, our feminine curves were masked in boyish combats and there was no scope for a sexy hip-flick on the march. Because when it comes to attracting the attentions of men in the military, the army girl is faced with a tricky quandary.

At the Academy you are surrounded by men daily, muscular, toned, handsome eligible men, that civilian girls beyond the gilded gates and barbed-wire fence would love to sink their manicured nails into. But these men are all colleagues, beyond the bounds of career decency. Flirtatious flutterings have no place on the parade square and the army girl is unflatteringly dressed up as a tomboy, not an inviting female seductress.

Late one Sunday evening after eight months at Sandhurst, I was signing back into the Academy still dressed for the weekend when one of the boys entered the corridor beside me.

'Ooo. You scrub up well,' he commented, as he looked me up and down.

What?

I'd been there for eight months and he'd never seen the real me, never peeled back the military mask and seen the girl beneath.

'Er, thanks,' I said. 'I guess that was a compliment.' I looked at him with a wry frown. He wasn't someone I knew. He wasn't in Imjin Company and I couldn't tell if there was an ulterior meaning in his remark so I received his compliment with suspicion.

'Of course it was a compliment. You girls don't get much chance to be ladies in here, do you?' he said as I passed him the pen. 'Sometimes we boys forget how different it must be for you.'

'Well, yes you're right,' I said, warming to him slightly. It was like living a double life I suppose. I had a split persona.

'I don't think I'd like the thought of my girlfriend going through Sandhurst,' he said, signing his name in the signing-in book.

'Really. Why not?' I asked.

'Well, it's not very ladylike, it is? Wearing the uniform and being out on exercise. She's too fragile and feminine for that. And I probably wouldn't fancy her if she was in the army. No offence, but no one wants to go out with an army girl.'

'Oh,' I said, a little put out by his hard words.

As we started to walk down the corridor, I thought about his prejudice. I wondered whether the thought of a robust girl who could succeed at Sandhurst was unattractive to him because in his eyes she had lost her femininity or if in fact he felt it threatened his masculinity. If a girl could do it, somehow Sandhurst lost its rugged notion.

As we reached the end of the corridor he held the door open for me, his chivalry saved for my civilian persona.

'Thank you,' I said as I walked through it, my heels clicking against the tiled floor on the other side as I began to walk away from him. I wondered whether he would dump his girlfriend if she decided to join the army. If he loved her it shouldn't matter what she did for a living. I am still the same person now as I was when I worked in the City, only my job has changed. I look the same; I have the same personality and character. In fact I'm much fitter and happier now. And in his compliment to me I had just proved his perception of the lost femininity wrong. As he disappeared behind me I seethed slightly; this narrow-minded view bothered me. It seems that at Sandhurst the selection may have been rich, but the pickings were poor. Perhaps he was just being young and naive. In my army career I have met plenty of young male officers with this prejudiced opinion, only to bump into them again years later and find that they have married a military girl.

There are some advantages to this lost femininity. When I get up in the morning, I don't fling open my wardrobe doors and sigh at the choice and decision to be made, because there is only one option. I don't waste time each morning styling my hair or applying make-up and instead set my alarm clock for the last possible safe minute. If I'm having a 'fat day' it doesn't matter, because underneath my combats no one can tell. And if I want my soldiers to take me seriously, it helps that they can't check out my ass.

And not all of the girls were interested in men anyway. In Eleven Platoon we had one unconfirmed lesbian. By unconfirmed, I mean she kept her sexual orientation to herself, but we all knew, and she now happily has a girlfriend. So despite the army's stereotyped reputation, our ratio of one in thirty seems fairly average for gay and lesbian numbers in the society we serve. Lesbians and gays have been openly accepted in the British Armed Forces since the ban on serving homosexuals was uneventfully lifted in 2000.

However, despite the firm establishment of women in the military, there continues a debate over their place and role. Many feminists see the continued exclusion of women from close-combat roles as one of the last bastions of sexual discrimination. At present women in the army are prohibited from serving in the forward echelons of the infantry and cavalry, where the job of close-up killing tends to be done. The officially stated reason for this surrounds the impact that a girl would have on the close-knit fighting units who do this task rather than any physical inability; the idea is that having a girl around in this small macho club would upset the balance and unfocus the mind. Although this debarring of women is not a globally held view as women currently serve in the infantry in countries like New Zealand, Denmark, Germany and Israel, but many civilized societies continue to find the concept of mothers, wives and daughters in the thick of battle unpalatable. Women are viewed as the more vulnerable sex and the idea of them thrusting a steely blade into another human being for a living doesn't sit well. As givers of life, it is felt we don't have the right to take it.

But none of the girls in Eleven Platoon had aspirations to get close up and kill anyway. None of us felt a need to break down this barrier to equality and take up arms. The infantry boys could keep their miserable crawling, digging and hiding in holes; for us the infanteering was just a necessity to get through Sandhurst and not a lifestyle choice. We ran around on exercises with guns and honed our shooting on the range but it was not what we joined the army to do. Only one third of the army is infantry, leaving the rest available to the girls – engineering, teaching, policing, intelligence gathering, communications, helicopter flying, logistics, bomb disposal and much, much more. I didn't join the army to go eyeball to eyeball with the Taliban (though it could happen), and the choice of alternatives was endless.

But it was a choice we had to start thinking about, because while it felt like the end of Sandhurst would never come, it was at a very early stage that we had to start considering where we wanted to go when we did eventually commission and had to set our designs on a future army home. With a third of the army off-limits to the girls this narrowing of choice should have meant for an easier decision, but it wasn't. While we'd all made the decision to join the army, what regiment or corps we actually wanted to join became a fluid, moving target as the year wore on.

In the first five weeks of Juniors, between room inspections and drill square humiliation, we had received presentations from each of our options, but I was so tired at this stage that my attention was focused more on fighting with my nodding head and drooping eyelids than absorbing any of the information I should have been, and my only lasting memory of this was the presentation we received from the cavalry.

For their presentation the cavalry had booked the most opulent of Old College's function rooms, the Wellington Room, which was situated at the front of the college. It had huge, towering windows which overlooked the parade square, offering views of the Queen Victoria statue and ornamental rowing lake. Inside, the walls of the Wellington Room were covered in elegant damask wallpaper over which hung rare gold-framed oil paintings of battle scenes, while in one corner of the room sat an impressive carved marble bust of Wellington himself, presiding over the room's events. It was in stark contrast to our Victorian schoolroom surroundings in New College and befitting of cavalry comfort and consuetude.

We attended these presentations as a platoon and although no one in Eleven Platoon was eligible to join the Royal Armoured Corps or Household Cavalry we still had to attend. On the day, we arrived early from the infantry presentation, another which the girls' platoon had pointlessly attended, gathering quietly in the corridor outside to wait for our time to go in. Waiting patiently we could hear cavorting laughter and guffawing coming from the other side of the double oak doors, like listening to the inner sounds of a gentlemen's club. The cavalry are an odd bunch. This collective of Flashman Army units are old and very traditional, still clinging to their glory days in Victorian battle with names like Hussar, Dragoon and Lancer. The typical officer has been bred from very good stock, with a top class private education, inherited wealth, a personal income and often land and a title too (both Princes William and Harry joined the Household Cavalry). Traditionally these swashbuckling types rode horses, but today they caper around in tanks, on Salisbury Plain or the Canadian prairie. Unfettered by financial constraints, cavalry officers are notorious for quaffing vintage champagne like water and wearing full black tie to dinner every night of the week in the Officers' Mess.

Waiting in the corridor outside the Wellington Room we heard the laughter eventually stop, and a latch clicked as the doors were flung open, revealing a floppy-haired gentleman, clad in burgundy cords and glossy leather riding boots. On his top half he wore a mustard-coloured heavy knit woollen jumper complete with elbow patches and tugged threads.

'Ladies!' he boomed at us. 'Come on in.'

And with a bowed flurry, Captain Flashman outstretched his arms and welcomed us inside. We filed past him through the doors for what we knew would be another pointless forty-five minutes of boyish bravado and a DVD of tanks to a Vangelis soundtrack, wishing we could just be allowed the sleep we so desperately needed instead. Inside the Wellington Room two further swashbuckling cads waited to greet us in equally vulgar cords and knitwear combo, their backs to a video projection of Challenger II tanks blowing smoke and dust across a German plain.

'So, ladies,' said number two Harry Flashman, clasping his hands together with a clap. 'Well, I guess none of you are actually allowed to join the cavalry, are you? So you won't get to know us by day, but by God I can tell you, you'll want to know us by night.' And at this he put his hands on his hips and thrust his pelvis towards us with a 'Woof!' (OK, all right, the 'woof' bit isn't strictly accurate, but the rest of his toady smugness genuinely occurred.)

*

One of the best examples of the differences between girls and boys in war at Sandhurst occurred on Exercise Dragon's Challenge, the next of the middle term's exercise thrashings.

Dragon's took us back on the coaches to Wales, but this time, with restrained relief, we weren't going to be staggering up the howling Black Mountains of Long Reach, or advancing to certain death across the ridgelines of Brecon, because Dragon's was to be our first foray into urban warfare (FIBUA) (Fighting In Built-up Areas) and would bring us out of the country and into the town. Into a mock West German town to be precise.

Cilieni village was a purpose-built, pretend hamlet of concrete buildings clustered around a church with a tall watchtower, from where the instructors could watch us breaking and entering in house-to-house combat. These bleak grey concrete chalets were constructed in the style of West German architecture and grouped together they smacked of the ugly communist dourness of a charmless ski resort. Steel shutters firmly covered up glass-less windows and, at the village's far eastern edge, the carcass of a burnt-out tank sat rusting under a cherry tree. This was to be our playground for the next five days, and play we would, because FIBUA turned out to be awesome fun. Like Quasar or paint-balling, it was the stuff of boy soldier dreams. The rough and tumble shoot-'em-up of boyhood war games played out at the bottom of the garden. We ran around with guns, leaping over walls and diving through windows in search of the enemy lurking around each corner and firing off loads of ammunition. We stormed houses with an SAS thrill, kicking down doors and lobbing in grenades, covering our ears and waiting for the smoky bang before charging in shouting and screaming with rifles to automatic, blazing the room with hot brass like a Sylvester Stallone character – our coolness marred only by the plastic safety glasses we had to wear.

The boys beamed as all their war fantasies came true and once we girls had got used to the concept of hurling ourselves through open windows and scrambling over corrugated-iron roofs, the inner tomboy burst free giggling. FIBUA was new and novel. It involved none of the slogging advances to contact, no death marches, or round-the-clock trench-digging, and it felt like playing a game, almost a sport. We snuck up to doorways, scurried down back alleys, crept through trap doors and loft hatches, armed with an 'urban assault kit' (ladder) and grappling irons, breaking and entering, clearing from room to room, house to house, seeking out surrendering Gurkhas. If it wasn't played out in a mock-up German village it would even have been relevant. And, unlike all our previous exercise experiences, FIBUA brought us indoors, so there was no lying in a muddy wet hole on stag trembling as the snow fell, or shivering in our sleeping bags as the wind whipped over us, because on Dragon's we were sheltered inside buildings, away from the harshness of Wales, in relative comfort and with dry pants on.

The exercise started with us capturing Cilieni village from the Gurkha enemy, chasing them out and then securing defensive positions in the buildings to wait for the inevitable enemy counter-attack. Eleven Platoon were assigned a three-storey house near the church to occupy and defend, and 4 Montgomery Drive was what an estate agent would probably have described as 'a well-appointed family home in need of some cosmetic improvement'. We set to work at it straight away with barbed wire, scaffolding poles, sandbags and sheets of corrugated iron, barricading doorways, blocking windows and constructing obstacles in the 'bijou' garden, building up a den and fortifying our new home. We became quite house proud of and even attached to the combat shabby chic decor, insisting on maintaining the integrity of a family home with a welcoming front door and even a dining room table. And this is where Eleven Platoon's home at 4 Montgomery Drive differed from the rest of the houses in Cilieni, because while the girls continued to keep a tidy organized home, even in war, the boys had ripped out all their furniture, barricaded their front door and were climbing in and out through a ladder propped against a first-floor window. It just didn't occur to us to be so destructive (and tactically astute). We still saw this pile of bricks and mortar as a house, something to covet and inhabit, whereas the boys were in role; they had made their house a fortress. So while at Number 4 we were measuring up for soft furnishings and arranging flowers, the boys were splintering tables and chairs into timber to block the stairs.

A girls' and a boys' castle are clearly very different creations.

As we were finishing off the final touches on the second morning, CSgt Bicknell came in to have a look around.

'Very nice, ladies. Very nice. I like what you've done here,' he said, taking a step back to admire our barbed wiring. 'Miss Wheeler, are you watching your arcs in there?' he hollered through to Wheeler who was sitting on some empty ammunition boxes at the window on stag, peering between a gap in the hessian curtain we had made to cover the window.

'Yes, colour sergeant,' Wheeler shouted back.

He continued on his tour upstairs, noseying around, checking sandbags and the steel picks we had used to block a window with. As he poked his head around a doorway on the top floor, a couple of us were sitting around a burning hexi stove making breakfast.

'Morning, ladies,' he said, coming into the room. 'So, who's going to make me a lovely cup of Rosie Lee this morning then?'

CSgt Bicknell had the endearing habit of sprinkling his speech with Cockney rhyming slang that often left us baffled as to his meaning. On the drill square, he'd chastise you for shuffling your 'plates of meat' or during a morning inspection he'd pick you up for mud on your 'daisy roots'. He'd learned his lesson about the peculiarities of dealing with girls and now understood our ways. As Merv leaned forwards and offered him a black plastic mug of hot tea he knew he had been welcomed back into the Eleven Platoon fold.

Unfortunately, the problem with FIBUA is that when war comes to town everyone dies, as the stakes go up at close quarters. History can testify to this overwhelming bloodshed with case samples from battles for Stalingrad, Budapest, Berlin and even Fallujah. And when the Gurkha enemy eventually returned for their counter-attack we got hammered. They stormed our stockaded buildings and flushed us out, crashing through our front door, storming the stairs and overrunning the village. Bodies lay everywhere – killed off by the directing staff – among the empty brass ammunition casings that carpeted each room of Cilienigrad. And when Captain Trunchbull started screaming at us to retreat to the hills, we had to take the wounded with us, and the resultant drudging withdrawal ranks as one of my top five worst moments at Sandhurst.

The woodblock we sought refuge in couldn't have been more than three miles away from Cilieni village, but getting there with bergens on, dragging the bodies of the wounded, was as emotional as childbirth, and the closest I ever came to public tears at Sandhurst. To get there we first slogged our way along a muddy flood plain, its river in full swell, schlepping in our heavy boots, drawing them deeper into the mire. With the weight of bergens and casualties dragging us down, we floundered dreadfully, stumbling and slipping like drunks on the greasy mud. We plugged onwards, as Captain Trunchbull hopped about with caged fury, screaming expletives and bawling senselessly at us to get a move on as the mud sucked us further in. The going was slow and demoralizing, each step getting harder and harder as cracks soon started to appear in the platoon.

Eventually, after a mile we turned left, moving away from the river's banks, heading upwards to join a narrow faded track that traced the steep slopes of a hill. The ascent to the top was utter agony. My bergen pressed down so heavily on my back I thought I might faint with fatigue and pain. I was by now completely exhausted from the mud plain march, my legs stung with an excruciating pain, which seared up through my spine and screamed at my brain to STOP. Which others did, only adding further to the suffering of those of us left on the march, since their bergens were handed to us to pick up and soldier on with. I was in astonishing amounts of discomfort, suffering under the weight of my bergen and struggling up the steep hill without the aid of crampons and a rope. Inside my head I was having a fierce mental battle to keep going, and using all my concentration to stop tears from welling in my eyes.

CSM Mockridge strode up next to me. 'Come on, Miss Goodley,' he said in a hushed voice. 'I know you can do this. You're not going to let yourself down. Keep going. Head up. Focus, Miss Goodley. Focus.'

I was on the verge of giving up. I couldn't see the summit and, as each crest ahead proved to be another false one, our goal remained tantalizingly out of sight. I knew I couldn't make it. At this Sandhurst had now pushed me too far. Here was going to be the point at which I finally broke and failed. As each step became more of a struggle and my legs trembled under the strain, failure looked more and more attractive. I could easily stop and give my bergen to someone else to struggle on with, and join the ranks of others who had already dropped out. I could shoulder the disappointment and shame of having let myself and everyone else down instead. While keeping my vertebrae intact.

Listening to CSM Mockridge I lifted my head and looked up from my boots to see the Platoon Donkey ahead of me wavering too. Faltering more with every step, she was crying freely with tears of pain and frustration. 'Come on,' I willed her on. 'We can do this.' I knew that if she gave up, her bergen would fall to me to carry, and that would be the final straw breaking over my back. If she went I knew I would too. And sure enough, she soon broke, collapsing to the ground in front of me, her cheeks streaked with tears, refusing to take another step. I went to her, hovering over the desperate heap lying in the grass, trying hopelessly to encourage her to her feet once more. The thought of having to take on her bergen as well as mine enraged me and I swore at her for being so selfish.

As she turned away from me, sobbing, Wheeler appeared and released the bergen from the Platoon Donkey's back, rolling it free. She lifted up one of the straps in her hand and, motioning for me to take the other, we lifted it off the ground between us. We shared the bergen like this as we continued on up, leaving the Platoon Donkey to stagger unburdened behind us. We moved in silence, struggling too much with our own mental battle to keep going to be able to speak to one another, resorting to just sideways smiles of encouragement. But it spurred me on.

From somewhere I found strength in pain, finding energy in not wanting to let the side down and a pride in being one of the few left. Somewhere inside my body a little box of reserve energy was found and opened, driving me to the summit, where finally I was overcome with relief, flopping down in the wet grass, as every muscle in my body flooded with elastic release. I had made it. I couldn't believe it. On my own there was no way I would have achieved what I had just done. As a pampered City girl, it would have been completely out of the question. Sandhurst was teaching me a stubborn resolve, a pride and bitter grit to keep fighting on, to battle with the pain and ignore my demons.

As I breathed in a light sigh of relief, CSM Mockridge appeared again and gave a gentle nod of his head in my direction, a rare smile spreading across his thin lips.

'Told you you could do it, Miss Goodley, didn't I. Well done.'

9

GAS, GAS, GAS

The middle term at Sandhurst was chaotically busy, with no chances to come up for air as our feet barely touched the ground. There was no time for a Kit-Kat break, no slippers-and-pipe moments, no opportunity to put our feet up and chill out; we sped from exercise, to war studies, to the assault course, to exercise, to international affairs lectures, to drill, to thrashing PT sessions, to the rifle ranges, to another exercise. All the while the instructors crammed activity after event into the timetable until it was bursting, and all along the standard Sandhurst nonsense continued too. Where room inspections and water parades had become a thing of our Old College past, a new method of messing around our days was introduced instead in the form of the 'show parade'.

The show parade was a punishment handed out by the CSgts for any minor indiscretion, and was given as freely as the kisses of a whore, as they sought to ensure every waking hour of our day was tied up with something. A show parade meant having to parade at nine o'clock in the evening, a time selected for perfect inconvenience, and involved, as the name might suggest, showing something, which usually was your indiscretion rectified. For example, if on the morning inspection parade CSgt Bicknell spotted mud on your 'daisy roots', you would be required to parade at nine o'clock that night with all the other day's 'defaulters' showing 'boots without mud'. Simple. But with all the other business in our days it was an annoyance you could do without. And there was plenty of scope for comic humour in this too, as the CSgts stitched each other up, as it was they who had to inspect the parade. I was once required to show 'ladder removed from tights' and paraded that night with a fresh pair of tights on and a step-ladder, along with 'show bed made', who had dragged his bed outside onto the parade square and 'show bright' who had come with torches taped to his body.

Another way Sandhurst used to occupy and waste our evenings was by employing us to guard the Academy. Since we had now learned weapon handling and visited the rifle range a couple of times we were deemed to hold the requisite qualifications to walk around the grounds at night armed, with real, live, bang, shoot-you-dead ammunition and a torch. We were after all trained and now equipped to kill, but God knows what would have happened if an intruder had actually tried to scale the fence because I didn't have it in me to pull the trigger. For the rest of the night, in between these armed-patrols of Surrey, we had to sit behind a desk in the College Guard Room and answer the telephone, and then when it rang we had to write out the account of the phone call in the

Daily Occurrence Book, but not in normal joined-up handwriting, but in BLOCK CAPITALS, against a ruler and only in black ink. (All army correspondence is only ever written in black ink. Colonels can write in red, and generals write in green.)

Squeezed around this hectic Intermediate Term timetable, we were also busy writing academic essays, one for each of the academic subjects: War Studies, Defence & International Affairs and Leadership Management. I liked the academic side of the commissioning course. I found it in complete contrast to the military skills and all the polishing-cleaning-shining-shouting-running-about that I was so useless at. Writing essays was the only prior skill I brought to Sandhurst. Instead of standing stiffly in the cold on a parade square or polishing brass buttons and doorknobs, the academic stuff was conducted in a serene, almost civilian environment. We sat in small groups in warm comfortable classrooms in a building called Farady Hall (nicknamed Faraway Hall), which was far away from the Colleges and gymnasium, far away from our cleaning products and far, far away from the CSgts' prying eyes. The staff who taught us were all academics, bespectacled civilians wearing cardigans and comfortable Hush Puppies, with not a combat trouser or polished boot in sight. The classroom atmosphere was relaxed and unpressurized, much like being back in a university tutorial. The academics didn't even mind if you closed your eyes and slept, taking pity on the thrashings we received elsewhere in the Academy. But what I loved most about Faraway Hall was the biscuits. The staff smuggled them in for us to have in the more than regular tea breaks (now CSgt Bicknell was our platoon colour sergeant the chocolate biscuits had stopped) and a charitable donation had to be made in exchange for them, raising thousands of pounds each term by doing this.

I can't remember what titles I chose for my War Studies or International Affairs essays, but I do remember the research I did for the Leadership essay, which dug up some rather frightening findings. I wrote my essay on transformational leadership in religious cults (Churchill or Nelson seemed a little too trite and military for me). And for the essay's research, I ventured, for the first time, into the Academy library, another of Sandhurst's CSgt-less oases. Today the library occupies the former Academy gym in what is a distinctly average building when settled alongside Old and New Colleges. Inside, this quiet, whispering sanctum was quite impervious to the shouting and marching that dominated much of the rest of the Academy's grounds, and the few moments we could steal in there were like dipping into the tranquillity of a health spa.

For my essay I plucked a dusty book on 'exploring the CULT in culture' from the shelves of books and between its musty pages found a list of the mind-control techniques used by cult leaders, some of which rang with sinister familiarity:[30]

---

30 *The Wrong Way Home: Uncovering the Patterns of Cult Behaviour in American Society* by Dr Arthur Deikman.

Sleep deprivation and fatigue: Creating disorientation and vulnerability by prolonging mental and physical activity and withholding adequate rest and sleep – typical brainwashing process

Dress codes: Removing individuality by demanding conformity to the group dress code

Verbal abuse: Desensitizing through bombardment with critical, foul and abusive language

Confusion: Encouraging blind acceptance and rejection of logic through interminable complex lectures on incomprehensible doctrines

Time sense deprivation: Destroying the ability to evaluate information, personal reactions, and body functions in relation to passage of time by removing all clocks and watches.

I was standing in the corridor in New College looking up at a noticeboard, flicking my eyes over the details on Company orders, checking for my name among the dentist appointments and timings for tomorrow's day on the pistol range. It was a Wednesday afternoon and I was wearing my Academy tracksuit, the staple blue baggy bottoms and red fleece-lined sweatshirt that was our only escape from army uniform. On my back was a little rucksack with my wet swimming kit rolled up in it, as I'd just finished in the pool. Around my eyes the red trace of where my goggles had been pressing against my cheeks was still visible and I smelled of chlorine. To my left a door suddenly swung open as CSM Mockridge strode out with some paperwork and drawing pins clasped in his hand.

'Ah, Miss Goodley. Just the person I wanted to see,' he said as he came to stand next to me and started pinning the pieces of paper to the noticeboard. 'How do you fancy being on a committee?'

'Er, what sort of committee, sir?' I asked, a little unsure what he was lining me up for.

'The Academy Adjutant is putting together a Mess Committee,' he said, finishing his pinning and turning to me. 'I thought you'd be the perfect person to represent Imjin Company,' he said. 'I need someone who won't take any crap in there. Someone who'll stick up for what the cadets want. You'll get stuck in and stand your ground, won't you, Miss Goodley? Give them some stick. Like Margaret Thatcher.' He chuckled to himself.

'Erm, yes, sir. I'll be happy to do it if you want me to,' I said, a little puzzled by his analogy. Where had CSM Mockridge got the opinion that I was like the Iron Lady from?

As he flitted back through the door to his office, Fergus came darting out through the brief gap and into the corridor beside me. Fergus was the dog belonging to the Officer in Command (OC) of Imjin Companys' and was having a great time at the Academy. Army officers and dogs go perfectly together, like cheese and pickle, and an army dog's life has to be one of the best. They can revel in plenty of open fields to run around, mud to roll in, and they get to come to work all day, where crowds of people fuss over them all day in the Mess. For a dog the army is a dream. But this dream is not open to all breeds, because officers' dogs typically conform to one of two types: Labradors or retrievers. A bit of variety can be brought into this by having a chocolate Lab rather than the standard black, but aside from this, army dogs come only in a standard issue. Although somehow Fergus had managed to buck this trend, as he was neither a chocolate nor black Lab, not even a retriever, for he was a scruffy little Border terrier and was totally apathetic to the importance of his surroundings. The complete antithesis of an officer's dog, he had flagrant disregard for the commands of his owner and the OC could regularly be seen standing on the steps of New College entrance calling Fergus's name as the little dog disappeared off into the distance with two fingers up to any promise of coming back. At home he had cunningly found a gap in the fence at the bottom of the garden through which he came and went as he pleased and we would often bump into him during a platoon run or loaded march as he went about his business on his own, returning home in time for his dinner. When he was in the mood to follow his master he would come along to Company meetings and sniff around at the back, looking for the best lap to curl up on. Though sadly for Fergus this treat came to a comic end one morning as he joined a gathering of Imjin Company in which the OC was handing out a Company-scale bollocking. That morning Fergus was obviously having a good day and feeling a little frisky, so while the OC stood gravely at the front raising his voice to us in a serious tone, Fergus was busying himself at the back of the room inappropriately humping the Yemeni cadet's leg.

I went along to the Mess Committee meeting as CSM Mockridge had asked, ready to fight a battle. In my mind my combats were a sharp suit once more as I felt all boardroom and power heels again. I hadn't lost my City edge. It was still there underneath the layers of green and boot polish. I relished being given a cause to pursue, a principle to stand up for. I may have even slammed my fist on the table at one point, frightening the Adjutant in his chair. And CSM Mockridge knew exactly what he was doing in selecting me to represent Imjin Company. He knew that I didn't shine on the drill square and got left behind when it came to exercise skills. He knew that digging trenches and leopard crawling were not my forte. He'd sussed out where my strengths did lie, then spotted somewhere I could prove them. I left the meeting triumphant, having successfully brokered the removal of yoghurts from our exercise packed lunches to be replaced with something sturdier. It wasn't a new corporate loan deal or rescue finance package that would have been an achievement in my former City days but it felt good to be in control of something again.

Things were now ticking along quite nicely at the Academy. I was comfortable with my surroundings, I was coming to grips with the military way and I'd made some good friends. I was even enjoying it. My early fears of incompetence had faded, and slowly I was creeping up the class. I no longer felt alone or useless and had earned my place in the platoon. In between the digging and crawling there was a lot of camaraderie and laughter too, as Eleven Platoon became a group of firm friends. The army is famed for its gallows humour and this is bred at institutions like Sandhurst, where often the only way you can get through the day is to laugh at it. When a CSgt is screaming at you on the parade square and threatening to flick you into the lake with his pace stick, chuckling behind fixed eyes is the only safe way to take it. Up in Norfolk as we had sat at the bottom of our trench, Allinson, Rhodes and I had howled with laughter at the ridiculousness of our situation: unearthing a Second World War bomb in sleeping rural East Anglia. In Cilieni village we had giggled between snatched breaths as we ran from house to house, leaping through windows and watching Captain Trunchbull getting stuck in the loft hatch, her bottom wedged in the square hole, legs kicking out for freedom.

We'd now spent a total of twenty weeks in training, and life had smoothed to a busy but manageable routine. We had learned to play the Sandhurst game, and were now quite good at it. We knew our way around and knew the shortcuts too. In CSgt Bicknell we had also found an ally at the Academy, having successfully converted him to the female approach, as he now embraced the subtle feminine touches with mugs of Rooibos 'Rosie Lee' (tea) supped from Cath Kidston china in the Pink Palace (the Pink Palace was Eleven Platoon's common room which we had painted a hideous, sickly Pepto-Bismol pink, in a bid to apply a feminine streak to our surroundings). And the platoon was settled. We were getting the hang of Sandhurst, but were nowhere near the finished article yet. We could dig trenches, fortify a house and advance to contact, but anything more complicated or contemporary was still beyond us. My initial terrifyingly steep learning curve had lessened and I was on the right course, although the thought of standing up in front of real-life soldiers and commanding them was still hugely daunting.

But by now real-life soldiers were already going to war. Because after just twenty weeks of their training, they were done. Trained. Good to go. From high school dropout to gun-wielding teen[31] in a mere twenty weeks. An infantry soldier spends just twenty weeks in training and some even graduate from the infantry training centre in Catterick and get straight on the plane to Afghanistan. It's a frighteningly quick process.

But I wasn't worrying about any of that, because at Sandhurst we were off to the pistol ranges.

There is something undeniably sexy about being armed with a pistol. Holding it tightly in your grip, clasping your fingers around the cool metal of its body and smoothly pulling the trigger towards you. Then feeling the power of the weapon as it kicks back and the round fires out, keeping your grasp steady and firm ready to aim for the next shot. Pistols feel racy and 007. Like being a Bond girl or one of Charlie's Angels. Its holster straps suggestively around your thigh and unlike a rifle there is no lying prone on the ground getting wet and muddy, shuffling about in the dirt

---

31 No soldier can deploy to war before his/her eighteenth birthday.

as you try to tuck the weapon into your shoulder. A pistol is small, sleek and pocket sized. It's a girl's weapon. Stylish and sophisticated, it's easy on the arm muscles and would slip nicely into a handbag. As I stood at the firing point on the pistol ranges, pointing the weapon at targets, I wanted a cape and eye mask, a black leather catsuit and Farrah Fawcett's flick. I felt the rounds spitting out, knocking down the life-sized figures twenty-five metres away and it felt so much more glamorous with a pistol.

In between firing, we sat in the little range hut cleaning the weapons, scrubbing away at the coated layers of carbon (Coca-Cola is a surprisingly good cleaning fluid for this, which is probably why it is also so effective at stripping the enamel from your teeth). We chatted and joked as we worked our way through the brown paper bag packed lunches, chewing on flaky sausage rolls and swapping crisp flavours. In the background, the firing of rounds could still be heard, interspersed with birdsong and the shouted orders from the CSgts in charge of the range. I was happy as I stripped down the weapon, smiling to myself as I removed the pistol barrel. This was a perfectly contented way to spend an afternoon, sitting in the sunshine having lunch in good company. I lay the pistol spring beside me on the wooden bench, appreciating the weapon's simplicity. It felt snug as it nestled in the palm of my hand and fitted back together effortlessly. I welcomed its small compactness, and the lightweight sensation as I held it. Handling the pistol felt simple and less complicated than a rifle. And unfortunately since our move to New College we had been spending a lot more time with our rifles and not necessarily for the most gratifying of reasons.

This extra rifle time came about because on our arrival at New College drill took a new and unpleasant turn, as now, having finally mastered the basic moves on Old College parade square, our first drill session in New College started with us queuing up outside the armoury. When I got to the front of the queue the armourer handed me my rifle as usual, lifting it out of its wooden bracket and passing it through the service hatch in the steel cage. From behind him he also picked a bayonet from a hook on the wall and handed it to me for the first time. I held them with awkwardness once more, harking back to that first time I had held my rifle in the Junior Term. This time I felt awkward because I was dressed for drill, not the ranges. I couldn't understand what we needed them for. Traipsing outside onto the parade square in my Blues with the rifle cradled stiffly in my arms, I clearly recognized the discordance. Rifles are not meant for drill, rifles are meant for killing. Rifles and drill do not go together like cheese and pickle. Rifles and drill go together like lemon juice and paper cuts. They smart and sting, bringing tears to your eyes. They are clumsy and graceless. Nothing about their design is meant for the parade square. When Heckler & Koch remodelled the SA80 army rifles there wasn't anything in their remit about ensuring they could be 'SEIZED', 'STRIKED' and 'GRASPED'. Rifles are designed for shooting, not holding to attention, but at Sandhurst we spent more precious time prancing up and down the parade square with them than actually pulling the trigger.

And the pain caused carrying this ridiculous 4 kg of pointless metal and plastic around in the sweltering sun was excruciating. Because, of course, during drill the rifle wasn't carried sensibly like on exercise or in Helmand. We didn't use a rifle sling or comfortable carrying posture; on the drill square the rifle had to be carried with one, just one, hand, as we switched it from the 'slope' to the 'shoulder' arms, balancing it against our shoulder, the rifle's weight held up by just a small group of quickly seizing muscles in your arm. A dull ache would spread its way up my arms, through biceps and triceps, from my gripped hand to my trembling shoulder.

And it was torturous.

The boys had cleverly worked out that if they slipped a small tin of boot polish into their right trouser pocket they could rest the butt of the rifle against it as they stood to attention, taking up the strain, but in Eleven Platoon we wore skirts and couldn't exploit such cunning tricks.

The very worst part of rifle drill however was the agonizing struggle of the 'present arms': standing motionless to attention with our arms extended forwards, holding the heavy rifle vertically out in front of us for inspection. This stress position could go on for tens of minutes, as we stood still under the burning glare of the sun, feeling beads of sweat trickling down our backs, pooling into a damp patch on our shirts, under the heavy woollen Blues jackets. The possibility of fainting loomed ever near.

Each time the rifle was part of a drill move it had to be grasped with an audible 'STRIKE' as we slapped it hard in unison. The CSgts wanted to see bloodstains on the white gloves we wore as we struck the weapon forcefully with our palms. And CSgt Bicknell joked that if anyone hit their rifle hard enough to break it, he would give them the rest of the day off.

CSgt Bicknell would stand out in front of the platoon, as we lined up in three ranks before him. Then when we were all ready, he would puff out his chest, angle his chin high into the air and, with his pace stick tucked under his right arm, he would bark out the first commands: 'Eleven Platoon. Eleven Platoooooooon. Shun!' And his voice would peak an octave higher on the 'shun' as in front of him thirty cadets stamped to attention, followed by a flutter of movement as we all tried to gain control of the rifles at our sides. More than once someone dropped their rifle to the ground with an exaggeratedly loud clatter and CSgt Bicknell would go berserk.

'Come on, ladies. Come on. Stand still. When you come to attention I expect you to stand completely still, I don't want to see a flicker of movement over there. Nothing. You are to just *freeze* as you are.'

Then he would puff his chest out once more and give the next command: 'Eleven Platoon. Sloooooooope arms!' And on the clipped shout of 'arms' there would be a ripple of clanging metal as we repositioned the rifle from down at our right side to resting against our shoulders, slapping hard at the weapon's side as we went, creating the audible strike CSgt Bicknell so desired.

'Come on, ladies. More strike. More strike. Let me hear some aggression in there.'

CSgt Bicknell loved drill. He was a proud guardsman and drill was in his blood. His heart pounded to the beat of the parade square drum, and he was in his absolute element on the drill square, spruced up in ceremonial dress with a brass band and expectant audience. Nowhere was he happier than out at the front, in command of a polished drill squad.

Except, unfortunately, Eleven Platoon was not yet a polished drill squad. In skirts it was harder to hide our drill errors, and the curve of our feminine figures prevented the robotic straight lines expected of marching troops. Hips swayed and their roundness prevented our arms from pinning straight at our sides, which frustrated CSgt Bicknell wildly.

For rifle drill we attached bayonets to the muzzle of the rifle, and their steely edges would glisten in the sunshine as we switched the rifle around, from 'slope' to 'shoulder' to 'present'. The clean, polished metal would catch the sunlight and remind any spectators that although we might look daftly unthreatening dressed in our formal uniforms, the rifles in our arms had a far more serious and sombre use. The sight of a parade square filled with over 200 cadets armed with rifles and this iconic blade must have presented a frightening proposition as one poor unfortunate discovered on a summer's afternoon after I commissioned.

On that day the entire Intermediate intake were on the parade square in front of New College being put through their paces by their respective CSgts when a coach slowly drove behind them and came to a stop at the college entrance. The coach was carrying a party of officers returning from a battlefield tour in northern France and, unbeknownst to anyone on board at the time, an Afghan refugee hiding in the coach's toilet. As the coach came to a stop for the first time since it had crossed the English Channel, the hydraulic hiss signalled the opening of the doors, and the Afghan stowaway spotted his chance, bursting free from the confines of his locked toilet. As he absconded onto the parade square, making a dash for freedom, he must have cursed his rotten luck when choosing his mode of passage at Sangatte, as he was confronted with the sight of over 200 armed cadets.

We had to get to grips with this new dimension to drill because in the Intermediate term there was another drill examination, and this time it was competitive.

Winning the Drill Competition was an accolade CSgt Bicknell so very desperately wanted. Drill was his thing, and while his brood of girls may not have been able to compete against the boys on the assault course or on exercise, the drill square was an equalizer. CSgt Bicknell believed that drill was about style and panache. That it was about putting on a show, and he felt that the girls would be best placed to do this. He was also a friend of the inspecting officer. So with a bit of dedicated practice our chances looked good.

But first, before CSgt Bicknell could have any crowning moment of glory on the drill square, we had something of more unfortunate relevance to attend to.

*

There is no doubt that the British Army produces among the best officers in the world. But now, over halfway through the commissioning course, I still couldn't see how. The stuff we were being taught still felt largely irrelevant to what we would be doing in Afghanistan or Iraq, which for some of us was less than a year away. The marching, the polishing, room inspections and water parades, digging trenches, assaulting East German villages and putting up bashas in woodblocks – I knew none of this was going on in Bastion or Basra, so why were we doing it?

My concern wasn't that Sandhurst was teaching us skills for all eventualities, but that so far it seemed these eventualities were not the Afghan and Iraqi realities. And while lessons from the past should not be ignored, the current wars staring us hard in the face were hard to ignore too.

Sandhurst justifies this lack of contemporary relevance in its training by pointing out that it is a leadership academy and that the mission-specific gloss is taught after commissioning, by the units and corps cadets commission into. Second-lieutenants leaving Sandhurst are not propelled into the wider army with just a pip on their chests and shiny shoes; instead they are taken deep into the bosom of their new cap badges, held away from real soldiers to be trained further on young officers' courses; the boys who sign up to the infantry pack their bergens once more and head back to Brecon for more crawling.

The engineers build bridges and then blow them up in Kent. The signallers fiddle with wiggly amps on the Jurassic coast and the pilots climb into the seat of a cockpit and try not to become too RAF.

As it was, on the few occasions we did receive some contemporary training at Sandhurst, it proved to be neither pertinent nor enjoyable. I could think of plenty of war skills that should feature higher up the Afghanistan checklist than dealing with NBC, but at Sandhurst it was the first modern-day training we were given.

NBC is Nuclear, Biological and Chemical warfare, and was undoubtedly selected to take prominence on the Sandhurst curriculum because of its eye-watering, lung-burning, head-boiling potential. I won't deny that for Saddam's Iraq this may have had some slim importance but Saddam was now dead, his weapons of mass destruction never existed and the only tasks left for the cadets from CC071 going to Iraq would be closing the doors and turning off the lights. Nevertheless, as we ran around the polo pitch panting and wheezing in our charcoal-lined chemical oversuits, I hoped to God that this wasn't relevant training for war.

We were playing NBC rugby, although there was no chance of me actually seeing the ball through the lenses of the thick rubber gas mask I had strapped to my face. The sweat from the mid-August sun had turned to steam inside my mask, misting the lenses and obscuring my sight, while the tight seal restricted my breathing, rendering me completely incapacitated for any form of sport. Despite these disadvantages the match was still equal, as the players on both sides were clumsily stumbling around in their NBC suits playing this mal-coordinated sado-sport, fumbling for the ball as if in the dark. And we were happy to stay here, out in the midday sun, running around in four layers of clothing, with rubber gloves and boots on, because we knew that when the final whistle blew something much, much worse was coming next.

It was the gas chamber.

We weren't allowed to call it that, but no matter how they dressed it up, as a 'respirator testing facility', or 'NBC confidence room', it was still a chamber in which we were about to get gassed. And the experience was as hideous as it sounds.

We'd long known that the little innocuous grey brick hut that was tucked away among the trees next to Range A would have to be visited at some point. And now, gasping and sweating, we queued outside it like condemned women, nervously waiting to see what would happen inside, each one of us hoping that we'd turn out to be in the statistical 1 per cent of people who are unaffected by the gas. The sweat we had worked up playing NBC rugby was part of the cruel conditioning before we went inside; the dampness on our skin and shortness of our breath would accentuate the symptoms caused by the gas, ensuring we could appreciate the full range of its effects.

And the full range of effects was utterly horrendous.

It was like being water-boarded with urine.

As the door shut behind us we held our breath and removed our gas masks, six of us standing inside a concrete bunker in the woods staring down at the small tablets of

CS gas burning on a breeze block in the centre of the room. In front of me, CSgt Rattray was covering the exit, blocking the way to clean, fresh, leafy Surrey air. He turned to look at me with his gas mask on, and I could see a smile forming across his eyes behind the glass lenses.

'Number? Rank? Name?' the Rat asked in a muffled voice, prompting me to think and speak in the gaseous fug. Straight away I could feel the surface of my skin starting to tingle with a wasabi sting, as the delicate skin around my lips and eyes started to burn.

'Whisky, one, zero, six, one, four, five, one. Officer Cadet Goodley,' I blurted out, trying to hang on to the reserves of my saved breath, so that I wouldn't have to draw any of the noxious air around me into my lungs.

'And what is your favourite colour?' he asked, attempting once more to make me gulp in a lungful of the potent gaseous cocktail.

'Blue, colour sergeant,' I said, my head starting to feel light, as the gas lingering in my nostrils slowly built from a gentle korma into the agonizing fire of a phall.

'And what is the square root of 206?' he finally quizzed. A small triumphant twinkle in his eye.

What? The square root of 206? How the heck was I supposed to know that? My brain had stopped working. My lungs were screaming out for air. I could feel the effects of the gas drowning every part of me. And then I lost it. My eyes and nose started streaming great swathes of snotty dribble. My ears burned. My skin inflamed. I needed to breathe. I desperately needed clean fresh air. Through streaked tears, I looked across the bare brick hut at the

Platoon Donkey. I could see her chatting away nonchalantly, remaining remarkably composed. At the Rat's request she was listing her top five Take That hits, and taking her considered time over it. I couldn't believe it; she was completely unaffected. She was immune. Of all people. Of all the personal attributes. The Platoon Donkey had finally found something she was good at, and it was just such a shame that this would be the one and only time in her entire military career she'd be called upon to do it.

Then just as I thought my lungs were about to collapse, the Rat stepped aside and bundled me through the open door, coughing and choking uncontrollably into the summer's air. I gasped at it, gulping in lungfuls between short snotty splutters. I wanted to curl up on the grass into a hugging ball and will the pain away, but outside CSgt Bicknell was shouting instructions for us to keep moving. Keep our arms outstretched to let the fresh air get in. So instead I stumbled blindly about, my eyes and nose streaming, waiting for the burning to subside, while those still left in the queue to go into the chamber watched in abject horror. And as the chilli sting finally mellowed, I prayed that God forbid we may never have to do this on exercise.

But of course we *were* going to have to do it on exercise; this was Sandhurst after all. Exercise was uncomfortable enough without the faff and sting of NBC, but now, at the hottest time of the year, we were deploying into the field once more and this time we would be digging holes, fighting Gurkhas and advancing to contact, all in two layers of additional clothing. The extra warmth I had cried out for during those shivering nights in Brecon and the Hundred Acre Wood now just became more junk that I had to wear and carry around with me, as NBC meant more stuff to squeeze into my bulging bergen.

And we soon discovered that, whereas in FIBUA everyone dies of gunshot wounds, in NBC everyone chokes to death instead. We sat in NBC lectures in Churchill Hall, absorbing the horrors of what Saddam Hussein did to his own people, and realizing that there was nothing at all sporting about NBC. We were taught about each of the possible agents in an evil villain's arsenal: nerve, blood, blister and choking agents, all of which were lethal. Gruesome pictures illustrated for us what would happen if we were exposed to them: first our pupils would contract then we'd experience profuse salivation and dizziness. This would be followed by convulsions, muscle twitching, involuntary urination, defecation. Then by asphyxiation and eventually death. None of which sounded like an agreeable event to have to deal with on the battlefield.

If we came under attack from any of these nasty agents we had just nine seconds to get our gas masks on. Nine frenzied seconds of hurriedly scrabbling at rubber, eyes screwed shut, breath held. In case of an attack our gas masks were carried around with us in a small bag strapped to our waists, like the bumbags that were popular in the eighties or with American tourists in London. Then when the chemical attack alarm sounded for us to put them on, we had to quickly remove our helmet and place it between our knees, rip open the Velcro fastenings on the gas-mask bumbag, pull out the gas mask, work out which way was up, grapple with the rubber straps, stretch them over our head and fix the mask into position. Then, when it was on and sealed to our cheeks we had to breathe out and shout a muffled, 'GAS, GAS, GAS,' to warn others. And all of this had to be achieved wearing large, thick rubber gloves on our hands, which meant it was like trying to thread a needle whilst wearing boxing gloves.

Making this nine-second deadline took lots of practice and all of Eleven Platoon would stand outside in a fumbling frenzy as CSgt Bicknell counted us down: 'GAS, GAS, GAS. Nine, eight, seven. Come on, ladies, you need to be quicker than this. Six, five, four. Come on, this needs to be faster, ladies. Three, two, one.'

At zero, half of us would still be grappling with the straps. The combat helmet that was supposed to be held between our knees would have dropped to the floor and rolled away, someone would invariably have their mask on upside down and those who had managed to get their mask on were slowly asphyxiating as it restricted their breathing.

In an NBC environment our chances would be slim.

Daily NBC life proved to be a complete faff too, as once the gas mask and gloves were on, everything became far more complicated. The mask narrowed your field of vision like a blinkered pony and with rubber boxing gloves over your hands the most basic of tasks became a muddled effort. I struggled with fiddly buttons and zips, while the logistics of eating, drinking and going to the toilet became an undignified and messy act. All required us to learn a complicated set drill; the defecation drill being of particular shameful indignity, and as I simulated trying to protect the toilet paper from contamination I hoped to God the constipating ration-pack biscuits never necessitated this become a reality.

My favourite NBC drill was the 'nuclear immediate action drill', which was quite possibly the most ridiculous thing I did during my entire time at Sandhurst, more bizarre even than looking for litter in the dark or singing the national anthem at dawn. The nuclear immediate action drill was to be carried out in the unfortunate event of being in the wrong place when a nuclear bomb is dropped. In this far from ideal situation, what we were to do was face the direction of the blast and lie down on the ground on our stomachs, head face-down, with our arms tucked underneath our bodies (the boys' hands invariably clutching their crown jewels). We were to lie there like this as the blast wave rushed over us, no doubt scorching and stripping the clothing from our backs, then we were supposed to continue lying there and wait for the returning second blast wave to come rushing back over us. Finally when both waves had passed, the drill was to stand up and brush the 'nuclear fallout' off our bodies with leaves and twigs plucked from nearby trees, like some sort of pagan self-flagellation ritual. That was if the explosion of a nuclear bomb hadn't turned you into crispy bacon and the surrounding trees still had any foliage left.

You don't need to be in the military to realize that all this is a completely fanciful notion, probably dreamed up to convince soldiers that in a nuclear attack they stood a chance, when in reality Hiroshima and Nagasaki conclusively attest otherwise. In reality, if a nuclear bomb does go off, any sensible soldier would be putting his head between his legs and kissing his arse goodbye.

I don't recall much of the NBC exercise; probably because my brain has elected to wipe most of the whole sorry experience from memory and possibly because with a gas mask on I didn't really see very much of it either. The exercise was called Marathon's Chase, named, I'm sure, because it was a long, miserable slog which would see us in considerable amounts of pain and, in my case, unable to walk by the end of it.

After the soggy suffering of Brecon, the third and final exercise of the Intermediate Term would be taking us back to the flat, featureless farmland of Thetford once more. To where our Worst Encounter trench demons lay and sadly I knew that this time there would be no swimming angels coming to rescue me. As the convoy of coaches pulled up on New College parade square for the pre-dawn start, the whole of CC071 piled onto them, bergens bulging with all the now well-worn exercise paraphernalia. This time for our East Anglia excursion the picks and shovels had been swapped for NBC oversuits, gas masks and a 'chemical warfare agent detector', which was a large cumbersome metal box that weighed a handy compact twenty-five kilograms and would have to be carried everywhere with us.

Despite NBC being of relative contemporary bearing, the exercise was still played out according to the now hackneyed Cold War template. And as dusk approached on the first night, we moved into the familiar routine of setting up a triangular home among the dense trees of a woodblock. This time I was sharing a shell-scrape with the Platoon Donkey and that night as we cooked our dinner and sorted ourselves out, I discovered in her someone even less suited to military service than myself as she produced a manicure set from a bergen pocket. I offered to dig our shell-scrape while she prepared the boil-in-the-bag ration-pack meals that would be our dinner (Tesco trips were now strictly out of the question), and I handed her my corned-beef hash to heat up while I attacked the topsoil.

'Can you stick that on for me, please?' I asked, throwing the dense silver foil packet to the ground beside her. 'There's some hexi[32] in the pocket of my bergen lid if you need it,' I said as I swept back a pile of leaves from the forest floor.

'OK. Thanks. I'll light it in a minute. Can I use some of your water too?' she said, filing the jagged edge of a broken nail.

'Yes, of course, it's in one of my webbing pouches, but there isn't much left, I need to fill up. Haven't you got any left?' I asked, as I shovelled the soil into a ridge around the outside of the shell-scrape hole, trying to create the illusion of a deeper excavation.

'Yes, I've still got lots of water left, but it's *Evian* and I don't want to cook with it.'

---

32 Hexamine is the waxy solid fuel tablet that we burned for heat to boil water over a small metal fold-out stove. It was smokeless but had a very distinctive smell that even now can transport me straight back to Army exercises and these woodblock moments.

'It's what?' I asked, swinging around to look at her, unsure that I'd heard correctly.

'*Evian* mineral water. I filled my water bottles with it back at Sandhurst before we deployed. If I only use it for drinking it'll last me till Wednesday. So can I use your water for the cooking?'

Oh good God. How had she managed to get this far into the course? I quietly shook my head and carried on digging, aghast at her utter illogic. It wasn't as though we had to go foraging for water on exercise, it was all provided readily for us in jerry cans to fill up from each time we stopped. But as I dug I thought about it more and in an odd sense I admired her; she had resolutely refused to give up her civilian girly ways, she was clinging on and dissenting, repelling the conversion to the army's sensible soldier approach. Except we all knew that at some point you had to give in, you couldn't fight the Sandhurst machine for ever and the earlier you relented the easier life became. Because once you understood that the Army has to operate within boundaries life made sense. To be an effective force there isn't scope within the army for wild individualism. You can't have ill-disciplined non-conformers. It would never work. It would be impossible to command an army of odd-bods and misfits and for this reason Sandhurst was pressing into us a method and way of doing things. Our personalities were not stifled (despite what I may have felt at times) but in uniform you can't go violently against the grain, and filling water bottles with *Evian* while relying on someone else to provide water for you to cook and wash with was actually selfish. The Platoon Donkey's fight couldn't last for ever, and she'd have to break at some point because the system wouldn't.

I dug away at our shell-scrape, finishing it off between spoonfuls of piping hot corned-beef hash, and as darkness finally fell I was looking forward to some brief snatched sleep at the bottom of it. In the army there is an exercise trade-off all soldiers face over the course of the year between warmth and sleep: during the cold winter months plummeting temperatures mean nights spent shivering in a sleeping bag, curled up into a foetal ball desperately seeking warmth, whereas the summer months bring more comfortable temperatures, but shorter nights, which reduce sleeping hours as dusk rapidly rushes into dawn. And as exercise Marathon's Chase fell over the summer solstice we had only a few hours of darkness each night, which meant there was little point in us having packed our sleeping bags at all, especially once the stag rota had been drawn up.

I was on stag with the Platoon Donkey and after just thirty minutes of shut-eye we were shaken awake by Merv to take our place at the sentry post, staring into the darkness. We were wearing our NBC chemical oversuits and I felt pleasantly warm in the extra clothing as I lay on the dirt, my head propped against my rifle. The unusual exercise warmth had a soporific effect and as we lay there battling the will to fall asleep I offered the Platoon Donkey a boiled sweet. We chatted in hushed whispers to keep ourselves awake, playing 'Snog, Marry or Strangle' to pass the time and give us something more exciting to think about than NBC.

'Brad Pitt, Daniel Craig or Justin Timberlake?' she said, sotto voce. 'Snog, marry or strangle?'

'Oh tough one,' I said, crunching on the remains of a boiled sweet as I mulled over my decision. 'I think I'd have to shoot Brad Pitt, to teach him a lesson for leaving Jennifer Aniston for Angelina Jolie. I'd snog Daniel Craig, definitely.' I closed my eyes and thought of the shirt-off James Bond moments.

'Good choice. Snog Daniel Craig, definitely,' the Platoon Donkey agreed.

'Oh, but hang on,' I said, trying not to raise my voice in the excitement of the memory. 'Do you remember that scene in *Thelma and Louise* with Brad Pitt, maybe I should snog him.'

'No, no. You should strangle Brad Pitt, for being an adulterous sleaze,' she said. 'Plus he's past his prime now anyway.'

'I suppose then that leaves Justin Trousersnake for marriage. I'm not happy with that. I don't like him. His music annoys me,' I said, taking my decision very seriously. 'OK, your turn to decide,' I whispered, turning the tables. 'How about Jeremy Clarkson, James May and Richard Hammond? Snog, marry, strangle?' I said, just as CSgt Bicknell emerged through the trees and appeared in front of us.

'Ladies,' he said as he strode towards us, giving the Platoon Donkey a fright.

'What's going on here? Were you asleep there?' he said, challenging the Platoon Donkey's startled reaction.

'No, Colour Sergeant,' she quickly responded. 'You just made me jump. Miss Goodley and I are keeping a vigilant watch out here.' She turned to look at me.

'Good, good. I wouldn't want to find you asleep on stag, would I? Did you know that it was the alert reactions of a young lance corporal guard commander in the middle of the night at Tern Hill barracks that saved lives?' he said, squatting on the ground beside us to tell us this fable lesson. 'He spotted the IRA planting a bomb, Miss Goodley. He wasn't asleep when he raised the alarm. It was his swift prompt reaction that stopped British soldiers being killed by the IRA as they slept in their own beds. Good vigilant soldier. So don't let me catch you sleeping on stag. You hear?'

'Yes, Colour Sergeant,' we responded in unison.

We'd heard this parable before. CSgt Bicknell told us the Tern Hill barracks story a lot. He liked the point it proved. And it was a true story. In 1989 a young Parachute Regiment soldier spotted two men acting suspiciously at Tern Hill barracks in Shropshire. He raised the alarm and evacuated the area just in time, before two home-made bombs exploded, destroying the accommodation block where fifty soldiers had previously been sleeping. I know this to be true because after I left Sandhurst I went to that guard commander's leaving lunch as he left the Army at the end of his twenty-two year career and felt a little pang of excitement at meeting this legendary man who had been so extolled to us by CSgt Bicknell.

With Marathon's being another Cold War scenario but with an NBC gloss, every now and then during the exercise we got gassed. Which was a thoroughly grim way to make a bad day worse. At completely inopportune moments, the CSgts would appear with small tablets of CS gas and let loose with them among us. Like someone farting in church. And this was why CSgt Bicknell had just popped out of the bushes and ruined our game of snog, marry or strangle. Very soon after his arrival on the scene someone in the Platoon Harbour area shrieked out, 'GAS, GAS, GAS,' sending us all scrabbling around for our gas masks, fumbling madly to get them on before the chilli sting kicked in. Being on sentry when this happened, as the Platoon Donkey and I were, came with an additional NBC farce, as it was our responsibility to give the camp the 'all clear' again when the gas had passed. And the way we had been taught to do this was by conducting the 'two-man sniff test'.

I would love to meet the person who drew up the British Army's NBC warfare guidelines. Because this man (and it was undoubtedly a man) had not only managed to pass the utterly ridiculous nuclear immediate action drill into military doctrine but trumped himself with a second madcap, away-with-the-fairies NBC practice when he created the two-man sniff test. A concept I can only think was dreamed up in the pub at the end of a heavy drinking session. The two-man sniff test was just that, two men, or in the Platoon Donkey's and my case, two women, sniffing. Like a dog at a lamppost. What was supposed to happen was that after a period of time sweating uncomfortably into our masks, the sentries would be tasked with testing the air to see if it was clear. And since in One Section we had managed to ditch our cumbersome 'chemical warfare agent detector' as broken, we had to check the Norfolk air for remnants of CS gas by tentatively removing our masks and sniffing it, sacrificially exposing ourselves to the gas so the rest of the platoon would know whether it was safe or not. Except for me there was one fundamental flaw in this set-up: I was partnered with the Platoon Donkey, who as we had all now discovered was immune.

Disaster struck for me on Marathon's Chase.

It happened as we were being gassed.

Again.

The entire contingent of Imjin Company had walked through the night, trampling across Norfolk farmland to assault an enemy village. Still in the darkness of early morning, we were at the end of the attack, reorganizing our fighting forces to extract, when suddenly a mortar boom thundered out across the quiet morning air, clearing my stomach and knocking the blood to my boots. Just as my eardrums recovered there came a second and third loud vibrating bang and then someone shouted the now dreaded words, 'GAS, GAS, GAS.' Utter pandemonium ensued in the morning blackness as the ninety cadets of Imjin Company hurriedly scrambled to put on their gas masks while the air around us began to fill with smoke. And within seconds the outside world became blocked out. My mask steamed up with sweat, and quietness filled my ears as the radio headset I was wearing became completely useless. I could hear nothing and couldn't speak into the microphone with my gas mask on. Straining to see through the misty lenses of my mask, I could see the faint silhouettes of people amidst the smoke and darkness. Everyone looked identical with their faces masked and finding the rest of One Section became impossible. Forget the difficulties of commanding odd-bods and misfits, here we were all identikit blind deaf mutes and it was far harder.

Using waving hand gestures, the whole company somehow came to be lined up in a semblance of order on the dirt track that led away from the village. At the front, people started moving forwards, trying to get away from the smoke and gas. With them the pace picked up and I found myself swept along, breaking my stride into a run as urgency dragged me forwards. I was still wearing full NBC clothing: the chemical oversuit, gas mask, rubber gloves and large rubber overboots, which flapped around at my ankles. The track beneath my feet was uneasy and I soon stumbled and fell in the confused melee, my ankle rolling over and out of joint at a divot in the path. The weight of the rucksack on my back propelled me forwards into the dirt, pinning and flattening me to the floor. Its force knocked the wind from my lungs and I struggled to gasp for breath as my gas mask restricted my breathing.

And then the pain hit me.

A searing, shooting pain that exploded in my ankle and flashed through my body to my brain, sending it screaming in torment. I let out a futile muffled yelp into my mask at the intense agony and lay there momentarily, sprawled on the dirt track, completely immobilized. I could feel chilling moisture begin to seep through the torn trousers of my chemical oversuit from the puddle of mud beneath me, and a tingling sting in my grazed palms. As blood began to trickle from the gritty open wound in my knee, I knew this was GAME OVER.

Around me time slowed as the stampede of people continued. The air was filled with muffled shouting and smoke as everything briefly became blurred. I lay there in a tangled sprawl on the ground for no more than five seconds before the Rat ran over to me. Grabbing hold of my rucksack, he hauled me to my feet in one swift movement, propelling me forwards, back into the migrating pack. Pain flared again from my damaged ankle as I put weight on it, but I began a limping run, swept along once more.

We ran like this for three miles before stopping. Running in full NBC kit, with gas masks on, rucksacks strapped to our backs and rifles cradled in our arms. An injection of adrenaline soon kicked into my bloodstream, which numbed the pain in my ankle, and for the three miles I ran regardless. Ahead of us dawn was approaching in the purple sky above but I couldn't see it through the smog and misted lenses of my gas mask. I sank into a trance, forgetting the pain and discomfort, just running. My mind was blank.

Finally, back at our harbour area, I unlaced my left boot and tentatively removed it to inspect the damage. I pulled off my black woolly sock and took a look at my bare foot. My ankle was swollen beyond all recognition, a bulbous pale ball. The knobble of my ankle bone had disappeared in the puffy swell and a tinge of black bruising was already forming in the arch of my sole. Now back inside the comforts of safety, the adrenaline that had kept me going on the march subsided and the pain returned, forcing me to limp to the medical tent.

If you were to ask any graduate of Sandhurst what their worst experience was at the Academy, undoubtedly the most likely response you would get would be the NBC extraction on Marathon's Chase. Eight miles in full NBC clothing, with gas masks, fully packed bergens and rifles, while also, unsportingly, being gassed. It is the sort of stuff that can bring grown men to tears and make the infantry hopefuls question their choice. The reputation of its horror and pain far preceded it and it was something everyone had been fearfully dreading on Marathon's Chase. We all knew that at some point the time would come and, as I sat there in the back of an ambulance, my leg elevated as a nurse filled out X-ray paperwork, it did. The call of 'GAS, GAS, GAS' came once more and the rest of Eleven Platoon, Imjin Company and CC071 masked up, grabbed their bergens and started the long gruelling march.

On Marathon's Chase I may not have been saved by my Worst Encounter swimming angel, but someone somewhere was still certainly looking out for me, because despite having a badly sprained ankle I was in far less pain than those on the NBC march.

Injury at Sandhurst is a fact of life. The intensity of the course means that bodies regularly get broken and there is a whole industry at the Academy devoted to putting damaged cadets back together again. If your injuries were serious and you couldn't continue with the training there was even a dedicated platoon where cadets went to convalesce and rehabilitate until they were fit enough to return to the course. Lucknow Platoon (or No-Luck Platoon as it was known) lived in Old College and, during my time in the Junior Term, they had paraded each morning beneath the window of my room. Each morning, I would see them line up, three rows of cripples on crutches, broken arms in slings, patched eyes and limbs, an assortment of woeful tales. As I made the final adjustments to my room before an inspection, I would look out at them, hoping to God that I would never have to join their ranks and spend any longer than necessary at the Academy. And thankfully I wouldn't, because my injury occurred so close to the end of term that there would be enough time over the summer holiday break for my ankle to heal.

Anyway, spraining my ankle proved to be the best thing that could have happened to Eleven Platoon, because as soon as we returned from Thetford, CC071 found themselves straight out of NBC and back onto the parade square.

No sooner had we handed in our rifles from exercise than they were all being signed straight back out again, along with bayonets, to be marched around the parade square in the baking August sun. CSgt Bicknell's moment of glory was now only days away and we could all feel the weight of apprehension, as he so desperately wanted to win. For a proud guardsman with an unhealthy passion for drill, the Drill Competition was certain to be the highlight of his time as a member of staff at Sandhurst, and you could sense the tension building as the big day approached. In readiness Eleven Platoon practised, polished, preened and prepared, making every effort to do CSgt Bicknell proud. Unlike most of the other Sandhurst competitions, the girls had a realistic fighting chance in the Drill Competition. We were now languishing at the bottom of the Sovereign's Banner competition, the year-long contest to find the best overall platoon in the intake, but there was the anticipation that in the Drill Competition we could redeem a modicum of pride in finally winning something. Especially with me injured on the sidelines, my sprained ankle strapped up. With me out of the competition, Eleven Platoon had their best chance yet, as my intractable legs and two left feet wouldn't be there to show them up.

Before the drill parade there was an inspection phase, which CSgt Bicknell fussed terribly over, clucking after us like a mother hen, checking the polish of our brass buttons and the shine of our shoes.

'Come on, ladies, I want those shoes so shiny the inspecting officer can see his very soul reflected in them,' he said, as he walked up and down the platoon lines checking our work. 'I want you to dazzle out there, ladies. I want you as smart as carrots, you hear? Smart as carrots.'

'Smart as carrots' was another one of CSgt Bicknell's favoured catchphrases that left us all baffled. By it he meant for us to be spruced to sublimity. I've never seen a 'smart carrot' but I'm guessing it would be organic and bought in Waitrose, so as the day of the Drill Competition arrived Eleven Platoon were clean, smart and organic fresh, ready to dazzle.

But we didn't win the Drill Competition.

We didn't even place second or third. Perhaps carrots and his reflected soul were just not what the inspecting officer was looking for. CSgt Bicknell was gutted; he'd done all he could. The whole of Eleven Platoon were gutted. We had tried, but heavy hearts lingered for the rest of the day as we dejectedly kicked off our polished shoes, and mulled over what went wrong. We took defeat so personally because it all mattered to us now. We wanted to win. We were ardent for some desperate glory. Because winning meant that we got it. That after two terms and twenty-eight weeks of training we could do it.

But what could we do? We could march. We could dig holes. We could crawl, polish and pick up litter. NBC may have been more relevant than First World War trench-digging but it was thoroughly miserable and the chances of any of us actually using the nuclear immediate action drill were slim. So as another term drew to a close, and we watched another Sandhurst intake commission on Old College steps, we got closer and closer to our own commissioning parade. Closer to the real Army. Closer to command. Closer to soldiers and war. Closer to Basra and Musa Qala, where we knew no one was using the nuclear immediate action drill. Ahead of us lay a month of carefree leave in the summer sun, but on our return the complex realities of what the Army were actually doing in Basra and Musa Qala awaited us, as finally the training got real.

10

I PREDICT A RIOT

My feet were killing me. These heels may look gorgeous but my God they were hurting my feet. I wanted to slip them off but we were standing in a bar and I might get thrown out for being barefoot. I peered down and slid one foot out of its high-heel hell to inspect the reddening around my scrunched toes. Ouch. Why did I do this? I was supposed to be on holiday. I suffered enough pain in my day job; I shouldn't be subjecting myself to more in my spare time too. I picked up my glass from the bar and lifted the straw to my lips, draining the remaining cocktail with a gurgling slurp; sucking at any trace of alcohol that could be remaining between the crushed ice. Perhaps more alcohol would numb the pain.

It was Ann's hen party, and there were a crowd of us, about thirty girls in total, all teetering in heels in the downstairs bar of Mahiki, the Mayfair nightclub. Ann and her fiancé George had been together for nine years now. They met on their first day at university and are a perfectly matched pair. Their eventual nuptials had never been in doubt, and their wedding would be the third I'd been to that year. As each invitation arrived in the post, I felt as though my personal life was frozen at Sandhurst. My friends were all busy moving on, getting married and having babies, while I didn't have time for anything else. On the few snatched weekends I got away from the Academy, I was too tired to start bothering with a boyfriend and army commitments had made me unreliable when it came to social engagements. Joining the Army had forced me to put my job first for a while, just as everyone else my age was settling down. Such is the nature of a military career. It is not a normal nine-to-five job. At junctures you are forced to put the Army first, while the rest of your life sits on hold.

Around us the club quickly filled with revellers and I found myself jostling for space, being bumped back and forth, which was not helping the high-heels situation. We moved to a standing table at the edge of the still empty dance floor and a couple of the girls made their way onto it, trying to get the party started. In the corner a DJ started his set and the speakers pumped out a good tune; I would've joined them in a dance if my feet could have borne the pain. Instead, I picked up my purse and headed over to the bar in search of another round of cocktails, squeezing my way through the throng to the end of the bar where the good-looking barman was working. He smiled and nodded as I arrived and I waited while he finished making someone else's drinks. Mahiki is Polynesian-themed and some of the exotic cocktails come in impressive pineapples and coconuts, complete with fruit slices and paper umbrellas. It's dreadfully kitsch, but somehow manages to pass off as cool.

As I waited I could see an argument erupting between a girl and her boyfriend at a small table beside the bar. She was getting animated and pointing her finger at him accusingly, flicking her long brown hair and shouting. She was clearly quite drunk and he tried to soothe her, but she was having none of it. Suddenly she stood up and threw the remains of her drink over his shirt, in a splash of ice and sliced lime. She then turned on her Jimmy Choos and stormed through the club, barging people angrily out of her way, knocking over a chair and Ann's drink as she went, which crashed to the floor behind her. She didn't care and didn't even stop to apologize.

How rude.

I'd forgotten how often I used to see this sort of obnoxious behaviour in London. Arrogant adults behaving like spoiled children in public. Acting with impunity, leaving everyone else to pick up the pieces after them. It used to exasperate me. As I watched her pass me I wished someone would do something about this petulance. And then before I knew it, I found myself walking towards her and grabbing hold of her wrist.

Oh my God. What was I doing?

'Excuse me,' I said, rather more confidently than I felt. 'You've just knocked over that chair and my friend's drink.' And I calmly pointed to the chair lying on the floor next to the broken glass of Ann's spilled drink. She lurched towards me, bringing her face up against mine; I could smell the Red Bull and vodka on her breath.

'So what,' she challenged. She snatched her wrist out from my grasp and glared at me. Behind her I could see her boyfriend walking towards us, a look of dread crossing his face. Perhaps I shouldn't have confronted her. I don't know why I did. This was not normally the sort of thing I would ever do. I hate confrontation. But I hated her loutish bad manners too. Plus the alcohol in my system had given me a little Dutch courage. For the first time in my life, I felt the need to intervene in something like this. Stepping in to defend the public order. Maybe this was because I was in the Army. I felt it was my public duty to police the situation.

'Well, I suggest you pick it up,' I said gently. 'And buy my friend a replacement drink.'

Her drunken eyes rolled around, while she took in what I'd just said to her. 'And who the fuck are you?' she demanded, as the boyfriend came over to take control of the situation.

'I'm a customer in here, the same as you,' I said, holding my ground. 'And I suggest you find some manners and stop tearing this place apart before you get thrown out.' I was on a confidence roll. Beside us, the boyfriend was apologizing to Ann and picking up the fallen chair, clearing up after her. He looked over to me, his eyes pleading for me to let it go. Over his shoulder, I could see a big burly bouncer by the door, with an earpiece in and his eye on us. I didn't want to ruin Ann's evening over this. The boyfriend reached for his girlfriend's arm, but she shrugged him away.

'Fuck off,' she said. 'Fuck off the lot of you.' And with that she continued to storm through the crowd and out of the club, her boyfriend chasing along behind her. I turned back to the bar, slightly incensed by her behaviour, but quickly forgetting it as the handsome barman came over to take my order.

In the Army we were expected to live our lives according to a set of values and standards that were being drilled into us at Sandhurst: selfless commitment, courage, discipline, integrity, loyalty and respect for others. In reality these are all common sense to decent well-meaning members of society, but to the officer class they are essential. If the Army are to trust us to command soldiers, it needs to know that we have the moral framework in which to do it. Evil triumphs 'when good men do nothing' as Edmund Burke said. But what I didn't realize was that applying these values in policing public order situations like Mahiki's drunks, was exactly the sort of soldiering that I would be doing once I returned to Sandhurst. Because when I got back the war finally got relevant, and a hell of a lot more complicated.

So much of the Sandhurst commissioning course felt entirely irrelevant: the marching, polishing, ironing, show parades, areas, lessons in waiting; none of this was going to help us command British soldiers to win wars. It might have given me a stubborn resolve and personal pride, but this alone was not going to defeat the Taliban. If blitzed in a nuclear strike I knew I would at least die with shiny shoes on my feet and a tidy bedroom, but I was still fairly confident that in Iraq and Afghanistan there were no nuclear weapons to worry about. But when I returned to Sandhurst for the third and final, Senior Term, it was as if the previous two terms of teaching hadn't occurred.

Because as I got back to New College, the last eight months of learning were effectively discarded, as finally the relevant lessons began.

Assaults on German villages, trench warfare, NBC drills, slogging advances to contact, all were parked to one side to make way for counter-insurgency ('coin') and peace support operations. Finally, we were going to be taught what the British Army really does. What the colour sergeants had actually done themselves. And what the British Army has largely been doing for the last fifty years, in Malaya, Northern Ireland, Bosnia, Iraq and now Afghanistan. From now on the enemy were no longer the formally organized Russians advancing from the east, but baddies in balaclavas and burkhas that were all around us. Whereas the Cold War had been all about chemistry and physics, now the clashing civilizations of modern war forced us to understand the social science of where we fought out battles, as we became 'nation-builders as well as warriors',[33] switching from what the United States Assistant Secretary of Defense called 'professional killers to armed diplomats'.[34]

And it was a hell of a lot harder than digging a trench.

The exercise where we applied all this new counter-insurgency teaching was Exercise Broadsword, which took place in a purpose-built village in Hampshire, or 'Hampshiristan' as it became in the scenario – the

---

33 General David Petraeus, Commander US Forces and the International Security Assistance Force in Afghanistan, previously Commanding General of the Multi-National Force in Iraq. A man who knows what he is talking about.

34 Bing West, United States Assistant Secretary for Defense.

'ungoverned space'. What had once been constructed as a mock-up of Bogside and the Falls Road to train troops for Northern Ireland had now been converted into an Afghan village. The pub and betting shop had closed, the end-of-terrace murals had been painted over, and instead there were prayer mats and tea drinking, while a dome had been placed on top of the church turning it into a mosque.

It was a total revelation.

Broadsword was nothing like the exercises we had done before. There were no slogging advances to contact, no digging shell-scrape coffins, no sleeping outside under a poncho or living in a woodblock triangle, because instead we occupied a patrol base next to the village, just like British troops do in Afghanistan. Living among the people and the enemy. The enemy had changed too, as the former clear-cut, black and white of previous exercises became a murky grey, blending and merging from nice convenient boundaries on the map into a less defined battle space. There were women and children to worry about. Fraught tribal divisions, important religious leaders to engage, corrupt governments, refugees, angry mobs, looters, and all to be dealt with under the scrutinizing glare of the media. Every action had a consequence, and for the first time each decision had a repercussion, as it was no longer about turning up and killing everyone. No more blunt military operations like the 'shock and awe' of the US Marines in Fallujah, destroying the city to save it. Now, it was about understanding the human terrain, engaging with the local civilian population and winning the war for hearts and minds.

Rather than the waving enemy Gurkhas that we had become accustomed to shooting at on exercise, there were actors playing starving refugees, rape victims, tribal leaders, hostages and rebel generals all thrown into an intense pressure-cooker of civil unrest for us to police (Mahiki's had just been a dry run). And it was all relevant, because unlike the other Sandhurst exercises, Broadsword had been written by the academic staff from Faraday Hall, who based it all on real-life incidents, using true scenarios faced by British forces during three decades in Northern Ireland, six years in Bosnia and the last four years in Iraq and Afghanistan. It was all the bad bits from the Shankill Road to Sangin, Pristina to Rumalia, and it couldn't have been more relevant without sand.

Patrolling 'softly' in berets rather than our normal hard helmets, we had to consider cultural sensitivities and tribal frictions, as counter-insurgency became a complex conflict 'amongst the people'.[35] Gunmen melted back into the populace just as farmers in Afghanistan put down their AK47s and return to their crops. The constantly changing situations we faced required the judgement of Solomon as one moment the locals liked you, and then the next they were throwing rocks. But Broadsword wasn't about killing everyone who stood in our way any more, because for every shot fired and innocent civilian harmed, more of the local population turned against us.

On our final afternoon in the village, I was patrolling through the increasingly hostile local population, trying to

---

35 General Sir Rupert Smith.

ignore their chants and taunts when I saw a large agricultural lorry arrive. The lorry was delivering a consignment of potatoes, and these were being distributed into small strategic mounds positioned around the streets. Tensions with the villagers had deteriorated since a hostage incident in the mosque and we all knew what this was building up to. A speaker outside the gates of our patrol base even played the Kaiser Chiefs' record to remind us. That night a large braying mob gathered outside the patrol base, hammering against the fence and launching rocks into the compound in protest at our occupation. They kicked loudly at the metal gate and tore down a road blockade like the frontage of a McDonald's in Trafalgar Square in a May Day "protest". Trapped inside, the riot gear was handed out and I braced myself for what was going to be a lot more than a pillow fight.

The public order riot is still the main event on Exercise Broadsword. A throwback from the days of training for Northern Ireland, it is an intense test of controlled aggression that cannot be qualified in any other environment. Pumped full of adrenaline and wrapped in riot gear, with batons and toughened plastic shields, the whole of Imjin Company finally left the patrol base in the dark hours of the following morning. Ready to face the music. The village was quiet. The previous night's protests had died down and everyone was subdued or sleeping. As we stepped outside into the murky darkness an eerie stillness hung in the morning mist. Nothing moved. Not a shuffle, nor sound. The leaves hung lifeless on the trees and clouds remained motionless in the sky above. Everyone and everything was waiting, savouring the last moments of tranquil calm. Inside my stomach was doing acrobatics the tension was so high, but around me not a word was uttered. Just the gentle sound of clomping boots on the wet road could be heard. We were in the eye of the storm. This was the calm before the fight, our backstage moment, and soon it would all be shattered.

As we marched over the brow of a hill into the village, I could see fires ablaze. Cars lay wrecked and burning, their flames glinting in our riot shields. At a street corner a cluster of people had assembled, gathered closely like a halftime hockey pitch huddle. We walked towards them line abreast, a six-foot high frontier of riot shields, visors and batons. Organized and trained. Psyched up and fizzing with aggression. Waiting for the crack of the first move. In the distance I spotted an ambulance arrive, parking ominously to a flank ready to patch up the wounded.

Ahead more hockey pitch huddles appeared as the villagers slowly came out of their homes and congregated, picking up potatoes and tossing them provocatively in their palms. The riot was being carefully choreographed by the Academy staff and as we straightened out onto the main street the first heckles began. Anti-army slogans were chanted by the growing crowd, gathering in pace and volume, getting louder and louder as the heat was turned up. My blood began to race as my heart pumped a heady mixture of adrenaline and fear, fear, FEAR.

Through my helmet visor I looked at their faces, picking out the whites of their eyes and seeing a maddening frenzy. Like football hooligans at a cup final, they had been whipped into a crazed rabble, braying for a battle. I could see the red mist of real unharnessed aggression in them, simmering, ready to explode. After advancing forwards, we eventually came to a stop at a T-junction and stood in organized ranks, holding the ground as a solid line. Waiting for the game to start.

Hearts quickened and then the green light came, bursting forth in a hail of potato missiles, fists and kicks. All hell broke free and I was pushed and shoved, back and forth, knocked off my feet as the force of the crowd took me with it, pulsing like the beat of a concert mosh pit. Rioters broke through the shields, charging and kicking their way, penetrating our organized front to be beaten back with batons. It was horrendous. The rioters showed no mercy, as we were kicked and beaten in the name of training. And then there was the sound of a whistle. Not Willy the whistle this time but worse, a high-pitched shrill, which caused the rioters to stop. They stepped back and cleared the area to our front. Momentarily we caught our breath and then the first petrol bombs were thrown, landing at our feet in a red and orange blaze of heat and shattering glass, causing us to dance on our feet and stamp them out before the next one came. Blasting again at our ankles, before the rioters were allowed back in.

It was terrifying.

The riot was essentially a legitimized fight; a scrap between two sides. One armed with potatoes and petrol bombs, the other with batons and shields. I had never before been involved in a fight. I have witnessed fights, usually on a Saturday at pub closing time, but I've always stuck to the avoidance technique I learned as a fourteen-year-old schoolgirl when confronted with the swinging fists of a brawl. Back then I was walking into town on a Wednesday afternoon with my friend Camilla. We had just finished netball practice and were wearing our compulsory school blazers that clearly marked us out as public school posh girls. Wednesday afternoon was one of the few occasions during the week when we were allowed outside the confines of the school grounds, and a hundred metres ahead of us another group of girls from the year above were also making the pilgrimage to Woolworths to buy Bootlaces and Nerds. They were much cooler than Camilla and me and were smoking casually as we crossed the park and calling to a group of boys who were lounging around a bench. The path wiggled its way across the park, around beds of rose bushes and a duck pond before joining the pavement that ran along the edge of a main road. We exited the park on to this pavement and followed it along towards a bus stop, located outside a supermarket where children from the local comprehensive school gathered, waiting for their ride home. None of them were wearing stupid blazers. As the girls in front of us approached the bus stop there was a shrieking shout as two girls leapt down from the low bus stop wall and grabbed their hair, pulling them down to the ground, where a catfight ensued. Camilla and I froze in our tracks. I'd never before witnessed such violence and didn't know what to do. As clawing nails and slaps rained in, my instincts told me to back away from the altercation and get the hell out of there. So Camilla and I did the most cowardly of acts, we crossed the road. We walked away, checking over our shoulder to see if the horror had ended, entering a sweet shop to report it to the owner. We didn't plough in. We didn't race over and help. We didn't attempt any form of heroics. Instead, we ran away, saving the hair on our heads and the flesh on our cheeks from the slashing of attacking nails. (Incidentally, Camilla later became head girl at our school and went on to study at Cambridge University so I take this cowardly response as the sensible, intelligent thing to have done.) Did we lack the moral courage the army so expects? Probably. But I was petrified, just as I was now on Broadsword. But I couldn't run away from the Broadsword riot. I was a coward caught.

I spent a feeble hour getting pummelled in the riot. Ducking to avoid the fast-bowled potatoes and wincing with each forceful kick. Blinded by confusion and the steam in my helmet visor, I felt helplessly vulnerable, brandishing only a baton gun and pointless blank rounds. I wasn't robust enough for a shield. I wasn't tough enough for the physical fight, like Merv, Wheeler and Gill. They were all in the heavy baseline, holding six-foot shields and feeling the full heat of the petrol bombs and brute force of each onslaught.

For the girls of Eleven Platoon the riot was an emotional and scary ordeal. But for the boys the riot was a wholly different experience. They loved it, relishing the thrill of the conflict and elaborate dance-off between the two sides. They revelled in the pleasure of a baton thwack against an aggressor's back and the satisfying self-justice in giving someone a good kicking. It was in their genetic make up to fight, because they dealt with the adrenaline kicking through our veins very differently from the girls. In me, it turned to fear but in them it became aggression. Our natural instincts were completely opposed; we girls cowered in fear while the boys confronted their aggressors in a descending red mist and beaming smiles on their faces.

Like my swimming interlude on Worst Encounter, Exercise Broadsword was not without its abstract moment. Later that afternoon while we packed up our patrol base home the exercise went into hiatus. Everything stopped. For two hours, batons and petrol bombs were laid down. Starving women and corrupt warlords came out of role, and radios were switched off, while England played Australia in the rugby World Cup. It was like a Christmas Day truce along the Western Front. We came out from behind the security fence of our fortress to walk freely through the village streets that only hours earlier had been the site of such violence. And support for the game was not compulsory either, so I chose to forsake the eighty minutes of unrequited pleasure admiring Jonny Wilkinson's bum and went for a shower instead.

As I stood in the queue outside the shower block next to one of the earlier rioters, he looked at my tired face. 'The riot was pretty full on, wasn't it?' he said.

'Yes.' I sighed. 'I won't ever be volunteering for public order duties after that,' I said, looking through the small plastic bag in my hand to see what toiletries I had brought with me.

'It was awesome though, wasn't it? I never thought it would be so much fun,' he went on.

'It wasn't fun,' I replied, a little too curtly.

'Yeah, true. It can't have been much fun for you girls out there,' he replied. 'You did look pretty terrified.'

'We were,' I said, trying not to engage him in a full post-match analysis. I wanted to forget the whole experience as quickly as possible.

'I got hit a few times myself,' he said, lifting up his shirt to reveal three large baton welts on his back, red and sore.

'Ouch. They look painful,' I said, wincing.

'Yeah. It was awesome though,' he said grinning as he reminisced. 'I suppose it won't be quite as harsh when you lot are the rioters though. I can't imagine the girls getting involved.'

'No. I think you're right. That sort of violence is not really my thing,' I said as I thought about how aggressive the rioters had been. I had never hit anyone, nor felt the need to in my entire life and couldn't see any reason for that to change at Sandhurst.

I was wrong.

Exercise Broadsword was split into three distinct phases: urban operations, rural operations and then the chance to join the actors, role-playing and creating havoc in the village as part of the civilian population. So having been the subject of a riot, it was soon our turn to join the mob throwing the potatoes at another company of cadets.

Initially I stood back. I have the aggression levels of a goldfish and chose not to get involved in the thrust of the riot, instead just shouting abuse and chucking the odd potato at the wall of plastic shields from a safe distance. I am lucky among girls to have a decent throw. When I was at school I had a boyfriend who was the school cricket captain. Each Saturday during the summer term, I used to sit in a deckchair outside the cricket pavilion in the sunshine and watch him playing in the distance. A little white speck in an open field. One afternoon after he had been batted out, he turned his attention to teaching me to throw a cricket ball, properly. Not a pathetic girly donkey drop but a decent full-armed launching lob, and it has proved to be a valuable life skill ever since (along with being able to whistle and wire a plug).

So as the riot kicked off I took to keeping back from the thick of things, but as the heat of the fight turned up everything changed. A red mist descended and I soon got swept along with the mob. As the violence developed and spread, I got infected. Drawn in by the pull of the fair, I abandoned my normal polite civilities and human kindness to make way for an evil Machiavellian streak. I found that with each potato propelled, I got a small kick as I watched it landing among the riot police. I found a strange satisfaction in seeing the minor devastation they caused, and drew cathartic warmth from watching them impact on a riot shield or helmet visor, fuelling the riot melee. As my violence grew, I joined the others in pelting the riot police with more and more potato missiles, understanding entirely the rationale of May Day protestors tearing up Oxford Street for no apparent reason. I became caught like a politician in a moment's madness.

Broadsword was the big Sandhurst test exercise. The crucial module we all had to pass. It was the most scrutinizing assessment of our ability to command and lead, and those who failed would have to face the music. And in Eleven Platoon this was the Platoon Donkey. Finally her time was up. She had bungled and blundered her way through two terms. Stumbling into trenches, mutinying in the Black Mountains and carrying Alpine mineral water around Thetford. But now was her final curtain call. As the 'ungoverned space' continued to take hostages on our return to Sandhurst.

As soon as we got back from Broadsword she was called into the Company Commander's office and 'back termed'. Booted out of Imjin Company, her bags were packed that very night. Tears were shed but good-byes were short, as she was too embarrassed and upset to linger. I popped my head around the door of her room as she was stuffing belongings into suitcases between sniffles.

'Are you all right?' I said, offering her a packet of chocolate biscuits as if that would make everything OK.

'Thanks, Héloïse,' she said, taking a biscuit and perching on the end of her bed to eat it, looking up at me for hope.

'I'll be sad to see you go,' I said, unsure of what I should say. I was sad. But I knew it was the right decision. 'Who am I going to play "snog, marry, strangle" with now?' I continued, trying to crack a smile on her sad face. She laughed.

'What do I do now?' she said, choking back tears.

'Things will work out. Don't you worry. Everything happens for a reason,' I said. 'And you'll come back stronger from this,' I added, clutching at straws. She would be better for it. She wasn't ready to commission with us in December, but she would get there eventually.

And we were sad to see her go.

For days we mourned her exit as her departure left a gaping hole in the platoon. The peals of laughter that normally rippled through the platoon lines were absent as the mood darkened and we grieved. It wasn't a surprise. And we knew it made sense, but it was still sad to see her go. Despite all her faults she had become one of us, a member our Army family. We had bonded through the nights of shivering on stag and chocking down boil-in-the-bag rations. Giggling at games of 'snog, marry, strangle' and marvelling at her CS gas immunity.

She didn't leave Sandhurst altogether. The army had already invested too much time, money and sweat to let her slip back into society. And instead she was sent back to the Intermediate term. Sliding down a snake to climb back up the commissioning ladder once more with another girls' platoon in the intake behind us. She would be given a second chance. Another shot at digging a trench. Another visit to the gas chamber. Another NBC extraction march and another drill competition.

There was no way I could have done it all again.

It felt good to finally be in the Senior Term. At last we had reached the top of the cadet food chain, moving from shorts to trousers, to applying for university places and meeting up in the pub. By now we knew it all, and we also knew that it was all nearly over. The Academy staff finally eased off, taking a step back and treating us more like the grown-ups that we were. The rigid reigns and suffocating control that had dominated the Junior and Intermediate terms were loosened as more personal responsibility was handed to us. We no longer had to march everywhere (not that I ever really mastered that anyway) and room inspections became a vague memory, although I continued to hide wine in my underwear drawer. In this newly relaxed regime, we were also granted the rare pleasure of some spare time, which became brief treasured snippets of freedom within the Academy fence. We became responsible for our own physical training too, which, thinking about it, was probably what the spare time was for, but instead we spent it drinking tea and relaxing for the first time in eight months.

Returning to New College at the end of summer leave, there was an air of nearly there, as the end was in sight. As I signed back into the Academy in my jeans, mindless of the consequences of being caught in the 'Devil's cloth', I felt as though the worst was behind me. Carrying my bags from the car park up to my room, I felt confident and almost at home in my surroundings. The light at the end of the tunnel I had once thought I would never see was now clearly visible, as the notion of commissioning became a veritable reality. A mere fourteen weeks now separated me from walking up the steps of Old College and receiving my Second-Lieutenant's pip. In Seniors our confidence had been built up again, we were no longer the floppy-haired civilians of the January frost, nervous, fearful and shy, unsure of where we belonged. Because the most significant change in Seniors was that finally we knew where in the army we were going.

It might seem odd that we had managed to get this far without actually belonging to an army home. Without knowing where we were going to end up at the end of it all. It should have been decided long ago, but Sandhurst was wary of removing this incentive carrot. The constant threat of receiving a negative report that failed to get you into the regiment of your choice was there to motivate us through the hours of pointless digging, crawling and polishing. Because throughout our time at the Academy our performance was ranked against each of the other cadets in the platoon and company, apportioning us by our shoe shining and marching abilities into thirds; namely top, middle and bottom. The constant danger of languishing in this dreaded 'bottom third' was intended to deter us from hopping in our cars mid-week and racing up the M3 to London for a night on the tiles, undoing all the indoctrination by fraternizing with carefree civilians and alcohol. For if your report placed you in the bottom third you would be overlooked by the more popular regiments, leaving you more than standing scruffily skewiff on parade the next morning, but potentially deciding the direction of the rest of your military life. Movement between these thirds was fluid and changed according to the season and Captain Trunchbull's whim. Some of those who had once shot to the top of the class for their folding and hospital corners in the Junior Term later found themselves battling it out at the bottom and being crossed off regimental visit lists.

The regimental application and selection process was like the university UCAS system – you applied to four regiments and then this got whittled down to two, with whom you interviewed. For a week these interviews consumed us, looming in the background as a steady distraction, hanging over each one of us like A-level results. The outcome would potentially dictate the rest of our lives, deciding where we would be spending our military careers and which Army family would be ours. The stakes were high and competition for top places was fierce. People withdrew into their rooms to prepare, closing their doors to sit in peace while they learned random facts like who the Colonel in Chief was, what battle honours had been won and what music accompanied the corps march.

I've had plenty of job interviews in my life, as I bounced unsatisfied between City employers, searching for something I would never find inside the Square Mile. I've even sat in the interviewer's chair too, recruiting the next graduates touting their souls into corporate slavery. When I worked at HSBC we received over a hundred CVs for just one place on our team. A pile of one hundred glowing, near-identical CVs to sift through, mounting in my boss's in-tray. And, when it came to choosing those he wanted to see for an interview, the boss simply picked up the top half of the CV pile and threw it in the bin, commenting that he 'didn't want anyone who wasn't lucky', turning to the 'lucky' remaining CVs to recruit from.

But interview experience didn't calm my nerves for the regimental selection board, as I stood anxiously in the corridor with seventeen other hopefuls awaiting the outcome of interviews for just eight available places in the Army Air Corps. The interview process that morning had been so quick, just ten minutes in the interview room. Ten short minutes to make my mark on the panel of officers who would decide my future. I had learned the Corps march (Recce Flight) and who the Colonel in Chief was (the Prince of Wales), I'd even learned the Corps battle honours, but I didn't know which third I was in, top, middle or bottom. Captain Trunchbull hated me so much she hadn't even given me a report. But as it turned out that didn't matter, because in reality the regiments already knew who they wanted. Because in reality the work had already been done months ago on visits to Officers' Messes and at hosted drinks evenings. In reality it was decided by how well you fitted in the mess bar with the other officers, and whether the recruiting Colonel thought your face fitted, rather than what Captain Trunchbull thought of you. The recruiting officers knew that being good at Sandhurst wasn't a measure of how well you would cope in the real army. With real command, of real soldiers, in real wars. It was not the same as shooting at Gurkhas in Brecon or digging a trench in Norfolk. And where I was going there wasn't going to be any crawling or digging, because I was joining the Army Air Corps.

The Army Air Corps was my first choice. Not because the sky blue beret complemented my blond hair, nor because I was seduced by the ego of a pilot, but because I quickly realised that being in the Army Air Corps would guarantee I would never spend another night shivering in a wet soggy hole. Because after eleven months of digging and crawling I wanted a military career that took me as far away as possible from cold showers and boil-in-a-bag ration pack horrors. Because in the Army Air Corps there would be no wary face paint, no sleeping in a shell-scrape hole. No shouting, no marching and no National Anthem at dawn. And because any time I had spent with the Army Air Corps I felt entirely at home, unlike I'd ever felt at work in the City.

With a confirmed regimental home we could start thinking about the future. About our first postings, our first operational deployment to Iraq or Afghanistan, our new homes and new lives. Behind closed doors those who had secured places began to shape their new berets, looking at the reflection of the final Sandhurst product in the mirror. I booked a fitting with the tailor to be measured up for my mess dress and Merv, Wheeler and I beamed with the excitement of a wedding dress fitting as we fingered fabrics and swished taffeta around the military tailor's shop, giggling excitedly.

Mess dress is the traditional evening dress worn at formal occasions, regimental dinner nights and balls, and is basically a very grandiose drinking suit. For the men it is the stuff of Jilly Cooper readers' fantasies, with high-waisted, very tight trousers worn over polished black riding boots complete with ornamental brass spurs. But although dashingly attractive, what Jilly Cooper doesn't divulge is that at the end of the night mess dress is also impossible to strip off a drunk man. Each regiment adopts a subtle variation on the mess dress theme, marking themselves out with differing coloured jackets and accoutrements.

Some, especially among the cavalry, are incredibly ostentatious and their mess dress can set a young officer back as much as £6,000, for the finest doe fur and gold thread weave.

For women, mess dress consists of a short woollen jacket that fastens at the neck and cuts away to reveal a Victorian style tea gown underneath, which is constructed from yards of billowing taffeta silk, and poufy netting to create a puffed-up meringue wedding dress effect. It was like something from a childhood princess fantasy, to be worn while trapped in a castle tower awaiting Prince Charming, and the whole outfit was beautifully tailor-made using rich fabrics. This was why we hadn't joined the RAF.

Standing on top of a stout wooden block in the centre of the tailor's shop, Mr Fitz Herbert fussed about me with a measuring tape, winding the long tape around me. Sucking between his teeth he made a whistling sound as he wrote my essential statistics down on a scrap of paper.

'We put plenty of extra material into the seams for future adjustments,' he said, jotting down my hip measurement in a squiggling scrawl with his pen.

'Oh,' I said, looking down at him from my podium. 'I hope I won't need to use any of that.'

'If I get posted to Germany the threat of beer and bratwurst might necessitate an adjustment,' Merv said, chuckling. Merv had been accepted into the Royal Signals and her mess dress was a modern slim-line fit, which would be less concealing than my acres of fabric.

'Have you seen these?' Wheeler said, pulling out a sliver of red silk from the puffed pagoda sleeve of her Royal

Artillery mess dress gown. 'The attention to detail is incredible. I'm never going to be allowed to take my jacket off, so no one will ever even see this.'

'And the silk buttons at the back,' I said, stepping down from the block to make way for Merv to be measured.

'Next up,' Mr Fitz Herbert said, drawing a line on his scrap of paper underneath my measurements as Merv stepped up onto the platform.

'It's such a lot of effort for something you're only going to wear just to get drunk in,' Merv said, frowning at me as Mr Fitz Herbert measured her bust.

'They're like blue wedding dresses,' Wheeler said, floating fabric through her hands.

'What happens with our pips?' I asked. 'The second-lieutenants' pips on the shoulders.'

'You cover them up,' Merv said. 'Until midnight. And then you can reveal them, as you commission.'

'We officially commission at midnight,' Wheeler said. 'Midnight on 14 December.'

I liked the sound of that.

All this meant that by the time we deployed on Exercise Broadsword we already felt tantalizingly there. My new Army Air Corps beret was perched on a shelf back in New College, I had my start date and a letter from the Regimental Colonel welcoming me to the fold. Which is why it was even more devastating to have the carpet now whipped from beneath your feet like the Platoon Donkey had. To have all this pulled away from you when it was so tangibly near, having been built up by the excitement of dress fittings and ordering corps socks. This foretaste and proximity to the final whistle made the disappointment of 'back terming' even more tragic.

I couldn't have joined the Platoon Donkey back in Inters again.

But I didn't need to, because I was finally on the home straight.

11

SERVE TO LEAD

'Miss Goodley, you take command for this one,' SSgt Walker said, as I stood lined up along with the rest of Eleven Platoon in three sweaty rows. 'You take the lead and we'll see if you can improve the time, this time around.'

'Yes, Staff,' I said.

We were at the start of the assault course, formed up as smartly as you can be when you are exhausted and just want to lie down. It was still early morning and weak late-autumn sunlight was filtering through the leaves of the tall trees around us, casting mottled shadows onto the muddy earth below. Rising out of the ground behind us were the high metal bars and rope nets of the 'confidence course': an array of knee-trembling challenges set three storeys above the security of the firm ground below. Beside lay the muddy shore of the lake around which the Sandhurst assault course was laid out, following a track that wound its way through the woodland trees.

We gathered ourselves and stood poised, at the start line. Through ten months of practice we had honed this down to a slick manoeuvre now.

Sgt Walker blew a short sharp blast on her whistle and like game-show contestants we were off. We raced up a ramp and onto the top of a six-foot wall then one by one we ran along it, leaping off at the other end like lemmings off a cliff. Then down the track to the next challenge, the rope swing, each person jumping forwards onto the end of a rope and gliding through the air over the cold waters of the stream below, sloshing onto the bank at the far side and then picking themselves up and running on again. Climbing, hopping, swinging, crawling, jumping, the whole platoon working its way over the obstacles and through the trees. Everyone called out as they went, like chimpanzees swinging in the trees, making noises of encouragement and instruction. We ran from the cargo net, to the monkey bars, to the stepping-stones and water tunnels. Dived through windows and crawled on our belt buckles under the cargo netting. We ran around the course with our helmets and webbing on and rifles strapped to our backs, adding a layer of awkwardness to overcoming each hurdle. It was like the final round of *Gladiators* but with firearms and mud.

SSgt Walker trotted along beside us, scrutinizing our technique and clasping a stopwatch in the palm of her hand. She shouted at us to keep up the pace.

As she had appointed me to command this attempt I too ran back and forth shouting encouragement to the platoon.

'Come on, guys. Keep going,' I called as each person ran over the see-saw bridge, dropped off at the far end and raced on towards the high-and-low beams. 'That's it, all the way. Come on, keep going.' This was the third time that we had been around the assault course already this morning. That was three times over the twelve-foot wall before most people had even finished their breakfast.

And it was the twelve-foot wall that was our assault course nemesis, our equivalent of the Gladiators' 'Travelator'. Our eliminator.

At five foot seven tall, I was slightly above average height among the girls of Eleven Platoon. The tallest was Wheeler at six foot and the shortest was Lea at just five foot one. So when faced with the brick face of the twelve-foot wall the sums just didn't add up for us. It may have been an attainable challenge for the strapping six-foot-tall boys at Sandhurst, but for us it was nigh impossible. We kicked and squealed, grunted and strained, before languishing in a defeated heap at the bottom. We lost our tempers with one another as people were left hanging, their muscles trembling as we tried to establish a technique that worked. After two terms and ten months of trying, the successful method the platoon eventually developed unfortunately involved me being pushed up first, much like my 'point man' experience when advancing to contact. Then, once I was in position at the top, it was my job to subsequently start hauling people up one by one until my arms had been drawn out of their sockets and I was left unable to raise them above my head the next morning. As a result the assault course was always where I discovered new muscle groups that I had never before known, and after a few rounds of tackling the obstacles like this they would subsequently ache for days, leaving me incapacitated and

struggling to put my hair back into its regulation bun the
next morning.

Once over the twelve-foot wall we were on the home
straight. A few ditch jumps, a long leopard crawl, then a
leap, skip, hop and sprint back to where we had started.
Each one of us came racing in, panting over the finish line.
SSgt Walker stood there with the stopwatch poised in her
hand and, as the last person came in, she pressed stop and
stared at the time, her expression giving no clues as to
whether we had beaten our target or not. The platoon
stood silently in front of her, puffing in the cold morning
air. Lined up back into three orderly ranks, our faces were
red as we wheezed for air. Our chests heaved up and down,
expelling hot breath that turned to mist in the morning
chill, forming an opaque cloud around us.

'Well done, ladies,' she said, looking up from the
stopwatch. 'Eleven minutes and forty-four seconds. That's
a big improvement.' There was a low murmur of approval
from the platoon as we realized that we had just cracked
the twelve-minute barrier. 'Now take on some water and
catch your breath, I want you to do it again in five minutes,'
SSgt Walker continued, and at that the murmurs turned to
sighs. We were used to this by now. SSgt Walker liked to
thrash us to within an inch of our lives. We were already
exhausted and knew that had just been our best effort
around the course, but this was how SSgt Walker liked to
push us, it was all part of the Sandhurst approach.

I glugged down some water from my water bottle,
feeling it quench my core, happy to let dribbles spill out
and cool my face. The sun was starting its climb in the sky

and below the tree canopy the shadows were shortening. It was going to be a beautiful crisp autumnal day, one where I would be grateful for a job like this that took me outside, away from the confines of a desk and grey office drudgery. I closed my eyes and tilted my face up towards the sun that was shining down on me through a crack in the leaves above. As the weak heat warmed my cheek, I smiled a satisfied smile.

'Miss Goodley, you can remain in command for this one,' SSgt Walker shouted over to me, snapping me from my pleasant moment back to the assault course.

'Yes, Staff,' I acknowledged again.

'And this time I want you to do it in silence, ladies,' she said, resetting her stopwatch with a series of audible bleeps. 'Happy?'

'Yes, Staff,' everyone replied in unison.

SSgt Walker waited until we were ready again, back into three orderly ranks on the start point, and then she put the whistle to her lips and blew a penetrating blast that sent us running once more. Up the ramp and on top of the six-foot wall, running along it, we then jumped down again, picked ourselves up and ran straight onwards to the rope swing. Grabbing hold of a rope, each girl glided through the air over the stream once more and splashed into the bank at the far side, then on again, hopping, skipping, jumping. Like last time I ran back and forth beside them calling out words of encouragement and giving instructions to coordinate the effort.

'Wheeler, left foot. Left foot lower and you're in,' I called, directing Wheeler to a foothold as she scrambled over the cargo net. This time everyone else remained silent as SSgt Walker had requested, and mine was the only voice heard. The lone voice of command. Rushing through the trees, the platoon continued to follow each other over the obstacles in convoy, like ants racing silently home to their nest. And as we completed the twelve-foot wall for the fourth and hopefully final time that morning, SSgt Walker stood waiting at the finish line with her stopwatch. And as the final girl stumbled in, crossing the finish in front of her, she pressed the red stop button with her thumb and stared at the digital figures on the watch face.

It must have taken us longer this time. Fourth time around was never going to be record-beating. She raised her head to look at us, a mordant smile on her lips.

'Twelve minutes ten. Slower, ladies, but still a good effort. Well done,' she said, dropping the stopwatch on its cord around her neck and walking towards us. She paced along the front rank until she reached where I was standing at the end, and there she stopped, her boots coming to a halt in front of me. She swung around and looked me in the eye, an evil grin crossing her lips. 'In the lake, Miss Goodley,' she said nodding her head towards the assault course lake.

What?

I didn't understand what she meant.

'Miss Goodley, I asked for that attempt to be completed in silence, did I not?' she said.

'Yes, Staff,' I replied.

'So why could I hear your shouting voice all the way around?' she asked.

'But—' I started to explain before she cut me off.

'Get in the lake, Miss Goodley,' she said, that sly grin returning as she nodded her head towards the lake once more.

Was she serious? I had been in command. How else was I supposed to command the platoon around the assault course? Using sign language? I had no choice. Shrugging off my webbing and handing my rifle to Merv, I walked towards the lakeshore. Looking back over my shoulder, I could see the platoon lined up, their heads moving and jostling, trying to get an uninterrupted view of the unfolding spectacle.

The lake was dark and still as I approached. Shaded by the surrounding trees, its surface was grey and uninviting. As I reached its edge, I took a step from the dry shore and lowered one of my boots into the murky waters, feeling it drawn into the fine squelching mud beyond the waterline. My boot easily sank into the sludge at the lake's bottom and, as I took another step forwards, I began to feel the cold water seeping in, trickling through eyelets and folds in the leather. As I continued further, I felt more water absorbing into my woollen socks, reaching my skin with a cold chilling sting.

I waded in until my boots were sodden and the water level reached my calves, then I turned around to look at SSgt Walker and the amused smiles of the rest of the platoon.

'Keep going, Miss Goodley,' SSgt Walker shouted, folding her arms contently across her chest.

She was enjoying this.

I carried on, feeling the icy water rise further up my calves and over my knees. How far was she going to take this? I thought wet boots would have been sufficient punishment for talking when I shouldn't have been, but SSgt Walker was making an example of me here. As I sank deeper, the murky lake water started to work its way up my thighs and I began to feel somewhat unjustly treated by this punishment. I stopped again as the water level lay just below my crotch, and hesitated, hoping this was enough to call me out now.

'All the way, Miss Goodley.'

Christ no. All the way in. I took another stride forwards and my boot got sucked further into the deep silt on the lakebed. Entering the slow chilling waters like this was like the agony of peeling off a plaster, the slower and more drawn out, the more pain I experienced. I should have just run straight in. Behind me I could feel thirty eyes on my back, watching as I lowered myself into the lake. This wouldn't have happened in my City job. The water was at my waist now, and I gasped as I felt the prickling bite of frozen water against the skin of my stomach.

'Keep going, Miss Goodley.'

Slowly the water rose up my torso, enveloping my body. Arms. Chest. Shoulders. Neck. I paused again, waiting for her to finally let me come out.

'All the way, Miss Goodley.'

And with that I held my breath and finally dunked my head below the water, springing back out again gasping for air as the cold shock flushed the wind from my lungs.

Behind me there was a round of applause as the girls of Eleven Platoon laughed and clapped at my misfortune.

I couldn't see the funny side.

I waded out and squelched my way back to the platoon where Merv patted me on the back and handed me my rifle with an amused smile. I took it and picked up my webbing, slinging it back onto my back and fastening it around my waist. Standing in a clearing among the trees, I could feel the sunshine on my face again, warming my shivering cheeks. I briefly closed my eyes and tilted my head towards it, letting out another satisfied smile. Despite the goosebumps and mud pooling in my boots, I still wanted to be here more than behind the desk of a London office.

Sandhurst ends on an exuberant high, with friends and family gathered around you, champagne corks popping, fireworks crackling and the sounds of a big band playing. The whole day was a jubilant, unforgettable occasion that is etched deep in the annals of my memory for me to reminisce about as I grow old. Clichéd as it sounds, the day I commissioned still remains one of the best days of my life. And it needed to be, because I required it to blot out our last final act at the Academy. Our farewell swansong. The final curtain call at the end of eleven long months. I needed it to exorcise my exercise demons, because before the extreme high of commissioning, came the low of Final Ex.

Traditionally the final exercise at Sandhurst is designed to simulate deployment to a theatre of war. Cadets board coaches and instead of travelling to Thetford or Brecon they arrive at Brize Norton to board RAF planes which take them to Cyprus, Canada or France, in the same way that months later these same planes will take them to Iraq, Afghanistan or beyond. Passports are added to the packing list and foreign currency drawn for nights of R&R celebration at the end. Because it doesn't matter how miserable digging a hole is, doing it abroad, on foreign soil, somehow brings a touch of glamour that extracting spades of clodded mud in Brecon can't. And we'd heard good things about the final exercise: barbecues on the beach in Cyprus, parties with American Marines in Edmonton, or wine rations in France. So spirits were deeply disheartened when we learned that CC071's final exercise wouldn't be taking us overseas. Nor in fact would we even be venturing across the border into Scotland or Wales, because our last act at Sandhurst would see us barely leave Surrey. And although technically new to us, Salisbury Plain was just as bleak and depressing as Brecon and Thetford had ever been. If not worse. And as soon as we'd seen the December weather forecast any remaining exercise joie de vivre was quickly erased.

It was miserable.

Wet, cold, frozen-solid misery. Ten unadulterated days of it. Ten days of eating rations and sleeping at the bottom of a muddy hole. No showers, no running water. No chance of warmth or thawing out. With exercise Broadsword, I thought we had turned a corner and left all that behind us. I thought that we had now grown up and graduated on to the important stuff, but as we received orders for the final exercise I was proved wrong. We were back at square one. Back in the Hundred Acre Wood, sleeping in waterlogged shell-scrapes, shivering in ambush hides and firing at waving Gurkhas all over again. It was as though Sandhurst was fondly musing over all the bad experiences from the last eleven months and rolling them up into one final hurrah, sending us out into the wider army on a climax of most-hated moments. The only thing missing was my gas mask.

My heart sank as we turned off the main A36 trunk road into Knook Camp. Peering through the rain-splashed window, I stared at the rows of neglected Nissen huts, their sorry state setting the tone for the exercise; they were sad and dejected, with curls of peeling paint, rusted metal window frames and drab prefabricated grey roofs. Still sitting in the warmth and comfort of the coach, I could tell that no fun was going to be had from this point forth. And I was right. Inside the mesh fence that surrounded the camp there was an absence of life. Not a flicker or sound. The mood hung, depressed and gloomy. As the coaches drew to a halt on an empty parade square a stray Coke can scuttled past, clattering its way in the gusting winds, bouncing off the potholes and cracks in the concrete. Stepping off the coach, I fought off sombre thoughts. I looked at the palette of grey around me as I gathered my bergen and webbing. Here the grey earth met with a grey sky, broken only by the grey roofs and my grey mood.

The exercise began with the worst thing I did during my entire time at the Academy. Number one of my top five horrendous moments. The whole ordeal lasted for four hours and eight miles, bringing tears to my eyes and nearly breaking me.

From our arrival point at Knook Camp, we walked through the night to Imber, a ghostly village in the centre of Salisbury Plain where we would be spending our first few days. Imber village was forcibly requisitioned by the War Office in 1943, evicting the villagers and leaving the buildings now spookily empty. It is a dead town. On the main street, the church and Bell Inn pub lie dormant. Cottages, a schoolroom and Imber Court manor house all sit vacated, their doors unlocked, opening into empty brick shells. As we arrived in the eerie darkness of early morning, mist hung hauntingly over the graveyard and a chill ran down my spine.

The walk there from Knook Camp was tactical, routing the whole of Imjin Company across country fields and track. Light rain was falling. We departed Knook at midnight, starting up the steep path that exited at the rear of the camp, loaded heavy with packed kit for the ten days ahead. Like pit ponies we carried everything, our bergens bulging with rations, ammunition, clothing, water, equipment, spades, a sleeping bag and the radio. With rifle and webbing, I carried over sixty kilograms that night, for eight miles across country. Four hours carrying more than my own body weight. It was crippling. I shudder still when I think of that long slow torturous march. The agony. It is a miracle that I made it to the end. Most didn't. Only nine girls in Eleven Platoon completed the entire march with their bergens like this.

I stumbled close to tears for the duration of the journey. The pain in my back was excruciating, stabbing along my spine with each laboured step. Each time we stopped for the leading person to check their map at the front, I would carefully lower myself to the ground. I lay in the grass beside a fence post or tree stump, which I would then have to rely on as a crutch to pull myself back to my feet once more as we continued on, because with sixty kilos on my back I couldn't stand up unaided. Vertebrae were crushed and discs slipped on that march. But it was realistic. This is how the Parachute Regiment got from Goose Green to Port Stanley in the Falklands conflict. Chasing the Argentinians for fifty miles over mountains with all their kit. But Parachute Regiment soldiers were not eight-stone girls.

I would sooner leave the army than anyone require me to make that walk from Knook to Imber again.

Once in Imber village, life didn't improve either.

Moving into one of the deserted houses, I made my home on the ground floor, in what had once been someone's kitchen. Slumping my bergen in a dank corner, happy to never lift it ever again, I wandered through the courtyard outside to the row of blue Portaloos. There were five of them lined up beside a wooden fence, a succession of blue Tardises standing in the countryside. Walking towards them I wished they were capable of time travel. I came to the first one and pulled at the black plastic door handle on the front, but it was locked. Moving along I tried the next one, but that too was firmly shut. Strange. Peering at it with my head-torch I could see that the occupancy window was green; it shouldn't be locked.

Maybe we weren't supposed to use them. I carried on and tried the next in line. That too wouldn't open despite showing it was vacant. I tugged at the door handle again, a little harder and this time the door broke free with a cracking sound, and then I realized why none of the doors would open – they were frozen shut.

Lit by the light of the moon I stood there outside the row of Portaloos close to tears. I closed my eyes and breathed deeply, trying not to scream with frustration.

What on earth was I doing here?

It was four o'clock in the morning; I was exhausted and famished. My back was in tatters, my feet were bloodied, I was cold and empty, and ten days of this misery lay ahead of me. Right now the rest of Wiltshire were tucked up in bed yet I was going on sentry. Why was I doing this? After eleven months I was still in Eeyore's gloomy place, which was still rather boggy and sad. Sandhurst hadn't improved. I'd made friends, I'd learned the rules, I'd even found my future army home, but I was still cold, tired, wet and hungry. I would still be shivering in my sleep tonight, still digging and crawling for the next ten days. And I couldn't even get into the toilet. I collected my thoughts and sighed. I couldn't stand a career's lifetime of this and so far every time I thought the hardship was over it came back with a vengeance.

In the field behind the Portaloos I spotted a cow, watching me. Standing still at the field's edge, her eyes fixed on my misfortune. The scene had all the surrealism of a Dalí painting, an incongruous gathering of a cow, a soldier and a Tardis at the edge of a field. I looked at the cow, watching her big dark eyes fixing on me, taking me in, and then I realized that it was me who was the silly cow here.

The frozen theme continued too as a few days later I was out patrolling along a ridgeline to the north of Imber village. Looking across Salisbury Plain to the north, I could see the city lights of Swindon sparkling in the night sky, its bars and clubs in full throng. It was a Saturday night and on the travelling wind I was sure I could hear the voices of drunken revellers spilling out of pubs, warmed by the festive spirit of Christmas work parties. I envied them. It was the weekend. A free time in the week that they probably took for granted. As I walked I could hear an odd rattling sound coming from my webbing. We weren't meant to make any noise as we patrolled as it might alert the enemy, and right from the start we had been taught how to pack our webbing and kit to ensure nothing rattled or shook. I couldn't work out what the rattling noise was. In my mind I was running through everything that was in there, I had packed it all as I should have, but with each step, there it was, an unwanted chinking sound. Eventually we stopped at a copse to check the map and drink some water. I reached into my webbing pouch and took out the black plastic water bottle that had accompanied me through so much of the last eleven months. Unscrewing the cap I put the bottle's rim to my lips and tilted my head backwards, but nothing came out. I shook the bottle in my hand and heard the now familiar rattle. And then I realized that even the water inside my water bottle had frozen solid, leaving me with a block of ice that was now rattling inside the bottle and nothing to drink.

Could this get any worse?

As it happened, yes it could.

I returned from the foot patrol with One Section and entered the once-kitchen of our occupied home. Living in Imber village, we were becoming quite spooked at night by CSM Mockridge's haunting stories about ghosts and headless horsemen among the gravestones in the abandoned churchyard outside. Now back from the patrol I had no idea what time of day it was. We were operating at all times of night and day, snatching sleep when we could, and the hours and days had begun to roll into each other. I stripped off my body armour and helmet, dropped my webbing to the floor and propped my rifle against it. I dug into one of the webbing pouches and pulled out a mess tin and stove. In my breast pocket I found a lighter and began to light a hexamine fire to heat up my boil-in-the-bag dinner. As I waited for the water to boil I decided to take my rifle apart and clean it.

Although strictly not allowed, we all used baby-wipes to clean our rifles and ourselves when on exercise. So I reached into my bergen and pulled out a packet of baby-wipes. I opened the plastic lid with a click, and realized that even my baby-wipes had frozen solid in Salisbury Plain's plummeting temperatures. Reverting to the fail-safe official army-issue weapon-cleaning kit, I cleaned my rifle with wire brushes as my dinner heated up. After a while I fished the foil bag out of the boiling water and placed it against my thighs, letting it warm them up and steam the moisture from my damp clothing. I tore the top off the foil bag and spooned mouthfuls of hot casserole into my mouth as I put the rifle back together: gas plug, cylinder, piston, the block, cocking handle, return spring, weapon housing and then I returned the magazine back into its slot. I pulled back the working parts and started to oil the inside, dabbing with a sponge swab inside the stock and entrance to the barrel. I felt the satisfying warmth as the hot food reached my stomach, taking away my hunger.

Things felt as though they were starting to improve on Final Ex. The extreme insertion march was becoming just a distant memory, the Portaloo doors had defrosted, I was settling into the patrol routine and was about to snatch a few hours' rest. Maybe this wouldn't be so bad after all. I sat on the floor with my rifle rested against my legs, and smiled contentedly for the first time in days. I finished oiling my rifle and released the working parts forwards, closed the dust cover and then pulled the trigger to fire off the action.

And that is when it happened. A loud unwanted BANG, which resonated around the bare brick room. It was like farting in bed with a new lover. Everyone heard it and it was completely unwelcome. I was struck by abject horror and shame. My heart leapt into my throat, and I sat rigid. Everyone in the room froze too, looking up, their eyes fixed on me. It was as if the world around me had suddenly stopped dead.

In pulling the rifle trigger, I had accidentally fired off a blank round, a 'negligent discharge' (ND) as it is known. I had thought the rifle chamber was empty, but my drills had been wrong, I had refitted the magazine and had now committed one of the most serious offences in the army. I was mortified. I couldn't believe it had just happened. For what felt like eternity I just sat and stared at the rifle in my lap, going over each of my actions in my mind. How had that happened?

Merv came through from the adjoining room with a look of concern on her face. 'Don't tell me that was what I think it was,' she said as she walked through the doorway.

'Yes it was,' Wheeler confirmed. 'Héloïse has just ND'd.'

'Oh shit. Are you all right?' Merv asked, knowing the grave consequences of what I had just done.

'Yes. Yes I'm fine,' I said, getting to my feet with the rifle still in my hands. 'I'd better go and tell someone.' I had to report it.

'Do you want me to come with you?' Merv offered, looking at the downcast droop of my shoulders.

So with Merv accompanying me, I went to the command post to confess, sending a message over the radio to tell the Academy staff, none of whom were present, what I had done.

NDs are a big deal in the army. With a live round or anything bigger, it could have had unimaginable consequences. Since I was still in training my fine would be lenient, but if this had happened at war, in Iraq or Afghanistan I would have lost my entire operational bonus (currently around £5,000 for a six-month tour) and with it my reputation. I was the fourth girl in Eleven Platoon to ND during our year at Sandhurst, and one of eight cadets in CC071 to do so during the final exercise. As I stood in front of the New College Commander back at Sandhurst along with the other seven, and graciously accepted my £200 fine, I thought back to those initial skill-at-arms lessons in weeks one to five. I thought about how tired I was when I was being taught such important skills. I remembered my head lolling with fatigue, as I hopelessly fought to keep my eyes open and mind focused in the warmth and comfort of the classroom, zoning out as sleep deprivation won over. And I thought how tired I had been on that day in Imber village on the final exercise when I pulled the trigger. Tiredness was not an excuse, but complacency was the cause.

It was the most important lesson I learned during my time at the Academy.

The final exercise dragged on for ten frozen solid days before eventually culminating with an assault on Cope Hill Down village in the centre of Salisbury Plain by the entire CC071 intake. Two hundred and forty cadets stormed the houses, diving through windows and kicking down doors, in an incredible full-scale military operation. But by now I just wanted it to end. I was only thinking about the shower at the finishing line, and a decent cooked breakfast, about pulling on fresh clean clothes and finally relaxing with a chilled glass of champagne. The armoured Warrior vehicles we rode in and the Apache helicopters that came and hovered over our heads for the final crescendo went completely unappreciated, as all we wanted to do now was fire our last rounds and hear the magic words: 'END EX.'

As the sun rose on that final day we stood along three sides of an open square in the centre of the village, the whole of CC071 grinning with relief. Piles of empty ammunition cases littered the rooms and stairwells of the buildings behind us, and the Gurkhas we had shot earlier were picking themselves up and coming to life again. Above the dawn sky, warming orange sunlight appeared through cracks in the cloud, casting a glowing hue over the gathered assembly. We stood smartly, lined up in rank and file, because in front of us stood the General, his hands clasped neatly behind his back. He was a short, jolly man, who, despite rank importance, we felt relaxed around. He lowered his head and looked soulfully at the ground, summing up his thoughts for our final address. Smiles of elation beamed across each cadet's face as we absorbed the fact that it was all finally over. We had finished. Sandhurst was over. Two weeks of term remained, but they were a mere formality now. The exams were done. We had reached the end.

I don't remember what the General said to us that morning. I was too giddy with excitement. He undoubtedly expressed his congratulations and spoke sage words to guide us through our officer careers; handing out nuggets of General's wisdom in the sort of profound speech that Generals are paid for. Whatever it was he said, he was completely eclipsed by what followed.

After he had finished speaking we took out our new berets that we had been moulding for weeks in the privacy of our rooms and officially put them on our heads for the first time. Beaming at each other like real, grown-up officers, not pretend cadets any more. Hands were clapped and shaken, backs slapped and mock salutes given, before chuckling and tittering in high spirits as we made our way towards a large empty hangar where breakfast was being served. Merv, Wheeler and I giggled with elated excitement, floating high on the satisfying drug of accomplishment as we drifted through the hangar entrance. Looking around inside, I noticed there were a number of fresh-clothed civilians expectantly milling around. They were wearing the usual black North Face puffer jackets and walking boots that non-military people adopt as suitable attire to blend in when working around people in uniform. Near the entrance a man was fussing around with a clipboard in his hands, directing us further into the hangar and towards the hotplates where a film crew were hovering.

I looked along the line of hotplates, hungrily eyeing up the food on offer. My first decent cooked meal for ten days. I was salivating at the thought of bacon and sausages. As I followed the buffet line of food, I realized that the normal Army chefs had also been replaced by North Face-wearing civilians. I couldn't quite work out what was going on. Why was a film crew recording our breakfast, and who were these chefs? As I collected my paper plate and plastic cutlery a blonde woman handed me a glass of champagne. I took a sip, and let the bubbles glide straight to my brain, feeling them instantly relax me, and that's when I saw him. Cheerily spooning kedgeree onto a paper plate ahead, smiling and chatting with the cadets. Andi Peters. I couldn't believe it. Was tiredness making me hallucinate? Why was Andi Peters serving us breakfast? Andi Peters who we had all grown up with presenting our children's television programmes. Andi Peters of Edd the Duck fame. What was going on?

The twitter of gossip travelled along the queuing line, sending word that these plain-clothed civilians were in fact celebrities taking part in the television programme *Celebrity MasterChef*. Apparently while we had been assaulting the village, Andi Peters and his group of Z-list celebrities, whom none of us recognized, had been under the heat in an army field kitchen preparing us a gourmet breakfast. And in front of us were trays of beautifully prepared smoked salmon, scrambled egg, kedgeree, pancakes and perfectly poached eggs Benedict. It looked delicious but was not going to be sufficient to feed our ravenous hunger right now, so at the far end of the hotplate lay trays of usual army fare: sausages, bacon, fried bread and gallons of baked beans. After ten days of shivering on Salisbury Plain the gastronomy was somewhat wasted as I politely accepted one of Andi Peters's lovingly prepared eggs Benedict and then smothered it in sausage and beans.

*

I was woken by the sound of bagpipes, the strangled screeching that had somehow become cause for nostalgia now I was in the military. I looked at my bedside clock, 05.27, army early. Outside in the corridor the bagpipe shrills drifted away, moving along to wake up someone else. I stretched my legs and spun out of bed, with all the excitement of a child at Christmas, leaping across the room and flinging open the door. Standing in the doorway I poked my head out into the brightly lit corridor, looking up and down, watching more heads popping out of the other rooms, each covered by a wide broad smile. The door opposite cracked open and Merv appeared in her pyjamas. Scratching her head she looked at me, grinning from ear to ear. Today was our last day at Sandhurst. Friday, 14 December 2007.

The day we finally commissioned.

For the preceding two weeks since the final exercise our days had been devoted to preparing for this – shining and smartening. Between final mess dress fittings and handing back kit, hours had been spent pacing the parade square, rehearsing and practising until every step of the final Sovereign's Parade was ingrained in our muscle memory. Each drumbeat, each halting step, every salute, all committed until they started entering my dreams at night. In our rooms each night we had polished and preened, shining shoes and buckles, buttons and brass, until everything was perfect. Because this time it wasn't just Captain Trunchbull who would be inspecting us, and it wasn't just CSgt Bicknell we needed to impress. It was the 2,000 spectating family and friends who mattered today.

As the preparations hit fever pitch, I finally understood why Sandhurst places such a high priority on drill. After eleven months at the Academy I realized that it was all about marketing the Sandhurst brand. It was all a show. It was about putting on a good performance for the viewing public, because for most people outside Sandhurst the pageantry of the Sovereign's Parade is the only insight available into Academy life. Three times a year, with each commissioning day, the gates are opened to family, friends and the national press to come and peer with their cameras. Getting a slim snapshot of life at this esoteric institution. Royalty arrive, foreign dignitaries, politicians and military chiefs, taking their places in the front row to watch the spectacle.

And before them a stately display is laid on, with a brass band playing and 500 cadets marching around Old College parade square in synchrony, showcasing the discipline and superior mettle of the British Army's Officer corps. This impressive display of pomp and ceremony masks the real blood, mud and grit that go into the commissioning course.

On that December morning, seated in stands at the edge of the parade square, were my parents, brother and Deborah, huddled in the cold with their cameras primed. My grandfather was the only regrettable absentee that day. As a former Second World War soldier, I desperately wanted him to be there. He would have appreciated the whole significance of my commissioning day the most, but at nearly ninety years old he was too frail to make the long journey south. Instead I phoned him the next day to tell him all about it. From his chair in a North Wales care home, he proudly saluted me down the telephone line and chuckled over the miracle that someone had finally forced his granddaughter to tidy her room.

Standing to a flank, formed up and ready to march I could hear the buzz of the crowd quietened as a brass band marched onto the parade square ahead of us. Smartly dressed in their red tunics, the splendour of Old College provided a stunning backdrop behind them as the drum beat out a military melody.

Da-da-da-dum-dum-dum.

The backing track for 500 cadets marching behind them. Now in the Senior Term, we had ditched the rifles that had been so cumbersome to march with in Inters, replacing them with far more stately swords. In the low winter light the rows of swords glittered, catching the sun and sparkling as we advanced to a cymbal clash. Stepping forwards, I could feel the pulsating resonance of the drum beating deep in the pit of my stomach.

Thump. Thump. Thump.

Setting the pace.

Filled with nervous pride and a stiffener of port, we were led onto the square by the Academy Adjutant mounted on his steady white stallion. I was tense and anxious. This was a big moment and not the time for one of my drill ineptitudes. For the Sovereign's Parade we didn't march in our usual platoons but as a half company, mixed up with the boys of Imjin. To my left was Officer Cadet Leroy from Ten Platoon, who took pride in his appearance and had kindly polished my shoes for me the night before. Leroy was commissioning into the Royal Logistics Corps and his family and friends were also seated in the crowd ahead.

As we marched forward and stepped onto Old College parade square I noticed something out of the corner of my eye on the ground next to Leroy's right foot.

'Leroy,' I whispered loudly over the drumbeat, 'your shoelace is coming undone.' At that Leroy tilted his head ever so slightly and glanced down. Sure enough his right boot was starting to unravel and a long black lace was starting to snake around his ankles. Next to me he bristled with the hideous reality of what was happening, of all the occasions, right now, here with 1,000 family, friends and dignitaries watching. The George boots the boys wore were laced with extraordinarily long laces too and by the time we reached the front of Old College for our first circle of the parade square Leroy's lace had now unravelled to a metre in length and was trailing like a whip behind him, kicking forth with each step.

It was catastrophic.

As we marched in circles around the parade square in front of the spectating crowd Leroy's lace flicked around out of control at his feet, baiting for one of us to stand on it and trip him up. And there was nothing he could do about it. I focused forward, minding each step but casting a sideways glance at the sea of spectators, searching for my parents among them. Eventually we came to a halt and turned to face the crowd standing to attention ready for inspection by the Queen's representative,[36] who today was the Chief of the Defence Staff, Air Chief Marshall Sir Jock Stirrup. Next to me Leroy was panicking. Glancing at the sight of his lace extending along the ground in front of us, he said to me in a hushed whisper: 'This is the worst moment of my life. I can't believe this is happening to me.' With my nerves this sent me giggling at the situation and I

---

36 The Queen doesn't attend every Sandhurst commissioning and in her place a Sovereign's representative is sent, varying from alternative Royalty to military Generals and even the Prime Minister.

started to choke as I held them back. 'I've got to bend down and do it up,' he said.

'No, no, no. Leroy, you can't do that,' I pleaded. We were standing in the front row. No one but the head of the British Armed Forces would see Leroy's lace, but the entire gathered crowd would see him crouch down and do up his laces. And the Academy sergeant major would probably have him shot on the spot for ruining proceedings. No, he had to leave it.

As the air chief marshall approached with his entourage Leroy began sweating. I could feel the tension and fear in him for what was about to happen. We were warned daily at Sandhurst by CSgt Bicknell and CSgt Rattray about the horrors of a stray lace. Then I heard a scraping sound, and felt Leroy fidgeting beside me. I heard it again and glancing down realized he was using his sword to scrape up the offending lace on the ground. Trying to drag it towards him, so that it didn't extend quite so obviously a metre in front of him. But it was futile. The air chief marshall was working his way along the front rank and was almost upon us.

Next to me Leroy stiffened and held his breath. Accompanying the air chief marshall was the Academy commandant (a major general) and the Academy sergeant major with his rack of campaign medals pinned to his barrelled chest glinting along with his brass buttons and shiny shoes in the sunlight. Everything about his appearance screamed perfection. If he saw the stray lace lying in a winding ribbon on the parade square I was sure he would rip Leroy's throat out.

The air chief marshall continued to move forward, stopping every third or fourth person to engage in pleasant chit-chat.

Christ, why did we have to be in the front row?

He moved nearer.

Standing to attention my head was thrust forward and my chin angled upwards but my eyes were stretched sideways in their sockets, focusing intently on the progress of the Academy sergeant major. Watching him as he looked around, taking it all in, absorbing the atmosphere and sense of occasion on this proud moment: his favourite of the term. A moment Leroy's lace was about to destroy.

The air chief marshall was steps away now and as he moved towards us from his conversation three cadets away he settled his eyes on Leroy and walked towards him. I became almost faint with fear on Leroy's behalf. This was horrible. The most important day of our year at Sandhurst, a day that would stick with him for the rest of his military career. As the air chief marshall stopped in front of Leroy his aide de camp hovered behind, and the Academy sergeant major stood back glancing around at the faces in the front row. He was bound to spot the lace trailing beneath his feet. He had the eyes of a hawk. He could spot a speck of mud on a boot at thirty paces.

'And are your family here today?' the air chief marshall asked Leroy.

'Yes. Yes, sir. My . . . my . . . my mother and father have travelled up from Devon, sir.' Leroy stammered out his response as, inside his heart was beating out of his chest.

'Goodness, that's a long way to have travelled,' the air chief marshall said. 'I do hope they have a lovely day.' And with that he turned and continued on, dragging with him the rest of his entourage including the Academy sergeant major. Leroy almost collapsed with relief. His lace had gone unnoticed and he remained unscathed.

As I continued to stand to attention holding my sword steady as the air chief marshall completed his rounds, I looked for the faces of my parents in the crowd, scanning the rows of faces watching. But there were too many people for me to find them. At the same time up in the stands my father was busy clicking away, watching the spectacle through his camera lens, eager to get a good shot of the day. When I later got home I looked through these images and was disappointed to see that I wasn't in a single one of them. Instead he had mistakenly snapped photographs of Wheeler, thinking she was me.

Completing the circle I finally walked up the steps of Old College, and through the Grand Entrance as I had done with Deborah on our arrival all those months ago. Slow marching to the heartening sounds of 'Auld Lang Syne'. Once inside, the doors closed behind me, marking the end to my journey. I stood aside to make way for the adjutant, who followed us up the steps on his horse, waiting again in the same corridor I had been so nervous in eleven months ago. But this time I was laughing. Whooping with joy.

I had done it.

I had commissioned.

And what came next was real.

12

TEA AND MEDALS

My eyes are closed. I can sense movement and hear voices around me but my eyes won't open. They are too tired. In the background I can hear the dull hum of aircraft engines, a loud constant whirring that I can't block out. My throat is dry and my head feels light; I should wake up to eat and drink, but it's too much effort. I'm so weary my eyelids hang like lead. I have no idea how long we have been travelling and flying for. I feel drugged, zoning in and out like this, doped on exhausted relief and jet lag. I recall the aeroplane landing at one point, but I don't know where; I must have slept through it. Maybe I dreamed it. We must have taken off again though because we are flying again now.

It is May 2009 and I'm coming home from Afghanistan.

I boarded a Hercules transport plane at Camp Bastion, and then the RAF Tristar at Kandahar again, making the same journey I took to Afghanistan but in reverse now. My hands and face are suntanned, and I have sand in my boots, but I don't have that end-of-holiday feeling which normally accompanies a flight home. I'm mellow. At the front of the plane the casualty stretchers are not empty this time, a final lingering reminder as we boarded in the middle of the night of the brutality of war. The blue curtain that separates 'first class' is drawn shut this time, shielding the patient, doctors and nurses from view.

At that point, I'm not aware that the injured soldier is Lieutenant Mark Evison. Mark was at Sandhurst with me. He was in CC071. Now shot in the shoulder, he lies fighting for his life less than eighteen months after the fireworks and joy of our commissioning. Sadly Mark died a few days later of his wounds in the military ward of a Birmingham hospital. His death was the first of our Sandhurst intake.

Slowly, I start to wake from my stupor as the cabin lights around me are switched on. I yawn and wince at the sudden discomfort in my back as I return my seat to its upright position in preparation for landing. Through the porthole window I can see flashes of green between gaps in the cloud below as the aircraft starts its descent. A flurry of white fluff obscures the view and then we are through the cloud, flying high over the Oxfordshire countryside and it is beautiful – lush and green and just perfectly lovely. Home has never looked so good. The trees are full of new fresh spring leaves, flowers are in bloom and Britain looks at its best. After the expansive dust of Afghanistan's desert the verdant splashes of colour are tonic to my eyes.

Out of the airport terminal and driving home, I can't help gazing with fixed eyes out of the window, observing the comings and goings of life as normal, taking it all in –

a mother pushing a pram, children in school uniform gathered at a bus stop, a painter up a ladder with paintbrush in hand. Over the last few months, daily life has carried on regardless, but for me it has been on hold. As I departed Brize Norton in January I pressed pause, freezing still the life I left behind, but everything has continued despite my absence. The seasons have changed and the news has grown old. I feel like I have woken from a coma and the last four months simply haven't happened to me. Around me the world looks the same, but after Afghanistan I feel it should somehow be different. A strange feeling lingers with me for days and weeks after I return, a heightened sense and emotion. Like walking out of the blackness of a cinema back into reality after a heart-rending film. I am giddy with unnecessary sentiments that those outside don't feel.

I stop at a set of traffic lights and two businessmen cross the road in front of the car, sweating in their woollen pinstripe suits in the May heat. My eyes follow them. I think back to when that was me, racing between meetings, and rushing back to the office to sit with a sandwich at my desk. I'm a different person now. Not fundamentally changed, but a better, more settled me. That something I was searching for when I worked in the City I have found now. The sense of purpose and worth. I stare out of the window at these mundane acts of normal everyday life and realize how much happier I am now. I have escaped. I am free of the London job I so hated. The ordinary. The grey. The bleak. Abandoning it all for the army was a great leap of faith but one I am grateful I gambled on.

Sandhurst was the best and worst experience of my life. It changed me. Subtly, not fundamentally. I'm still the same person, with the same manners and methods, but the experience improved the basic template of me. So much of what I was taught there seemed irrelevant: the marching, crawling, trench-digging and nuclear immediate action drill. I won't use any of it again (technically I should use the marching again, but it will be to everyone's benefit if I don't). But it was the stuff I wasn't taught that I learned at Sandhurst: the personal pride and stubborn resolve to keep going, to hold my head high and carry on because I can do it, whatever it is. The confidence and fierce self-belief that give drunk army officers in London nightclubs their arrogant name. The standards and morals to make the right decisions. Because Sandhurst can't teach you how to solve every situation, but somehow when a soldier is in court for assaulting his neighbour, or on his knees because his wife has just left him, you know what to do. Because through all the room inspections, water parades and lessons in waiting Sandhurst actually works. It is 'the finest command and leadership training course in the world'.

And at the end of it all I did OK.

Though traumatic and painful I successfully made the transition from civilian to soldier. I learned how to iron my uniform, fold hospital corners, dig a trench and survive a nuclear strike. And I wrote it all down too. Because throughout Sandhurst every Officer Cadet was required to maintain a diary of their experience, usually written in incoherent scrawls at bedtime between when the ironing stopped and my head hit the pillow. These personal memoirs were then periodically collected in and read by the directing staff, presumably to look at our inner thoughts and check how we were coping.

I had never before kept a diary. I spent an entire Gap Year travelling around the world and never once kept an account of it for posterity. I went through the hormonal development of my teens and turmoil of boarding school but never at any point wrote it down. But under orders at the Academy I chronicled it all and at the end of Sandhurst when the prizes were handed out I received the diary prize. Not a sword like the best cadet, or the trophies presented to the sportiest, but a certificate and handshake from the General, leaving a piece of silverware locked in a cabinet somewhere with my name engraved on it; a legacy of my time at the Royal Military Academy. The accolade was much mocked at the time, diaries are for girls and none of the boys wanted the honour, but that diary has now become this book, and I hope it has given you some insight into the behaviours and customs of the military.

As I stepped outside the familiarity of Sandhurst I realized that in many ways being there had been like looking through a letterbox at the real army. Peering through at a slim snapshot of army life. The morning after I commissioned I drove through the Academy gates for the final time, my head fuzzy with the after effects of champagne and my small Volkswagen Polo, crammed once more with my belongings. As the noise of the Commissioning Ball fireworks still rang in my ears, I watched Old College grow smaller and smaller in my rear-view mirror and looked ahead to my biggest challenge yet.

Soldiers.

Not the colour sergeants or sergeant majors we had met at Sandhurst, but real soldiers. Soldiers that I was expected to command and lead. Soldiers that would make me proud and let me down. Soldiers that would make me laugh, and make me want to bang my head against the wall with frustration. Soldiers that would introduce me to life's rich tapestry and teach me more about command, leadership and the pornography industry in just five minutes than any Sandhurst lecture.

A few months after returning from Afghanistan I am back inside the Square Mile again, sipping a cup of tea on Old Broad Street in the City, while I wait for Ann and Deborah. I'm feeling reflective as I watch the corporate slaves dashing back and forth. A copy of the FT tucked under one arm, a mobile phone glued to an ear. Occasionally one will pop out of an office doorway and scurry across the road to get a steaming corrugated card cup of takeaway coffee, before scampering back again like a mouse into its hole.

Not me. I have time to linger.

I stretch out my legs and cross them again beneath the coffee table, feeling mildly smug. I've escaped all this. I am no longer in captivity here, enslaved to the bonus pool, mortgage and share prices. I bit the bullet and made the change. I gambled with my future and it was worth the risk. However, it could so easily have all gone horribly wrong. I had known nothing about the military when I joined. I just knew I needed to get a grip and do something with my life, and fortunately I landed on my feet on the other side of the twelve-foot wall. For me the army fits.

Warming my hands around my teacup, I realize that joining the army hasn't just been about a job either, it has become a way of life too. A way of life I am happy to be part of. In the forces I am now a member of a close-knit community in a way that employment in a London job never could be. The Army is more than just nine to five and a pay cheque at the end of each month. It defines who I am. And I'm proud to be part of it.

With the army I have rediscovered the passion that I lacked. The joie de vivre that had lain dormant since I left university. My confidence and the energy that faded as each City year ticked by is back now. I feel alive. I have that sparkle in my eye and a reason to get out of bed each day. Because my raison d'être is no longer to make rich people richer. And my perceived happiness and success is no longer measured in money and material gain.

I jab a fork into the corner of my chocolate brownie, breaking off a piece and popping it in my mouth, just as Deborah arrives. She dumps her laptop on the sofa beside me and apologizes for being late.

'So sorry, Hel. The meeting dragged on. All I wanted to do was just get the hell out of there, but the client was insistent we go through all the numbers one more time.' Throwing her jacket over the laptop bag she heads over to the coffee counter. 'Do you want anything else?' she says over her shoulder.

'No thanks,' I call after her, just as Ann walks in with her BlackBerry to her ear. She gives me a little wave and points to the phone with a shrugging gesture that I take to mean the person at the other end is rambling tediously. Blowing me an air-kiss, she joins Deborah at the counter and I quickly eat another mouthful of my moreish chocolate brownie for fear of having to share it with them when they sit down and join me.

'So? How was it?' Ann says, sitting down next to me with a skinny decaf macchiato.

'Come on. Tell all,' Deborah adds. 'Did you meet Charlie Boy? What was he like?' she asks, plonking down her vanilla white caffé mocha on the coffee table in front of me so that she can rearrange her laptop bag and jacket on the sofa. I look at the two coffee mugs with their frothed milk and sprinkled cocoa. When did drinking coffee become so complicated? I think.

'Yes. Prince Charles was there,' I say. 'He even gave me my medal. My dad was so proud. He absolutely loved it. I couldn't tear him away at the end. He was busy taking photographs of everything.' I undo the clasp on my handbag and open it up. 'I've got something to show you,' I say to them as I pull out a small black box with a crown printed in gold on the lid. I hand it to Ann and she opens it up. I watch her face as she looks inside with an affecting broad smile.

'Wow. That is so awesome,' she says. 'Your bling. Can I touch it?'

'Yes, of course you can. Take it out of the box,' I reply. Deborah leans in towards Ann and looks at the medal sitting inside the little box.

'Oh, Hel, that's so special. Well done you.'

I stab at another piece of chocolate brownie with my fork as Ann lifts the silver medal out of its case and holds it up by the colourful ribbon.

'"For operational service. Afghanistan",' she says, reading the inscription. 'And it's got your name on it too: "CAPT H. V. GOODLEY". That's pretty cool, Héloïse.' She hands it to Deborah.

'Oh it's quite heavy, Hel,' Deborah says, weighing it in her hand. 'Wow. Your very own bling.'

And this wasn't the only 'bling' I now owned.

When I returned home from Afghanistan there was a parcel waiting for me. I unwrapped the brown paper and inside found a similar small plastic box to mine. Inside it, beneath layers of tissue, was one of my grandfather's Second World War medals. At the age of ninety he had sadly died while I had been away in Afghanistan and I had been unable to return home for his funeral, instead standing at a memorial service in Camp Bastion for two more soldiers who had died in Helmand action. The medal he left me was his Burma Star, won fighting at a place called Kohima. During his life, my grandfather spoke little of his time in the army, joining in the silence of old soldiers, part of an entire generation who tried to forget by erasing the memory and deleting time. But he did once mention Kohima, a city that now lies in India but was viciously fought over in the Burma Campaign. Before I had started Sandhurst, he told me of Kohima and a carved stone memorial that now stands there, inscribed on which are the words of the Kohima epitaph:

> When you go home, tell them of us and say,
> for their tomorrow, we gave our today.

Holding my grandfather's war medal, I realized that it would be a complete injustice to the men and women who sacrificed their tomorrows, not to make the most of our todays. They fought and died in the battles of the World Wars, not so that I should be trapped in a City job and London life I so loathed, but so future generations could live life to the fullest and make the most of opportunity.